AF737334

State Capitalism under Neoliberalism

State Capitalism under Neoliberalism

The Case of Agriculture and Food in Brazil

Edited by Alessandro Bonanno and
Josefa Salete Barbosa Cavalcanti

LEXINGTON BOOKS
Lanham • Boulder • New York • London

Published by Lexington Books
An imprint of The Rowman & Littlefield Publishing Group, Inc.
4501 Forbes Boulevard, Suite 200, Lanham, Maryland 20706
www.rowman.com

6 Tinworth Street, London SE11 5AL, United Kingdom

Copyright © 2019 by The Rowman & Littlefield Publishing Group, Inc.

All rights reserved. No part of this book may be reproduced in any form or by any electronic or mechanical means, including information storage and retrieval systems, without written permission from the publisher, except by a reviewer who may quote passages in a review.

British Library Cataloguing in Publication Information Available

Library of Congress Cataloging-in-Publication Data

Includes bibilographic references and index.
ISBN 978-1-4985-8989-5 (cloth) ISBN
978-1-4985-8990-1 (Electronic)

Contents

Acknowledgments vii

Introduction: The Research Question, Its Significance, and the Debate 1
Josefa Salete Barbosa Cavalcanti and Alessandro Bonanno

1 State Capitalism in Neoliberal Agri-Food: The Case of the Brazilian Company JBS 17
Alessandro Bonanno

2 From the Neoliberal to the Developmental State?: The Ambiguous Political Paradigm Shift in Brazil 43
Paulo Niederle and Catia Grisa

3 March of the Daisies: Subject, Agriculture, and the State 59
Andrea Butto

4 State Intervention in Agri-Food: From Implementation to Maintenance of Irrigated Fruit Production for Export in the San Francisco Valley 77
Cinthia Regina Nunes Reis and Stéphane Gérard Emile Guéneau

5 Oil Palm Cultivation in the Brazilian Amazon: State Actions, Interest Groups, and Conflict 93
Dalva Maria da Mota, Moisés Mourão Júnior, and Heribert Schmitz

6 State Intervention and Irrigated Agriculture in the San Francisco Valley, Brazil: Productive Transformations and New Organizations of Work 113
Guilherme J. Mota Silva

7 Family Farmers Besieged between Neo-Developmentalism and Neoliberalism: The Role of the State in Agriculture and the Contradictions of the Present Time 133
Beatriz Medeiros de Melo

8 Neoliberalism and Neo-Developmentalism as Promoters of Capitalist Aquaculture in Brazil: The Case of the State of Pernambuco 147
José Ignácio Vega Fernández

Conclusion: The Political and Structural Limits of State Capitalism in Brazil 161
Alessandro Bonanno and Josefa Salete Barbosa Cavalcanti

Index 179

About the Editors and Contributors 183

Acknowledgments

Earlier versions of the chapters contained in this volume were presented at the international seminar "The Emancipatory Role of State Capitalism in Brazil" that was held in November 2017 in Recife, PE. Brazil, and sponsored by the Graduate Program in Sociology of the Federal University of Pernambuco (UFPE) and the CNPq research groups "Globalization of Agriculture and Laboratory of Rural Studies." Our thanks go to these institutions for permitting the realization of the seminar. We are also grateful to those who attended it and participated in the discussions on these chapters and other themes and papers discussed in that forum. We would also like to acknowledge the support of the CNPq and the grant program *Programa de Bolsas de Productividade* that financially assisted the empirical research that resulted in these chapters. We are also in debt to the program of internationalization (PRINT-CAPES/UFPE) of CAPES, the UFPE and Sam Houston State University for their support for the work of the editors. Additional thanks go to Ana Maria Costa for her technical support for the realization of the seminar and Marnie Hageman for her assistance during various phases of the writing of the English text.

Alessandro Bonanno
Josefa Salete Barbosa Cavalcanti
May 15, 2019

Introduction

The Research Question, Its Significance, and the Debate

Josefa Salete Barbosa Cavalcanti
and Alessandro Bonanno

This book is about the role of the Brazilian State in the recent evolution of the agri-food sector. In particular, it answers the research question of whether the type of state capitalism implemented in Brazil between 2003 and 2016 represented an emancipatory alternative to the neoliberal globalization that has dominated the economy, society, and agri-food since the early 1980s. Employing eight original research chapters and an original conclusion, this edited book's analysis of the intervention of the Brazilian State in agri-food is specifically directed toward an international audience that is familiar with the general trends of global agriculture and food but has only a relative understanding of the socio-economic and political situation in Brazil.

The scientific, but also socio-political, relevance of this research question rests on the significant problems that the evolution of the neoliberal version of globalization has engendered in society, in general, and in agri-food in particular (Bonanno, Busch, Friedland, Gouveia, and Mingione 1994; Bonanno and Cavalcanti 2011; McMichael 2004). Agri-food products are more than ever global commodities whose production and consumption count on the development of global networks controlled by large transnational corporations (TNCs) and an emerging transnational capitalist class (Robinson 2014). As decisions about production strategies and their implementation are increasingly centralized at the corporate level, the ability to democratize the use of natural and human resources and achieve transparency in the production and distribution of agri-food items is proportionally declining (Bonanno and Constance 2008; Howard 2016).

To be sure, the corporate neoliberal globalization of agri-food is resisted. One of the most common forms of resistance consists of the actions of responsible and conscientious consumers who demand quality products grown with the overall respect of the environment and labor (Carolan 2013; McKeon 2015; Wolf and Bonanno 2016). Shifting attention to "short value chains" and community-based alternative agriculture, this pattern of resistance calls for the establishment of alternatives to industrial agri-food and the generation of products that are locally grown by employing traditional techniques and farmed without the use of chemical inputs (Renting, Marsden and Banks 2003; Bonanno, Sekine, and Feuer 2019). Instances of these consumer-oriented programs include organic farming, civic agriculture, biological production, and farmers markets.

While often commercially successful, these initiatives are criticized. First, critics of this type of resistance contend that by promoting marked exchange-based consumer behavior, these programs are charged with reproducing the same ideological and behavioral dimensions that characterize corporate neoliberal globalization (Guthman 2008; Johnson 2008). Second, these critics question these initiatives' anti-corporate efficiency, as their growth has failed to reduce not only the expansion of corporate agri-food but also the ability of TNCs to co-opt them. In effect, a number of the features of these programs are now practiced by TNCs that have established systems of quality control designed to capture the demands of reflexive consumers (Lawrence and Dixon 2015; Cavalcanti and Krone 2015). Third, these initiatives' reliance on the market and their relatively small scale expose them to the negative effects of market competition and fluctuations (Bonanno and Wolf 2016). Finally, because they require the production of more expensive quality products, these programs often discriminate against low-income groups that do not have the economic resources to participate. Additionally, their local nature further precludes the participation of distant groups or those located in areas with limited access to food retailers (food deserts). In essence, because the underlying political economy foundations of neoliberal globalization are not addressed, consumer-based alternative forms of agricultural production address the symptoms rather than the causes of the problem (Bonanno and Wolf 2016; Guthman 2008; Johnson 2008).

In pertinent literature on resistance to global neoliberal agri-food, a second group of scholars focuses attention on the enormous amount of power gained by transnational corporations. In their view, a way to address the negative consequence of neoliberal globalization is to limit the actions and significance of TNCs (Friedland 1991; Heffernan 1998; Heffernan and Constance 1994). Beginning in the late 1970s, they contend, agri-food TNCs took advantage of the neoliberal deregulation of global markets to create transnational networks of production and consumption. These networks count on the hypermobility of corporate capital whereby TNCs are able to move their production sites to convenient locations around the world. Global sourcing, or the global search for convenient factors and conditions of production, accompanies the hypermobility of capital. The application of hypermobility of capital and global sourcing created production and consumption systems that are difficult to oppose as they allow TNCs to relocate production in the event of local opposition and/or declining availability of convenient factors of production. In addition, TNCs' hypermobility has motivated local political authorities to offer incentives to attract direct investment in their districts. Accordingly, TNCs, this group of scholars argues, can count not only on convenient and discounted factors of production but also on the financial support from local governments in terms of tax abatements, infrastructure building, and labor force training and education. In terms of labor relations, TNCs have been able to use immigrant and undocumented labor to control wage levels, split the labor movement by pitting workers in different production sites against each other, and adopting other strategies of labor management that reduce wages such as the feminization of labor in farming (Cavalcanti and Krone 2015).

In pertinent debates, this group of scholars is criticized at two different levels. First, their illustration of the power of TNCs depicts corporations as virtually invincible, discouraging initiatives that can limit their power. In the same vein, they fail to acknowledge the actual boundaries of corporate power and their weakness concerning consumer initiatives, public opinion, anti-corporate sentiments, and the regulatory actions of nation-states. Second, critics argue that the exclusive focus on corporate power is actually counter-productive (De Lind 2011). This is the case because the many existing forms of resistance, the activities of militants at the local level, and instances of resistance that affect corporate behavior influence the political economy of agri-food.

A third group of researchers stresses the opposition to neoliberal globalization represented by a movement that contends that access to food is a "right" (Carolan 2013; McMichael 2014; Wittman, Desmarais, and Wiebe 2010). The project of "Vía Campesina" is arguably the most eloquent example of this form of resistance. For Vía Campesina small-scale agroecological farming is socially and politically emancipatory as compared with other forms of production. It permits food sovereignty that consists of the ability of those who produce and consume food to control these and associated processes. In this context, the identification of food as a right contrasts with the neoliberal proposal that sees food as a commodity that is best managed through market competition. Critics, however, suggest that smallholder production is not equipped to deliver a sustainable, just, inclusive, and global food system. They argue that agroecological, local smallholder production cannot provide a sustainable and sufficient quantity of food for the growing world population that does not have access to land. Moreover, critics state that the pre-capitalist nature of smallholder agriculture is difficult to reproduce in advanced capitalist societies (Bernstein 2014).

A fourth type of critique maintains that some modes of resistance may give the illusion of opposition while, in reality, they are part of projects that support the status quo (Bonanno and Wolf 2016). Bonanno and Wolf employ the concept of "Artificial Negativity" to stress the limits of existing forms of resistance and, in particular, consumer- and community-based opposition. Artificial negativity, they explain, is a concept that finds its roots in classic Critical Theory. First formulated in the late 1970s by Paul Piccone (1977), it borrows from the twentieth-century analyses of classic critical theorists such as Marcuse, Adorno, and Horkehimer who stressed the controlling power not only of culture and consumerism but also of state bureaucracy. These theorists contended that the exploitation of the working class by the ruling capitalist class is displaced from the sphere of the economy to that of culture. Stressing the growth of mass consumption, they maintained that consumerism—the purchase of goods and services in ever-increasing amounts—and the increasing intervention of the State created a "totally administered society" that features a "one dimensionality" whereby the instrumental rationality of capitalism has erased and replaced alternative forms of thinking (Horkehimer and Adorno 1969 [1944]; Marcuse 1964). In essence, for critical theory, as advanced society is based on instrumental rationality and consumerism, all actions, including opposition, are part of the fostering of capital accumulation.

Following this understanding, Bonanno and Wolf contend that advanced capitalism has eliminated substantive forms of opposition and that the corporate appropriation and reinterpretation of historically progressive concepts such as justice, ethics, responsibility, and regulation define contemporary social arrangements. In this context, progressive ideas that motivate alternative initiatives in agri-food are reconfigured in ways that satisfy corporate interests while fostering the actions of political militants. In this context, alternative forms of agri-food production and consumption such as fair trade, organic, eco-certified, geographic identification, civic agriculture, and more fit the rationality and assumptions of market capitalism and are transformed into instruments that promote capital accumulation while simply appearing as an alternative. These actions are part of a protest (negativity) that is artificial, as it has lost the ability to critique or the capacity to show the limits of dominant discourses and structures. These authors further contend that theoretical formulations based on the poststructuralist views of Michel Foucault allow the identification of individuality, market competition, and responsibilization (or consumers' internalization of the requirements of market capitalism that diffuse political critique), as dimensions that, while appearing to be emancipatory, contribute to the strengthening of the power of the neoliberal regime.

A final group of researchers focuses their attention on the theme of the "retreat of the State" (Bowen 2015; Denny, Worosz, and Wilson 2016; McKeon 2015). They stress that the reduced intervention of the State in the regulation and control of agri-food production is a feature of neoliberalism and a situation that creates significant negative consequences for consumers, family producers, and farming communities. In previous eras of the evolution of agri-food and in particular under Fordism (1945–1975), they contend, the State operated not only as a promoter of agri-food research and the dissemination of its results among producers but also as a guarantor of the quality of products and the effectiveness of the distribution process. The latter includes the implementation of welfare programs aimed at addressing hunger and malnutrition. The rolling back of these programs along with the withdrawal of the State from the regulation of production and consumption created conditions that affect the well-being not only of weaker segments of society but also of the rest of consumers and small-scale family producers and their communities.

The regulatory role of the State under Fordism, critics of this neo-Fordist position suggest, was not free of problems that are not resolved under neoliberal globalization. First, the regulatory intervention of the State engendered a fiscal crisis, as finite state resources had to cover the expanding costs of maintaining a regulated economy and agri-food sector. Second, the ruling capitalist class resisted the use of state resources for programs that did not directly benefit it. This opposition of the ruling class made the fiscal crisis of the State more difficult to manage. Third, state management of the agri-food sector engendered a number of contradictions. These included the creation of surpluses that brought down commodity prices and created the impression of mismanagement and inefficiency and the allocation of the majority of resources to large operations. The latter discriminated against small and family farms that were often indicated as the primary beneficiary of state intervention. Third, state intervention in the economy, in general, and in agri-food, in particular, engendered a crisis of social legitimation, as the State was not always capable of justifying its decisions to the general population. Finally, critics of neo-Fordist proposals contend that the state-corporation dichotomy is a false one as the State does not necessarily oppose corporations and, in effect, often supports them (Bonanno and Constance 2008; Fridell 2014; Wolf and Bonanno 2014).

THE CASE OF BRAZIL

Despite the criticisms that the intervention of the State has engendered within academic and political circles, it remains an important tool in emancipatory struggles. This is particularly the case in Brazil as the State has historically occupied a central role in the development of capitalist social relations in the colonial, post-colonial, modern, and contemporary Brazil. This is certainly the case in agri-food as a strong interaction between the State and relevant social groups has persisted through the decades. In effect and regardless of the sharp ideological differences among the various Brazilian governments of the contemporary era, major changes in agri-food could have not occurred without the intervention of the State.

Following Brazil's independence in 1822, the relative weakness of the domestic bourgeoisie allowed a pre-capitalist class of landowners to remain politically prominent. This situation translated into greater power for the officialdom of the State that assumed a position of control over the local classes and the economy (Bieber 1999; Kerr 2014; Kirkendall 2002). As its power remained intact, in the first half of the twentieth century the Brazilian State fostered economic growth by investing in domestic companies. Its strategy included an intervention to assist struggling firms but also to control essential economic sectors. Continued after the end of World War II, state intervention escalated with the establishment of state-owned and operated companies following the then established theory of import substitution (Bieber 1999; Kerr 2014; Kirkendall 2002). Import substitution policies were aimed at diminishing the dependence of Brazil on expensive imports from the advanced North and reducing the unequal exchange that characterized its interaction with more developed economies (Furtado 1967).

As Keynesianism and Fordism dominated at the economic and social levels in the Western world, the Brazilian State increased its intervention in the economy. The creation of state-owned companies such as *Petrobrás*—the energy giant that would become the symbol of the Brazilian State intervention in the economy—and institutions such as the *Economic and Social Development Bank* (BNDES)—the investment bank that became the financial arm of state interventionism—defined the time's state policy. The period of the military dictatorship (1964–1985) featured the virtual suspension of political and intellectual freedom and a top-down authoritarian approach to socio-economic development. Yet, it also saw an increase in the number of state-owned companies and their expansion to the status of conglomerates (Bear 2008). Concerned with these companies' profitability, the authoritarian Brazilian State paid only formal attention to socio-economic development as economic contradictions and social problems did not improve. In agri-food, this intervention involved investment in infrastructure, research, and extension that increased the production and productivity of the sector. As it will be described in a number of chapters contained in this volume, state initiatives for the irrigation of the semiarid San Francisco Valley—in the less developed Northeastern portion of the country—laid the foundations for the economic growth of one of the most productive agri-food regions of Brazil and the entirety of Latin America (Marsden, Cavalcanti, and Ferreira Irmão 1996; Cavalcanti 1999).

In the mid-1980s, the return to democracy was supported by a strong socio-political mobilization that centered on the right to directly elect the President of the Republic (or the *Directa Ja* movement). It was followed by an equally strong mobilization for the creation of a new and democratic constitution that included a significant number of rights and entitlements for the working class and the poor. Initiated in 1986, this movement culminated with the promulgation of the constitution in 1988 (Saad-Filho 2008). At the socio-economic level, the late 1970s worldwide end of Fordism translated into a severe economic crisis that affected all sectors of the Brazilian economy and society. Additionally, high levels of inflation hampered the success of corrective measures as the status of the economy continued to deteriorate. To be sure, inflation was an international problem in the 1980s. In the United States, under the leadership of Paul Volker, the Federal Reserve initiated a process of tightening interest rates that rapidly curbed inflation but also made access to capital for investment and spending very difficult. For Brazil, the significant increase of interest rates made the repayment of international loans tough to accomplish, a difficulty that was compounded by the existence of a great number of these loans that Brazil had previously contracted to support the State's socio-economic programs. To be sure, the indebtedness contracted by Brazil in the previous decades was, to a significant extent, the result of the pressure that developed countries—led by the United States—exercise on emerging economies to borrow from them. Developed countries promoted borrowing by offering low-interest rates and used it as a convenient way to invest surplus capital. However, as this condition changed, it favored harsh economic adjustment programs and loan repayment plans (Harvey 2003; McMichael 2004).

The destabilization of the economy, the reduced cash flow, and the incapability to borrow internationally, de-facto paralyzed the ability of the Brazilian State to continue its policy of high intervention in the economy. As in the rest of the world, the solution to the crisis was identified in the implementation of neoliberal measures. Centered on the end of state interventionism and the privatization of state-owned companies and assets, neoliberalism became a buzzword in Brazilian political circles at the outset of the 1990s. This climate allowed Fernando Collor de Mello—a neoliberal—to win the presidential elections in 1990 on a program that abandoned the long-standing principle of state-supported economic and social growth. Conversely, Collor de Mello selected privatization as the anti-crisis feature policy. He divested the portfolio of BNDES, privatizing, however, mostly profitable companies. This divesting move financially hurt the Brazilian State but benefited the domestic and global bourgeoisie that was able to acquire excellent financial and productive assets at convenient prices.

Despite these problems, the privatization policy continued first under the administration of Itamar Franco (1992–1994) and later under the presidency of Fernando Henrique Cardoso (1995–2002). A former leftist sociologist, co-author with Enzo Faletto of the seminal book "Dependency and Development in Latin America" (1971) and later supporter of the "Third Way" policy of Bill Clinton and Tony Blair, Cardoso endorsed the privatization of not only state-owned firms but also public services such as electricity, communication, transport, and mining (Baer 2008; Musacchio and Lazzarini 2014). In agri-food, the neoliberal wave dovetailed with the expansion of globalization and mandated the virtually uncontested acceptance of the requirements of large transnational corporations (TNCs) (Cavalcanti 2015; 1999; Bonanno and Cavalcanti 2011). The expansion of corporate agri-food profited from the growth of the global demand that, in the case of Brazil, signified primarily the export of basic commodities, such as soybeans, and high-quality products such as fresh fruit and vegetables. The latter occupied a segment of the market propelled by consumer demand for tasty and healthy food. Appropriated by corporate producers and retailers, the expansion of quality agri-food production engendered significant changes in the organization of production and the use of labor (Cavalcanti 2015; 1999; Bonanno and Cavalcanti 2014; 2011). Ultimately, the export of agri-food commodities became one of the major components of the Brazilian economy and defined its position in the global division of labor (Cavalcanti 1999).

The implementation of neoliberal measures did not improve the socio-economic conditions of Brazil (Baer 2008). As economic and social instability remained, left-leaning protests gained traction and materialized in the campaign that led to the electoral success of the PT and the concomitant election of Luís Inácio Lula da Silva to the presidency in 2002. Lula proposed an end to the privatization process and issued statements about the emancipatory role that the Brazilian State would carry out under his administration. In effect, during the administrations of Presidents Lula and Dilma Rousseff, the number of state-owned companies increased at a significant rate and progressive policies were implemented. However, the case of the PT administrations presents a unique characteristic that sees pronouncements and actions in favor of small family farming, landless peasants, indigenous communities, and food deprived poor urban groups co-existing with actions in support of corporate agriculture. This contradictory posture was difficult to navigate as it engendered splits internal to the State itself and overt conflicts in the civil society. Accordingly, the pro-small scale family farming Ministry of Agrarian Development was pitted against other branches of the State that resisted policies that promoted food security, land rights and the eradication of hunger such as in the case of the program *Fome Zero* (no more hunger). Simultaneously, the implementation of these and similar policies was opposed by affluent segments of the agri-food sector that succeeded in appropriating resources earmarked for subordinate groups.

In effect, the domestic literature on the emancipatory role of the Brazilian State under the PT administrations is split into two camps and this split reflects precisely the double axis of the intervention of the state just described. At one pole of the debate, we find analyses that underscore the progressive side of state interventionism (e.g., Carneiros dos Reis 2018; Haddad 2009; Mueller and Rossi de Oliveira 2009). They accentuate the element of wealth redistribution of the PT policies that ultimately benefitted the working class, the poor, and residents of rural regions. In the case of farming, this literature refers to the struggle of social movements that the PT administration supported and whose demands it included in its program. They stress that the Brazilian governments sought to introduce in their policies measures that addressed calls for the distribution of land, the recognition of occupied lands, the just remuneration of labor as expressed by movements such as those of the landless peasants (*Sem Terra*), indigenous and quilombolas groups, and other rural settlers.

At the opposite pole, left-leaning critical views of the role of the State see PT policies as a continuation of the Third Way approach followed by Cardoso (Arestis and Saad-Filho 2008; Saad-Filho 2008). This group of scholars indicates that the policy of the PT State was ambiguous and ultimately benefited the domestic and global bourgeoisie more than the local working and middle classes. In the case of farming, the TNCs' abilities to control quality production and the retailing sector are identified as instances of the way the progressive Brazilian State was incapable of halting the corporate expansion in the sector and country. They conclude that the PT employed not only neoliberal policies but also was affected by internal problems (Paulani 2008).

THE ORGANIZATION OF THE BOOK

These problems and the overarching research question on the emancipatory role of state capitalism are discussed in the next eight chapters of the book. Following this introduction, chapter 1 by Alessandro Bonanno is entitled "State Capitalism in Neoliberal Agri-Food: The Case of the Brazilian Company JBS." Bonanno studies the case of the agri-food corporations JBS, one of the largest agri-food companies in the world. His objective is to address the research question of the extent to which state capitalism is an emancipatory tool that can oppose neoliberal globalization. He contends that state intervention in the economy and ownership of companies has been common in previous eras of contemporary capitalism. However, this has changed under neoliberalism as the State retained only the minority equity ownership, leaving the company's management in private hands. In Brazil, this new form of state capitalism has been employed by the PT Administrations of Lula and Dilma Rousseff as tools to foster emancipatory socio-economic development. The analysis of the JBS case shows that state funding was instrumental in the global expansion of this company. However, its economic behavior followed patterns typical of large global companies, resulting in economic expansion but limited contributions to the wellbeing of workers, communities, and the environment. Moreover, corruption has characterized the relationship between this company and the institutions of the state. The author concludes by questioning the emancipatory effectiveness of new forms of state capitalism experimented in Brazil.

Chapter 2 is entitled "From the Neoliberal to the Developmental State: The Ambiguous Political Paradigm Shift in Brazil" and authored by Paulo Niederle and Catia Grisa. Nierderle and Grisa probe the way in which the paradigm shift that characterized the PT administration has affected agriculture and rural development. In particular, they investigate the changes that occurred from the neoliberal administrations of the last decades of the twentieth century to the PT government of the early portion of this century. They document that the electoral victory of the PT in 2002 translated into the introduction of a neo-developmentalist model of development that replaced the neoliberal model adopted by the Cardoso administration. However, they continue, rather than a rupture, this change is better described as a transition whereby the neo-developmental paradigm adopted by the PT was much more similar to the neoliberalism of Cardoso than the early "developmental approach" employed from the 1940s to the 1970s. Responding to the research question of the book, Niederle and Grisa conclude by stressing the contradictory nature of the policy employed during the 2003–2016 period. The PT policies opened spaces for the valorization of family agriculture through the implementation of socially oriented and redistributive measures. However, they also introduced macro-structural policies that benefited corporate agrifood and export agriculture and ultimately jeopardized the well-being of family farmers, traditional communities, and their social reproduction.

Chapter 3, "March of the Daisies: Subject, Agriculture and the State by Andrea Butto analyzes the March of the Daisies" (Marcha das Margaritas), is the largest social movement of rural women in Brazil. The chapter probes not only this movement's establishment and growth but also its actions, paying specific attention to the struggles for the distribution of land, the adoption of agroecology, and the availability and conservation of water. These topics are discussed in terms of the claims proposed by this movement in the five marches that it organized between 2000 and 2015. In addition, the role that the diffusion of feminist ideas played in the evolution of the March is presented. The chapter stresses the positive role that the Brazilian State under the administration of the PT played in the struggles of rural women. While some contradictions remain, the analysis underscores the positive impact that the PT administrations had for the democratization of labor relations in agriculture and the conditions of rural women. The chapter concludes by contending that the recent abrupt end of the PT administration of the country and the concomitant establishment of conservative governments represent serious setbacks for the struggle of women in agriculture and rural areas. In this respect, the chapter maintains that the emancipatory dimension of the PT administrations compensated for the contradictions of some of their policies.

Authored by Cinthia Regina Nunes Reis and Stéphane Gérard Emile Guéneau, chapter 4, "State Intervention in Agri-Food: From Implantation to Maintenance of Irrigated Fruit Production for Export in the San Francisco Valley," discusses state actions in the production of fresh fruit and vegetables in Brazil. It employs the case of the San Francisco Valley that is a region that accounts for more than 90 percent of the Brazilian exports of fruit. Interpreting this success as a sign of the reduced state intervention in the economy, the author continues, pertinent studies stress the positive impact of the actions of the private actors and, particularly, the adoption of private certification systems that are considered fundamental for increasing international market share. Adopting Michel Foucault's concept of governmentality (*gouvernementalité*) as a specific way of exercising power by governing from a distance, the chapter contends that the actions of the State are redefined by the implementation of direct and indirect forms of governmentality. Accordingly, the system of agricultural production in the Valley of San Francisco is shaped not only by the actions of private actors but also by state intervention that promotes production for export. Addressing the research question of the book, the authors conclude that the role of the State in the neo-developmentalist era is contradictory as its actions are intended to benefit actors with contrasting interests.

Framed in the context of the PT governments' effort to diversify energy sources and through an analysis of pertinent public programs, chapter 5 investigates the actions of the State aimed at expanding palm oil production in the Brazilian Amazon. Dalva Maria da Mota, Moisés Mourão Júnior, and Heribert Schmitz are the authors of "Oil Palm Cultivation in the Brazilian Amazon: State Actions, Interest Groups, and Conflict." Focusing on the multifaceted postures of relevant actors, they stress the central role played by the State in the diversification of energy sources and the power that agri-food special interest groups have on it. The State and agri-food special interest group interaction spans different scales of the social construction of new productive spaces and involves issues concerning the environment, economy, and society thus encroaching the resistance of social movements. Specifically, the authors contend that the State assisted the expansion of oil palm production by providing scientific and technical support that generated favorable economic conditions for corporate groups. This action, the chapter concludes, was part of a broader process that saw the joint effort of federal, state, and municipal institutions in support of the cultivation of palms for oil production.

Focusing on fruit production in the San Francisco Valley of Brazil, chapter 6, "State Intervention and Irrigated Agriculture in the San Francisco Valley, Brazil," by Guilherme J. Mota Silva proposes an analysis of state intervention in the creation and development of irrigated agriculture. In the middle of the twentieth century State intervention strengthened the local productive structure and provided technical assistance in support of irrigated farming. Beginning in the 1990s and under the aegis of the neoliberal model, State intervention changed. It focused on providing financial and tax incentives to large agri-food companies in order to attract them to the region. Starting in 2003, Brazil initiated a new economic policy defined by the doctrine of neo-developmentalism. It allowed the growth of irrigated fruit production, the expansion of rural employment, and the establishment of a new growth pattern marked by specialization, financialization, the intensification of productive activities and state programs for "citizenship territory" and the reduction of rural poverty. This move, however, engendered contradictions that affected the achievement of heralded objectives as the State was incapable of reconciling pronouncements in favor of subordinate groups and actions that supported the expansion of agri-food firms.

Beatriz Medeiros de Melo is the author of chapter 7, "Family Farmers Besieged between Neo-Developmentalism and Neoliberalism: The Role of the State in Agriculture and the Contradictions of the Present Time." This chapter analyzes the efforts that the Brazilian State has taken to promote agricultural production since the 1990s. In particular, its objective is to illustrate the contradictory actions of the Workers' Party (PT) that governed the country from 2003 to 2016. These contradictory actions rest on the PT administrations' implementation of popular income redistribution policies in favor of family farmers and their evident commitment to support corporate agri-food. The latter consisted primarily of significant financial support, infrastructure building, and deregulation measures that permitted agri-food corporations to increase their power. This analysis is employed to discuss the conditions of family farmers in a context characterized by the rule of a progressive government. The contradictory nature of this proposal, the author concludes, consists of the simultaneous support of two very different groups and the lack of a project that would balance the divergent objectives of these two groups.

Chapter 8 by José Ignácio Vega Fernández is entitled "Neoliberalism and Neo-Developmentalism as Promoters of Capitalist Aquaculture in Brazil: The Case of the State of Pernambuco." Based on an analysis of the expansion of capitalist aquaculture in Brazil and in the state of Pernambuco in particular, this chapter contributes to the academic discussion on the globalization of food production and the relationship between the State and the agri-food system. To this end, it stresses the strategies that capitalist aquaculture has used to legitimize its interests, ensure its expansion, and neutralize possible opposition. The ideological assumptions accompanying the capitalist aquaculture rest on the neoliberal globalization project. They center on the defense of this sector that is considered capable of ensuring the continued growth of fish production and meeting the demand of a growing national population. Paralleling the claims of the global neoliberalization of agriculture and its "green revolution," the capitalist aquaculture sector portrays itself as the promoter of the "blue revolution" in world fish production in conjunction with different state institutions that promote its growth. In addressing the book's research question, the chapter concludes that the policy implemented by the PT administrations shows a significant degree of continuity with the policies of previous administrations as it continued the support of the expansion of capitalist aquaculture.

"Conclusion: The Political and Structural Limits of State Capitalism in Brazil" ends the book. Its authors, Alessandro Bonanno and Josefa Salete Barbosa Cavalcanti, employ the analyses presented in the book to reach a set of conclusions about this book's research question. They identify seven pertinent conclusions. The first states that neoliberal globalization is an unsustainable regime and that this unsustainability promoted the demand for change that provided impetus for the constitution and strengthening of the social movements that supported the electoral victory of the PT and its 2003–2016 administrations. Their second conclusion indicates that the PT created expectations that were too unrealistic in regard to the historical and structural problems that faced Brazil, but simultaneously, its administrations were willing to propose solutions to address these problems. The authors' third conclusion is that the intervention of the Brazilian State in favor of small family farming and the peasantry contributed to the improvement of the socio-economic conditions of these social groups. However, and as indicated in their fourth conclusion, these actions of the State were not free of problems as financial and technical support earmarked for family agriculture went, to a significant extent, to larger farms and monoculture production for export and that, as expected, the land reform was actually never implemented. The fifth conclusion indicates the PT government's support of Brazilian corporations and their insertion into global circuits generated contradictory results and ultimately did not achieve the desired objectives. The sixth conclusion is about state efforts to offer alternatives to the dominant agri-food system. As the conditions of family farmers and other subordinate groups improved, the authors contend, the structural conditions that generated their status were not altered. The seventh and final conclusion stresses that the contradictory actions of the Brazilian State cannot be simply attributed to the will of the PT administration itself. Instead, they are the product of existing structural conditions and the global social groups that control them. In effect and despite improvements in the living conditions of significant segments of the population, the reduction of inequality, the recognition of the rights of subordinate groups and the access and regularization of occupied land, the Lula and Dilma governments were not able to contain the power of large landowners and global corporations. As conservative forces took control of the Brazilian State, the dismantling of the Ministry of Agrarian Development and the reversal of the gains obtained by subordinate groups represent, with symbolic force, the limits of the resistance to the neoliberalism.

BIBLIOGRAPHY

Arestis, Philip, and Alfred Saad-Filho (Eds.). 2008. *Political Economy of Brazil*. New York: Palgrave-Macmillan.

Bernstein, Henry. 2014. "Food Sovereignty: A Skeptical View." *Journal of Peasant Studies 41*(2): 1031–63.

Bieber, Judy. 1999. *Power, Patronage, and Political Violence: State Building on a Brazilian Frontier, 1822–1889*. Lincoln: University of Nebraska Press.

Bonanno, Alessandro, Lawrence Busch, William H. Friedland, Lourdes Gouveia, and Enzo Mingione (Eds.). 1994. *From Columbus to ConAgra*. Lawrence: University Press of Kansas.

Bonanno, Alessandro, and Josefa Salete Barbosa Cavalcanti (Eds.). 2014. *Labor Relations in Globalized Food*. Bingley, UK: Emerald Publishing.

———. 2011. *Globalization and the Time-Space Reorganization: Capital Mobility in Agriculture and Food in the Americas*. Bingley, UK: Emerald Publishing.

Bonanno, Alessandro, and Douglas H. Constance. 2008. *Stories of Globalization: Transnational Corporations, Resistance, and the State*. University Park, PA: Penn State University Press.

Bonanno, Alessandro, Kae Sekine, and Hart Feuer (Eds.). 2019. *Geographical Indication and Global Agri-Food: Development and Democratization*. New York: Routledge.

Bonanno, Alessandro, and Steven A. Wolf (Eds.). 2016. *Resistance to the Neoliberal Agri-Food Regime: A Critical Analysis*. New York: Routledge.

Bowen, Sarah. 2015. *Divided Spirits: Tequila, Mezcal, and the Politics of Production*. Berkeley: University of California Press.

Cardoso, Fernando Henrique, and Enzo Faletto. 1971. *Dependency and Development in Latin America*. Berkeley: University of California Press.

Carneiro does Reis, Márcio. 2018. "Reflecting on Counter-Hegemonic Strategies of Food and Nutritional Security: Notes on the Brazilian Case." In Alessandro Bonanno and Steven Wolf (Eds.), *Resistance to the Neoliberal Agri-Food Regime: A Critical Analysis*, pp. 95–105. New York: Routledge.

Carolan, Michael. 2013. *Reclaiming Food Security*. New York: Routledge.

Cavalcanti, Josefa Salete Barbosa. 2015. "Globalization of Food and Labor: Challenges for Sociology. *Sociologies in Dialogue 1*: 64–78.

Cavalcanti, Josefa Salete Barbosa (Ed.). 1999. *Globalização, Trabalho, Meio Ambiente. Mudanças Socioeconômicas em Regiõnes Fruticolas Para Exportação*. Recife, Brazil: Editora Universitaria UFPE.

Cavalcanti, Josefa Salete Barbosa, and Mónica Isabel Bendini. 2014. "Globalization and Change in Labor Relations in Fruit Regions of Brazil and Argentina." In Alessandro Bonanno and Josefa Salete Barbosa Cavalcanti (Eds.), *Labor Relations in Globalized Food*, pp. 3–32. Bingley, UK: Emerald Publishing.

Cavalcanti, Josefa Salete Barbosa, and Evander Eloi Krone. 2015. "Brazilian Farmers, Quality and Markets." In Alessandro Bonanno and Lawrence Busch (Eds.) *Handbook of the International Political Economy of Agriculture and Food*, pp. 110–30. Cheltenham: Elgar.

Denny, Riva C. H., Michelle Worosz, and Norbert L. W. Wilson. 2016. "The Importance of Governance Levels in Alternative Food Networks: The Case of Red Meat Inspection." *Rural Sociology 81*(4): 601–34.
De Lind, Laura. 2011. "Are Local Food and Local Food Movements Taking Us Where We Want to Go? Or Are We Hitching Our Wagons to the Wrong Starts?" *Agriculture and Human Values 28*(2): 273–83.
Fridell, Gavin. 2014. *Coffee*. Malden, MA: Polity Press.
Friedland, William H. 1991. "The Transnationalization of Agricultural Production: Palimpsest of the Transnational State." *International Journal of Agriculture and Food 1*(1): 48–58.
Furtado, Celso. 1967. *Development and Underdevelopment*. Berkeley: University of California Press.
Guthman, Julie. 2008. "Neoliberalism and the Making of Food Politics in California." *Geoforum 39*: 1171–83.
Haddad, Monica. 2009. "A Spatial Analysis of 'Bolsa Familia' Is Allocation Targeting the Needy." In Joseph Love and Werner Bear (Eds.), *Brazil under Lula*, pp. 187–204. New York: Palgrave-Macmillan.
Harvey, David. 2003. *The New Imperialism*. New York: Oxford University Press.
Heffernan, William D. 1998. "Agriculture and Monopoly Capital." *Monthly Review 50*(3): 46–59.
Heffernan, William D., and Douglas Constance. 1994. "Transnational Corporations and the Globalization of the Food System." In Alessandro Boanno, Lawrence Busch, William H. Friedland, Lourdes Gouveia, and Enzo Mingione (Eds.), *From Columbus to ConAgra*, pp. 29–51. Lawrence: University Press of Kansas.
Horkehimer, Max, and Theodore Adorno. 1969 [1944]. *The Dialectic of the Enlightenment*. New York: Continuum.
Howard, Philip H. 2016. *Concentration and Power in the Food System*. New York: Bloomsbury.
Johnson, Josée. 2008. "The Citizen-Consumer Hybrid: Ideological Tensions and The Case of Whole Food Market." *Theory and Society 37*(3): 229–70.
Kerr, Gordon. 2014. *A Short History of Brazil: From Colonial Peoples to the Modern Economy*. Harpenden: Oldcastle Books.
Kirkendall, Andrew. 2002. *Class Mates: Male Student Culture and the Making of a Political Class in Nineteenth-Century Brazil*. Lincoln: University of Nebraska Press.
Lawrence, Geoffrey, and Jane Dixon. 2015. "The Political Economy of Agri-Food: Supermarkets." In Alessandro Bonanno and Lawrence Busch (Eds.), *Handbook of the International Political Economy of Agriculture and Food*, pp. 213–31. Cheltenham: Elgar.
Marcuse. Herbert. 1964. *One-Dimensional Man*. New York: Routledge.
Marsden, Terry K., Josefa Salete Barbosa Cavalcanti, and José Ferreira Irmão. 1996. "Globalization, Regionalization, and Quality: The Socio-Economic Reconstitution of Food in the San Francisco Valley Brazil." *International Journal of Sociology of Agriculture and Food 5*(1): 85–114.
McKeon, Nora. 2015. *Food Security and Governance: Empowering Communities and Regulating Corporations*. New York: Routledge.
McMichael, Philip. 2014. "A Comment on Henry Bernstein's Way with Peasants and Food Sovereignty." *Journal of Peasant Studies 42*(1): 193–204.
———. 2004. *Development and Social Change*. Thousand Oaks, CA: Sage.
Mueller, Bernardo, and André Rossi de Oliveira. 2009. "Regulation during the Lula Government." In Joseph Love and Werner Bear (Eds.), *Brazil under Lula*, pp. 93–114. New York: Palgrave-Macmillan.
Musacchio, Aldo, and Sergio G. Lazzarini. 2014. *Reinventing State Capitalism*. Cambridge, MA: Harvard University Press.
Paulani, Leda Maria. 2008. "The Real Meaning of the Economic Policy of Lula's Government." In Philip Arestis and Alfred Saad-Filho (Eds.), *Political Economy of Brazil*, 42–54. New York: Palgrave-Macmillan.
Piccone, Paul. 1977. "The Crisis of One Dimensionality." *Telos 35*: 43–54.

Renting, Henk, Terry K. Marsden, and Jo Banks. 2003. "Understanding Alternative Food Networks: Exploring the Role of Short Food Supply Chains in Rural Development." *Environment and Planning A 35*(3): 393–411.

Robinson, William I. 2014. *Global Capitalism and the Crisis of Humanity*. New York: Cambridge University Press.

Saad-Filho, Alfred. 2008. "Neoliberalism: Democracy and Economic Policy in Brazil." In Philip Arestis and Alfred Saad-Filho (Eds.), *Political Economy of Brazil*, pp. 7–23. New York: Palgrave- Macmillan

Wittman, Hanna, Annette Aurélie Desmarais, and Nettie Wiebe (Eds.). 2010. *Food Sovereignty, Reconnecting Food, Nature and Community*. Oakland, CA: Food First Books.

Wolf, Steven A., and Alessandro Bonanno. 2014. *The Neoliberal Regime in the Agri-Food Sector: Crisis, Resilience, and Restructuring*. New York: Routledge.

Chapter One

State Capitalism in Neoliberal Agri-Food

The Case of the Brazilian Company JBS

Alessandro Bonanno

The study of the role of the State in the promotion of socio-economic development has a long history in the social sciences and sociology in particular (Aglietta 1979; Harvey 1990; Musacchio and Lazzarini 2014). In Brazil, since the election of President Lula of the *Partido dos Trabalhadores* (PT or Workers' Party), the State has actively intervened not only in the promotion of economic activities but also, and more importantly, in the expansion of local companies through forms of direct ownership. In essence, the Brazilian State has been active in promoting socio-economic development through the transformation of Brazilian firms into companies that operate transnationally (Arestis and Saad-Filho 2008; Musacchio and Lazzarini 2014). This new wave of state ownership of firms, however, differs from early forms of state intervention because it often sees the State as a minority equity owner. This situation leaves the control of companies in private hands with the State providing public funds to support investments and industrial strategies (Kurlantzick 2016; Musacchio and Lazzarini 2014).

In this context, this chapter addresses the research question of whether or not this new form of Brazilian State capitalism is an effective instrument to achieve socio-economic development that benefits the working class and the poor. This type of emancipatory development is in line with the programmatic pronouncements of the PT and its recent leaders Lula and Dilma Rousseff (Carneiro dos Reis 2018). To achieve this objective, the case study of the agri-food transnational corporation JBS is presented. JBS is a Brazilian agri-food company that started as a small local enterprise. However, thanks to significant investments from the Brazilian State, it eventually acquired the status of transnational corporations with operations in many countries and economic sectors. In recent years, it has experienced a significant crisis due to allegations of corruption and mismanagement that cast doubt on the effectiveness and desirability of state capitalism.

The chapter opens with a discussion on the historical forms of state capitalism. It first reviews classical forms of state intervention in the economy and ownership of firms implemented in the pre–World War II years and in the postwar Fordist period. It illustrates the manner in which the State established ownership of companies in strategic sectors to promote development and direct its trajectory to desired objectives. Introduced in intra-war authoritarian regimes such as Fascist Italy, state intervention and company ownership were strategic tools also employed in democracies, such as the United States and Great Britain. In Brazil, the presence of a relatively weak national bourgeoisie and its subordination to international capital had required state support since the time of independence in the first part of the nineteenth century. In the twentieth century, the Brazilian State was active in the acquisition of companies and the control of key economic sectors. In the postwar Fordist era, the adoption of Keynesian economic policies favored the further development of state ownership of companies. In this case, the State often acted as an entrepreneur and directly operated firms and appointed their leaders. In the case of Brazil, the State established the Economic and Social Development Bank (BNDES), an institution designed to support the development of local companies. It heavily invested in the creation of state-owned large companies in strategic sectors, such as *Petrobras* in the oil sector and supported the creation of industrial conglomerates or companies that own enterprises in a number of different industries.

This section continues by briefly illustrating state ownership of companies in the neoliberal era (from the 1980s to the present). As Fordism entered its final crisis in the 1970s, processes of liberalization of the economy became dominant. Liberalization policies involved the deregulation of the economy, the drastic reduction of state welfare spending and social programs, and the privatization of state-owned companies. In Brazil, the crisis of Fordism coincided with social unrest and the democratization of society that further weakened the ability of the State to intervene vis-à-vis increased expectations for the betterment of socio-economic conditions. The application of neoliberalism translated into the reduction of the number of state-owned companies. This process extended through the 1990s and the presidency of Fernando Cardoso. The continued existence of socio-economic problems and social protest led to the presidential victory of Lula in 2002. The new economic policy of the PT promoted state intervention and a return to the policy of state ownership of companies. In this last wave of state acquisitions of firms, the section concludes, the State often acted as a minority equity owner allowing private ownership of firms.

The second section presents the case study of JBS. JBS is an example of a state-supported company that received public funds during the Lula and Dilma Administrations. The section chronicles the humble origins of this company and its gradual growth through the mid-2000s. During this period, however, JBS never transcended its domestic status despite its acquisition of the largest beef company in Argentina. In 2007, due to massive state support through the intervention of BNDES, JBS initiated a very ambitious expansionist strategy that led to the acquisition of a number of domestic and international companies in the agri-food sector. This expansion catapulted JBS to be one of the largest agri-food transnational corporations in the world. Recent charges of corruption engendered a crisis and a restructuring program that contemplates the liquidation of some of its subsidiaries that characterized the current situation of the company. This section of the chapter also offers a brief review of the evolution of BNDES, illustrating some of the criticisms that its actions elicited. In particular, despite the PT Administrations pronouncements in favor of the improvement of the socio-economic conditions of the lower and working classes in Brazil, the actions of BNDES have been consistently aimed at supporting large corporations concentrated in a handful of sectors.

The last two sections of the chapter illustrate the analysis of the case study and the conclusions. The analysis underscores three points. The first indicates that the growth of JBS as a global company was possible because of the financial support that it received from BNDES. The second point stresses that while BNDES' intervention to promote the global expansion of JBS was justified publically as part of the Lula Administration plan to promote socio-economic development, the primary result of this intervention was the expansion of JBS without any contribution to the wellbeing of workers and communities and the protection of the environment. The third point underscores the lack of transparency that characterized the relationship between state intervention and JBS. These analytical points allow the conclusion that recent state capitalism in Brazil is, at best, a highly problematic way to employ public funds to promote development.

STATE CAPITALISM AND THE NEW STATE CAPITALISM OF THE NEOLIBERAL ERA

The Early Years and Fordism

State capitalism is one of the historical forms of the organization of the economy and society that stands between the two extremes of pure free laissez-faire—the absence of state intervention in the market—and socialism—the abolition of the market system in favor of state planning of the economy (Bremmer 2010). Musacchio and Lazzarini (2014, 2) define state capitalism as: "the widespread influence of the government in the economy, either by owning majority or minority equity positions in companies or by providing subsidized credit and/or other privileges to private companies." As such, state capitalism is not a new phenomenon. However, it has undergone a significant evolution since its inception in the early portion of the twentieth century (Kurlantzick 2016; Musacchio and Lazzarini 2014).

Early forms of state capitalism emerged out of the failure of laissez-faire models and involved the direct control on the part of the State of enterprises and sectors (Gerschenkron 1962). This state-owned enterprise system (SOES) was first introduced in corporatist intra-war economies as a way to promote economic development through industrialization and the availability of public stimuli to economic actors. In addition, it was employed as a system to control labor and the expansion of labor unions and movements (Tarrow 2011). The case of Fascist Italy in the 1930s is an eloquent example of this type of SOES. The Italian State created "mixed" enterprises that operated in the market as private entities and were not only under the direct control of the State but also subsidized by it (Amatori 2017). Moreover, the State appointed the company managers and supervised industrial strategies (Amatori 2017). Also, in the case of fascist Italy, SOESes were an instrument of labor control (Harold and Tanner 2017). In this scheme, the State exercised anti-democratic, violent, and repressive forms of social control that eliminated the ability of labor to challenge management (Amatori 2017).

In non-totalitarian regimes in Europe and elsewhere, state control and financing of enterprises and sectors were also common. For instance, in the 1920s, the British government nationalized a number of key companies including the BBC and the Central Electric Board. In France, the State took control of all major private airlines and established the state-owned Air France. Additionally, it created a state-owned railway system by nationalizing five private companies (Musacchio and Lazzarini 2014). In the United States, the Roosevelt administration combatted the Great Depression by implementing the New Deal, a set of policies based on state intervention for the revitalization of the economy. In this context, in 1933, the US government established the Tennessee Valley Authority (TVA) that is described as "a corporation clothed with the power of government but possessed of the flexibility and initiative of a private enterprise" (TVA 2017: No page number). The TVA was charged with the task of creating economic activities that would "lift the nation out of the depths of the Great Depression" (TVA 2017: No page number). The Great Depression also promoted experimentations with new economic theories. Symbolized by the development of Keynesianism, the notion of state intervention to stabilize economic supply and demand was complemented by policies of the direct intervention of the State in the ownership and management of firms. These new theories and policies prepared the ground for the Fordist socio-economic system of the post–World War II era (Aglietta 1979; Harvey 1990).

After the end of the war, the US-led international division of labor, Pax Americana contemplated an even greater role of the State in the coordination and regulation of the economy and society. Processes of reconstruction in Europe and Japan, as well as modernization schemes in less developed countries, involved plans for state direct ownership and/or indirect control of a variety of enterprises (Kurlantzick 2016). In this Fordist system, the State, rather than the market, was the primary regulator of the evolution of the economy, the resolution of crises, and the maintenance of socio-economic stability (Streeck 2014). While often contradictory, this system allowed sustained growth for more than three decades and made state regulation of the economy and participation in the ownership and control of firms accepted and a common economic policy (Kurlantzick 2016; Musacchio and Lazzarini 2014).

In Latin America, growing state ownership of firms was primarily associated with two conditions typical of local economies: recurrent crises and socio-economic underdevelopment. As far as economic crises are concerned, the State provided firms with financial resources as a way to solve crises and address poor economic performances. In this context, it also promoted public-private partnerships to create new firms but also strengthen existing economic initiatives (Musacchio and Lazzarini 2014). As for the issue of underdevelopment, import substitution strategies were accompanied by state intervention in the economy that included the nationalization of private enterprises, acquisition of strategically important firms, and the creation of new firms in sectors deemed central for growth (Galeano 1997). Simultaneously, as crisis resolution required forms of social control, Latin American nation-states were often the theater of military coupes d'état that translated into prolonged fascist dictatorships. The result was the establishment of undemocratic forms of governance that de facto eliminated labor militancy and political opposition (Galeano 1997).

Brazil in the Early Years and Fordism

These patterns applied also to the case of Brazil. Like in other Latin American countries and since its independence in 1822, the Brazilian economy and society have been characterized by the presence of a relatively weak national bourgeoisie (Bieber 1999; Kerr 2014). The domestic pattern of development followed a trajectory that was different from that of more advanced capitalist countries where the bourgeoisie was able to defeat the aristocracy and take control of the economy and the polity (Bieber 1999; Kerr 2014; Kirkendall 2002). In Brazil, conversely, precapitalist classes continued to maintain a relevant amount of power that, eventually, translated into not only the persistent lack of independence of the domestic bourgeoisie but also a greater power of the officialdom of the State (Kirkendall 2002). The political class, therefore, assumed a position of control over the relatively weak endogenous bourgeoisie (Bieber 1999; Kerr 2014). According to this view, the recurrent cases of corruption that affect Brazil are, to a significant extent, the result of the existence of a state-dependent economic class that operates with the controlling support of the State (Little and Posada-Carbó 1996).

Following this historical pattern, in the first four decades of the twentieth century, the Brazilian State left its imprint in the economic development of the country through the support and eventual ownership of key companies. First, the State intervened to save struggling companies from bankruptcy. Later, as these companies endeavored to survive, the State acquired them (Topik 1987). Similarly, the government took progressive control of key sectors, such as the railway system and hydroelectric power. In the case of the railway system, state acquisitions began in the late 1800s and, by the 1940s, more than 80 percent of the entire system was state-owned. This percentage increased to more than 90 percent in the early 1950s. In the case of hydroelectric power, the administration of President Getúlio Vargas, a free market politician turned nationalist and protectionist, nationalized the waterways and later, through a number of legislative measures, forced private companies to sell hydroelectric facilities to the State (Baer 2008). Moreover, Vargas was instrumental in the creation of the national steel mill industry (Baer 2008). This pattern continued during the World War II years with the establishment of a number of state-owned companies in relevant economic sectors, such as mining (Companhia Vale do Rio Doce or CVRD), automotive (Fabrica Nacional de Motores or FNM), and electricity (Companhia Hidroelectrica do São Francisco or CHESF).

In the postwar decades, state control of domestic economic activities and companies increased primarily due to the implementation of import substitution policies (Bieber 1999; Kerr 2014; Kirkendall 2002). As the Fordist system of socio-economic development was promoted by the United States, the Brazilian government escalated its presence in the economic sector and its ownership of firms (Baer 2008; Musacchio and Lazzarini 2014). In particular, in the 1950s, the government institute *Petrobas* that would become the most visible state-owned company in the future economic history of the country. Similarly, the *Economic and Social Development Bank* or BNDES was established (then BNDE) with the specific objective of directing funds to the creation of state-owned firms (see below). This posture of the State continued during the years of military dictatorship (1964–1985). The period between 1970 and 1974 represents the time when the greatest majority of state-owned firms were created (Musacchio and Lazzarini 2014: 87). This process engendered the establishment of state-owned industrial conglomerates (Baer 2008). Industrial conglomerates are companies that, originally established in one sector, acquire firms in other sectors in order to diversify their portfolios. In the 1960s and 1970s, a number of state-owned firms reached the status of conglomerates and acquired companies in sectors that were outside their original spheres of action (Musacchio and Lazzarini 2014). Additionally, a good number of state-owned enterprises established a significant degree of independence from the government. Mostly because of their profitability, they were given greater autonomy as opposed to firms that, due to poor economic performances, received government guidance in return for new influxes of state funds (Baer 2008). Through these years, the declared objective of these firms was profitability. Social concerns such as socio-economic development and social stability received lip service but, de facto, occupied only a marginal position in the agendas of these state-owned companies (Musacchio and Lazzarini 2014).

Neoliberalism

In the 1970s, the Fordism system entered its final crisis (Bonanno 2017; Harvey 1990; Streeck 2014). This crisis was complex and involved a number of converging factors. First, over the years, the expenses associated with state intervention grew significantly. These expenses were necessary in order to promote capital accumulation and maintain social stability. Simultaneously, however, they created inflation that was one of the major factors for the destabilization of the economy. Second, sustained state expenses required increased fiscal pressure that was highly resisted by the entrepreneurial class. Third, the inability to increase fiscal pressure engendered a fiscal crisis of the State. Because of its fiscal crisis, the State was unable to effectively regulate the economy and maintain social stability. Finally, as world instability altered economic and political equilibria (oil crises, labor unrest, anti-establishment movements in the South, and more), state intervention in the economy became ineffective and inefficient (Bonanno 2017; Harvey 1990; Streeck 2014).

Affected by the crisis of Fordism, governments across the globe abandoned long-standing policies of direct regulation of the economy and adopted free market-oriented postures. The idea that the economy should be guided by the free functioning of the market was not new as laissez-faire economic policies had characterized the economies of many nations for significant portions of the 1800s and early 1900s. In this case, however, the liberalization of the economy was based on a new version of Liberalism—Neoliberalism (Bonanno 2017; Mirowski 2014; Crouch 2011). For neoliberals, state intervention in the economy, as well as its ownership of firms, is one of the most significant reasons for economic instability and crises (Friedman 1982

[1962]). Accordingly, neoliberals promoted state intervention that was aimed exclusively at the creation of new markets and the deregulation of existing ones. They further contended that the free functioning of the market is the most desirable instrument for the allocation of resources and the tool that generates economic growth and social stability.

At the political level, the crisis of Fordism was followed by at least two important changes. The first involved the advent of neoliberal governments in many countries, including the United States and Great Britain. In the United States and United Kingdom, the electoral victories of Ronald Reagan and Margaret Thatcher inaugurated the adoption of neoliberal policies and the concomitant deregulation of the economy. The second change refers to the neoliberalization of left-leaning parties that increasingly incorporated basic tenets of neoliberalism into their agendas. Again in the case of the United States and United Kingdom, the administrations of Bill Clinton and Tony Blair proposed the so-called "Third Way" that supported the liberalization of the economy, the restructuring of the welfare system, and the abandonment of the historical support of the cause of labor and its organizations (Mirowski 2014; Crouch 2011). As a result, neoliberalism informed the organization of the economy and society for the next four decades before entering its mid-2010s crisis (Bonanno 2017; Mirowski 2014).

The implementation of neoliberal policies promoted the deregulation of the economy and the rollback of welfare measures that were based on policies of economic austerity, budget cuts, and the rollback of all types of public intervention in social and economic spheres. Multinational companies became transnational companies by severing the Fordist connection between the nation-state and firms. In this new regime, companies bypassed undesirable state requirements and, simultaneously, assumed new nationalities to receive state support and take advantage of convenient socio-economic and political conditions: a phenomenon known as *global sourcing* (Bonanno 2017; Streeck 2014). This process entailed the creation of global circuits of production and consumption that fostered a system of global governance based on free trade agreements, the liberalization of the circulation of commodities and capital, and the enhanced exploitation of labor. As immigration restrictions and laws—rather than the market—controlled labor, this neoliberal globalization promoted a discourse of "there are no alternatives" or TINA that equated socio-economic development with participation in global production and consumption circuits and the adoption of neoliberal policies (Bonanno 2017; Streeck 2017).

Coupled with significant tax cuts that favored the rich, this neoliberal restructuring resulted in the growth of inequality and the concentration of wealth in the hands of a very small minority of rich people, the so-called 1 percent (Piketty 2014; Langman and Smith 2018). Additionally, the enhanced exploitation of labor, the defeat of unions, the new neoliberal postures of political parties of the left, and global sourcing translated into the creation of precarious and poorly paid jobs, the expansion of subcontracting, and the ability of companies to control labor by moving operations in other and often distant locations. The latter is a phenomenon known as the *hyper-mobility of capital* (Bonanno 2017; Streeck 2017). The neoliberal proposal of *trickledown economics* impoverished members of the working and middle classes who accumulated huge debts to be able to afford housing, education, health care and, in many instances, basic necessities such as food, clothing, and transportation (Lazzarato 2013). As the accumulation of profit was de-coupled from socio-economic development for individuals and communities, resistance to neoliberalism developed. In advanced and developing countries worldwide, episodes of resistance and anti-neoliberalism movements developed. Associating neoliberalism with globalization, these oppositional movements promoted alternatives and denounced the limits of the market-based system. In Brazil, the electoral victory of the PT in the 2002 presidential election is part of this process of global opposition to neoliberalism (Carneiro does Reis 2018).

Neoliberalism and Brazil

The crisis of Fordism in Brazil accompanied the struggle against the military dictatorship and the process of the reestablishment of democracy. Two primary sets of events marked the evolution of these processes. The first set is economic in nature and refers to the particular severity with which the economic crisis associated with the end of Fordism affected the country in the late 1970s and early 1980s. As inflation became widespread, the United States initiated a process of tightening the interest rates that made international loan repayments very expensive. In the case of Brazil, this situation was particularly serious, as the government had borrowed heavily to support programs of socio-economic expansion. Additionally, the crisis affected the profitability of firms and the overall tax base. Accordingly, the government experienced a severe fiscal crisis that, in turn, signified limited availability of funds to shore up state-owned firms. The combined result of these factors ignited an economic downward spiral that crippled the Brazilian economy (Baer 2008; Keer 2014; Harvey 1990).

The second set of events refers to the political struggles that affected the country. Two specific struggles deserve mention. One was that for the direct election of the president that culminated with the victory of Trancredo Neves in the presidential vote of 1985. While Neves was never sworn in as president due to his sudden death, this episode was the culmination of a strong social mobilization in favor of democracy known as the *Directa Ja* movement (Keer 2014). The second struggle was the campaign for the drafting of a new and democratic constitution that took place between 1986 and 1988.

The significant mobilization of the labor movement and trade unions that took place resulted in the writing of a progressive constitution that ratified a number of entitlements for the lower and working classes (Saad-Filho 2008).

All these events, however, destabilized the government and hampered the ability of the State to intervene in the economy as a series of anti-crisis economic plans failed. Their Fordist style was ultimately ineffective against a declining rate of profit, continuous inflation, reduced investment, and the impossibility to mobilize adequate quantities of new capital (Musacchio and Lazzarini 2014). As the fiscal crisis worsened and the State could no longer support the companies that it owned, the neoliberal strategy of privatization emerged not only as plausible but also highly supportable (Saad-Filho 2008). In 1990, privatization programs marked the presidential campaign and later program of the new President, Fernando Collor de Mello. Breaking the long-standing shared principle that socio-economic development requires state intervention, Collor de Mello pursued neoliberal policies that identified the market (privatization) rather than the State as the engine of development (Fishlow 2011).

To be sure, there was some privatization in the 1980s as part of the anti-crisis restructuring introduced by the military government first and by President Figueiredo later. However, as indicated above, the most decisive push toward privatization occurred under the presidency of Collor (Fishlow 2011; Baer 2008). In the 1990s, this President implemented the National Program of Privatization that contemplated the divesting of BNDES-controlled firms (Musacchio and Lazzarini 2014). However, rather that privatizing underperforming companies, privatization involved the most profitable and productive firms and those operating in strategic sectors, such as petrochemical and steel (Baer 2008). This policy was continued after President Collor was impeached and Itamar Franco assumed the presidency of the country (1992–1994). As Fernando Cardoso became President in 1995, the privatization process continued. A supporter of the Third Way, Cardoso promoted not only the privatization of state-owned firms but also public services such as electricity, communication, transport, and mining (Baer 2008; Musacchio and Lazzarini 2014).

Liberalization and associated neoliberal strategies hardly solved the socio-economic problems of Brazil (Baer 2008). Because of the difficult economic situation and the unfulfilled promises of this policy, the left-leaning oppositional movement that accompanied the democratization of the country in the 1980s and 1990s continued to gain strength and eventually gained the control of the government with the election of President Lula in 2002. As the leader of the radical PT, Lula proposed a reversal of the privatization policy by identifying the State as an agent of emancipation (Arestis and Saad-Filho 2008; Carneiro dos Reis 2018). Accordingly, the decline of the number of state-owned companies was reversed and by 2009, this number had increased by almost 60 percent (Musacchio and Lazzarini 2014). This posture continued with the election of Dilma Rousseff in 2011. Analyses of the resurgence of state-owned companies indicate a new and different type of partnership. Differently, for the classical Fordist system, the new system sees the State as a minority equity owner with company leadership remaining in private hands (Musacchio and Lazzarini 2014). The case discussed in this chapter is an example of minority participation in which, however, state funds played a fundamental role in the development of the company.

In addition to these observations about the development of the state-firm partnership, the literature stresses two opposite evaluations of state intervention. One pole of this debate includes analyses that point out the progressive role of the intervention of the State in the economy and society (e.g., Carneiros dos Reis 2018; Haddad 2009; Mueller and Rossi de Oliveira 2009). According to this view, the PT Administrations and, in particular, the Lula Presidency, achieved not only the further democratization of the country but also implemented a substantive redistribution of resources that benefited the working class and the poor. Based on the enhanced participation of subordinated groups in political debate and calls for empowering the civil society and transparency, the socio-economic conditions of the poor and the working class improved. Moreover, these pro-poor and -working class policies established programs and implemented actions that stood in alternative to those that guided Brazil in the Fordist and liberalization eras (Nylen 2000). On the opposite pole, there are studies that stress the limits of state intervention (Arestis and Saad-Filho 2008; Saad-Filho 2008). According to this position, the Lula and, later, the Dilma administrations followed policies that were more in line with the "Third Way" of Clinton, Blain, and Cardoso rather than proposing an effective left-leaning political change. They suggested that while paying lip service to a left-leaning agenda and the substantive fight against poverty and underdevelopment, these administrations were friendly to transnational capital and the global neoliberal establishment. Ultimately, they ended up adopting not only neoliberal postures but also succumbed to corruption and a lack of transparency which they once identified as serious problems to be eliminated (Paulani 2008). In the case of corruption, however, both schools of thought stress the negative effect that this phenomenon has played in the evolution of the role of the State in the development of Brazil. Given this historical and theoretical background, the case study presented in the following pages provides an instance of state intervention in the neoliberal global era.

THE CASE: JBS, ITS GROWTH, AND CRISIS

The Early Years

Headquartered in Sao Paulo, Brazil, JBS is the largest company in that country and one of the largest agri-food transnational corporations in the world with revenue surpassing 55 billion USD in 2016 (Blankfeld 2011; JBS 2017). As of 2017, it employs 235,000 men and women in more than 20 countries where its presence consists of both production facilities and commercial offices. Its plants produce primarily processed beef, pork, chicken, and related byproducts (JBS 2017). It controls more than a dozen world-renowned brands including Pilgrim's (formerly Pilgrim's Pride), Seara, Swift, Friboi, Doriana, Moy Park, Primo, Gold KistFarms, and Pierce. Its activities transcend agri-food, however, as they include sectors such as leather, biodiesel, soaps, glycerin, and waste management. Its products reach more than 300,000 customers and are available in 150 countries (Trevisani 2017). The Batista family, headed by the bothers Joesley and Wesley Batista, owns the company and the investment holding company, J&F Investimentos SA, that controls this and other firms across a number of industries such as food and beverages, financial services, consumer goods, electricity, retail, and manufacturing (J&F Investimentos 2017). Since 2007, JBS has been listed on the Brazilian stock exchange, BOVESPA, with plans to be listed on the New York Stock exchange by 2018 (Mano 2017). The planned IPO may be delayed, however, due to ongoing legal problems that will be illustrated below (Mano 2017; Trevisani 2017). JBS USA, its American subsidiary, was established in 2007 after Swift & Company was acquired in a 1.5 billion USD cash deal that propelled JBS to be the then largest beef processor by sales in the world (Trevisani 2017). In the United States, JBS controls 22 percent of the beef processing market-share in the country and 18 percent of the market-share in poultry processing that generate about 70 percent of its total revenue from the US beef market (Blankfeld 2011: Runyon 2017). As of 2017, JBS remains the largest world meat producer while JBS-owned Pilgrim's is the second largest poultry producer in the United States (Runyon 2017). However, also in 2017, legal problems forced the company to undergo a restructuring process that involved the sale of a number of assets and the reorganization of its industrial plan (Runyon 2017). At the time of writing this chapter, the direction and extent of the company's restructuring remain undetermined.

While globally large, JBS has a relatively short history as a transnational corporation. It was established in 1953 by José Batista Sobrinho in Anápolis, Goiás, Brazil and named after the initials of the full name of its founder, JBS (Blankfeld 2011). José Batista Sobrinho worked as a rancher and took advantage of the 1956 establishment of the new capital of Brazil, Brasilia, that was located only 200 kilometers (125 miles) away from his ranch. The proximity to this growing market gave him the opportunity to expand his beef production by supplying butchers and restaurants of this newly established metropolitan area (Barreto 2007). Yet, for many years, JBS remained a "one man show" with José slaughtering only a few heads of cattle a day. In 1968, he bought a slaughterhouse that allowed him to slaughter 100 heads of cattle daily with some additional acquisitions in the following years that brought the number of heads slaughtered to 500 (Barreto 2007; Blankfeld 2011). As the business grew so did the family, and José Batista Sobrinho's three boys, José, Wesley, and Joesley, became involved in the company as soon as they finished high school (Blankfeld 2011). In the 1980s and 1990s, while marked, JBS's growth did not transcend the national scope as it acquired a few Brazilian companies that despite this, secured its presence in the domestic beef market (Blankfeld 2011). The eldest of Sobrinho's three sons, José, oversaw this early development as he led the company for 20 years after his father retired in 1985. But in 2005, he left JBS to pursue a career in politics that, however, never took off. Despite these events, José remained on the company's board of directors along with his three sisters—Vanessa, Vivianne, and Valere—and the father José, who while technically retired, continued to advise his sons on business matters (Blankfeld 2011). José's two brothers, Wesley and Joesley, took control of the company in 2005 and led its global expansion that rapidly evolved after the 2007 acquisition of Swift & Company. The same year, Wesley became the CEO of JBS USA and moved from his native Brazil to Greeley, Colorado, where the headquarters of JBS USA were located. Joesley remained in Brazil as JBS's CEO and took control of the company's finance division. In 2011, Wesley left the United States and relocated to São Paulo to become JBS's new CEO while Joesley was named the company chairperson. Don Jackson, formerly in charge of the reorganization of Pilgrim's Prime, took over the duties of CEO of JBS USA. This division of labor characterized the management of the company until May 2017. At that time, Joesley resigned from his chair position, leaving Wesley as the CEO of the company (Runyon 2017). By 2017, the company was engulfed in financial and legal problems. Following charges of corruption, both Wesley and José were arrested on September 13, 2017, and remain in custody at the time of writing this chapter. This situation prompted the Board of Directors of JBS to name the company founder, José Batista Sobrinho, CEO of JBS a few days later on September 17, 2017.

BNDES

Despite its continuous growth, by 2005, JBS was still a relatively unknown family-run Brazilian company whose business was primarily domestic (Blankfeld 2011). Plans were drawn to expand to adjacent Latin American countries and, for this purpose, JBS acquired Swift Armour S.A., the largest beef producer in Argentina in 2005. Yet, no other international acquisitions took place until 2007. In that year, a significant change occurred that, promoted by the assistance of the Brazilian state-controlled Economic and Social Development Bank (BNDES), formerly the Brazilian Economic Development Bank (BNDE) (BNDES 2017a), propelled JBS to its status as a large agri-food transnational corporation. In effect, the support of BNDES was the primary reason for the explosive growth of JBS in the 2010s. Simultaneously, however, it represents one of the factors that would engender the most significant crisis of the company's history in 2017.

Established in 1952 with the objective of promoting economic development, in 1971 this state agency was transformed into a state-owned company in order to have "more flexibility to raise and invest funds . . . [and] less political interference (BNDES 2017b: no page number). During the first two decades of its existence, BNDES operated primarily in agriculture through the financing of farming and ranching activities, the support of mid-sized operations, and the creation of infrastructure (BNDES 2017b). In the 1970s, sharing the then-popular import substitution policy and the idea that industrialization signified economic development, BNDES was active in the development of the industrialization of Brazil and the creation of companies in the manufacturing sector. Surviving drastic political changes in the governing of the country, BNDES's support of import substitution policies involved investment in consumer goods firms along with the backing of initiatives for the development of information technology and microelectronics. In the same decade, the then BNDE established a subsidiary to operate directly in the financial market which transformed it into a major financial actor in the Brazilian economic panorama.

At the outset of the 1980s, the bank took its current name of the Brazilian Economic and Social Development Bank to stress its commitment to not only economic growth, but also social development. Its current mission statement reflects this pronouncement as it states that BNDES wants "to foster sustainable and competitive development in the Brazilian economy, generating employment while reducing social and regional inequalities" (BNDES 2017a: no page number). This commitment continued in the following decades and, by the 1990s, projects to reduce social inequality and protect the environment received formal attention. Additionally, investments that promoted Brazilian culture and history were declared relevant as well (BNDES 2017a). Named as a bank, BNDES is not a commercial bank for it does not accept deposits nor does it perform many of the operations customarily associated with a bank (Cardim de Carvalho 2013). Additionally, it does not have private shareholders, as the Brazilian State fully owns it. Its budget, therefore, is derived from public funds that the Brazilian government makes available to it. To be sure, over the years, BNDES has accumulated its own capital and it is required to exercise compulsory savings. Yet, most of its money comes from the Brazilian Treasury that also intervenes in case of crises such as those experienced in 2008–2009 and beyond. Similarly, its directors are political appointees selected by the Brazilian president (Cardim de Carvalho 2013). Some argued that this organization is not linked to party politics and that both President Lula and President Dilma Rousseff used nominations prudently. However, other observers concurred with the statement that: "[f]or years, different administrations used the bank to lend money at low interest rates to businessmen with close ties to the sitting government" (Biller 2017: No page number; Cardim de Carvalho 2013). In support of this latest position, in May of 2017, President Temer, de facto, ousted the then BNDES president, Maria Silvia Bastos. This move was justified on grounds that her attempts to alter the long-standing bank policy that favored economic elites was opposed by the business community (Biller 2017). Quickly, Temer appointed as president of BNDES the economist Paulo Rabello de Castro, a graduate of the University of Chicago and a student of Milton Friedman, whose support for neoliberal economics is well known.

These achievements notwithstanding, the actions of the bank are widely criticized. One type of criticism refers to the bank's overt support of large corporations and their transformation into transnational corporations (Nunes Costa, Bravo, Borin and Pereira Filho 2017). Most developmental banks around the world serve small- and medium-size businesses. BNDES, instead, operates primarily with large companies, such as JBS, and promotes these companies' acquisitions of foreign firms and the establishment of plants in countries other than Brazil (Cardim de Carvalho 2013). More relevant for the discussion at hand is the related criticism that President Lula actively promoted this strategy during his administration (Cardim de Carvalho 2013). Specifically, the Lula Administration initiated the Productive Development Program with the stated objective of transforming national companies into transnational corporations. These companies were commonly referred to as "national champions," and their expansion was justified as a tool to engender socio-economic development (Nunes Costa et al. 2017). Moreover, this justification included the argument that state direct investments were necessary due to the lack of private capital in Brazil. In advanced countries of the North, companies could access private capital and through its availability finance their business activities. Lacking an effective private market for capital, the Brazilian State was compelled to intervene and support domestic companies by promoting their investments and business activities (Cardim de Carvalho 2013). As this position of the Brazilian State fits the logic of increasing profitability for these companies and dividends for their shareholders, the criticism remains of how it improves the well-being of Brazilian communities, curbs unemployment, reduces social inequality, and ultimately generates socio-economic development (Nunes Costa et al. 2017).

Germane to the above is the observation that BNDES' activities are highly concentrated and, therefore, benefit only a few companies (Torres and Góes 2013; Contantino 2017). Torres and Góes (2013) report that according to a 2013 study, oil and gas, mining, and power industries received about 54 percent of BNDES's investments in 2002. Ten years later, in 2012, this quota jumped to 75 percent. Additionally, by including the food and pulp and paper sectors to this list of industries, the 2012 quantity of BNDES' investments devoted to this small group of industries reached almost 90 percent. In monetary terms, this process indicates that 66.3 billion reals [or 21.4 billion USD in 2012 reals] of the 74.5 billion reals [or 24 billion USD] invested by the bank went to members of these industries. The rest of the industries operating in the Brazilian economy received 8.2 billion reals in total. Given the fact that BNDES finances almost exclusively large companies, the charge that BNDES acts like the financial institution of a small elite of enterprises remains particularly relevant.

Another type of criticism refers to claims that developmental programs supported by BNDES damage the environment and the well-being of local communities and indigenous people. In this regard, NGOs, pro-environmental organizations and local indigenous groups contend that, over the past two decades, the bank has operated in ways that go against its stated objectives. One such case is the funding of the construction of the Belo Monte dam. Some of the charges related to this project indicate that it created the dislocation of more than 40,000 local residents, involved the reduction of biodiversity in the region, promoted the destruction of land and bodies of water used by local communities, and when local residents protested its construction, their actions were violently repressed by police (Brandford 2016). The entire project was also charged with limited technical and financial viability as the high economic, social, and environmental costs could never be compensated by the quite limited amount of electricity generated by the dam. Last but not least, the financing of the project involved episodes of corruption as members of the then PT government received payment to allow the massive BNDES financing of the process to take place (Brandford 2016).

The Global Expansion of JBS

2007 represents a pivotal year for the transformation of JBS into a major transnational corporation. Supported by BNDES, that year JBS launched an IPO (Initial Public Offering) in the Brazilian stock exchange and became a public company traded in the BOVESPA. Simultaneously, it received 390 million USD from BNDES (Blankfeld 2011). With these funds, JBS acquired Swift & Company, the third largest US beef and pork processor, for 225 million USD (Runyon 2017). After the acquisition, Swift & Company was renamed JBS USA and remains one of the most lucrative units of JBS, propelled by the expansion of the beef business in North America (Mano 2017). Under the new ownership, Swift & Company, however, underwent a significant restructuring based on JBS's evaluation that its poor management significantly hampered the potential for growth (Blankfeld 2011). This acquisition allowed JBS to enter the pork meat market and obtain control of a number of beef and pork processing plants not only in the US but also in Australia. At the time, it was estimated that JBS acquired the ability to slaughter more than 51 thousand heads of cattle per day (Blankfeld 2011). Additionally, this acquisition permitted JBS to follow the action of other transnational corporations and bypass nation-state regulations, such as in the case of the June 2017 US ban on Brazilian beef. Imports of Brazilian fresh beef were halted for sanitary reasons (Polansek 2017). However, JBS continued to export to the United States taking advantage of its international subsidiaries.

In 2008, JBS acquired the beef business of Smithfield Foods, a major US meat packing company that employs more than 52,000 workers in plants located in North America and Europe (Smithfield 2017). Like in the case of Swift & Company, the acquisition of Smithfield Foods was accompanied by the renaming of the company to JBS Packerland. In September 2009, JBS consolidated its position in the Brazilian and world beef market by acquiring the Grupo Bertin, a leading Brazilian beef processor. At the time of the acquisition, Grupo Bertin was experiencing a financial crisis that allowed JBS access to this company's stocks at a highly discounted price. In 2016 and because of the discounted price paid for it, this acquisition became the subject of a criminal investigation by the Brazilian government (see below) (Reuters Staff 2016). On the same day of the Grupo Bertin acquisition, JBS announced the acquisition of the American company Pilgrim's Pride that signaled JBS's entry into the chicken meat market (ABC News 2009). Even in this case, this acquisition was supported by BNDES and based on Pilgrim's Pride financial difficulties. In effect, on December 1, 2008, Pilgrim's Pride, the large US chicken producer, filed for Chapter 11 bankruptcy (Associated Press 2008). This filing was the result of a misguided expansionist strategy that included the acquisition of the rival Gold Kist in 2007, the concomitant increase of the price of feed and, ultimately, overproduction (Associated Press 2008). By 2007, Pilgrim's Pride's total assets were estimated at 3.75 billion USD with 2.72 billion USD in debts. While the bankruptcy was described as a part of a process of restructuring, the financial weakness of the company was evident. In the original bid, JBS acquired 64 percent of the company. However, only one year later, it increased its control to 75.3 percent (Mano 2017). As in other instances, after the acquisition, the company was renamed to Pilgrim's.

This powerful entry into the poultry sector was the first of a number of additional acquisitions in the Americas. In July 2014, Pilgrim's announced a bid to acquire *Tyson de México*, one of the three largest producers of chicken meat in that country (Gyton 2015). One year later, after receiving approval from the Mexican anti-trust commission (The Federal Economic Competition Commission), the vertically integrated 400 million USD company was acquired positioning Pilgrim's to be the second largest supplier of poultry products in the growing Mexican market. Simultaneously, JBS foods acquired Tyson operations in Brazil, *Tyson de Brasil*. This company controlled three integrated production plants in the states of Santa Catarina and Parana and employed more than 5,000 workers. Also, in this case, the purchase was made official after it received regulatory approval from the Brazilian government. In the United States, JBS acquired Cargill Meat's pork business: Cargill Pork (Ryan 2015). With the purchase, JBS obtained two meat processing plants in the pork division of Cargill for 1.45 billion USD in 2015 located in the US Midwest and five feed mills located in the Midwest and also in the Southwest. At the time, the estimated revenue generated by these plants exceeded 6 billion USD with a production capacity of over two million pounds of bacon per week (Ryan 2015). In 2014, a bid to acquire Hillshire Brands, formerly Sara Lee, failed as the company was acquired by rival Tyson Foods.

The state-supported growth of JBS was justified not only in economic terms but also from a social point of view. The state's strategy to legitimize its intervention in the global economy remained constantly linked to the issue of local development (Cardim de Carvalho 2013). However, analyses of the specific consequences of JBS acquisitions of facilities in various parts of the world indicate that it followed practices of global sourcing and subcontracting that rely on precarious and poorly paid employment (Aboites, Bonanno, Constance, and Martinez 2014). Additionally, as in the case of the beef and poultry industry, the negative impacts on the environment, labor, and communities of this type of production are well documented (Martinez, Constance, Aboites, Sosa, and Almanza 2016; Constance 2016).

Charges of Corruption and Crisis

Fueled by the financial support of BNDES, the expansion of JBS appears to be one of the success stories of the corporate world in the neoliberal global economy. However, 2017 marked the beginning of a financial, ethical, and economic crisis that, at the time of writing this chapter, is not yet resolved. The crisis is linked to the wave of scandals that have affected JBS's home country of Brazil in recent years. Symbolized by the "Car Wash" (*Lava Jato*) and the Joy Train (*o Trem da Alegria*) scandals, corruption probes have characterized the recent political and judiciary events in Brazil. In the case of JBS, there are at least three types of accusations of corruption. The first type of charges refers to allegations of corruption in connection to the original

BNDES investment that propelled JBS's global expansion (Runyon 2017). In May 2017, the government of Brazil indicated that JBS received illegal financial benefits from BNDES. Because of this irregular financing, BNDES lost about 385 million USD of public taxpayer money. As the investigation continued, the Batista brothers denied these accusations (Runyon 2007). In August 2017, BNDES sued JBS, alleging mismanagement by the Batista brothers (Mano 2017).

The second type of corruption involves a continuous wave of bribes paid to politicians and government officials over an extended period. In particular, JBS, through its financial holding J&F Investimentos, was accused of paying bribes to the last three Brazilian presidents, Lula, Rouseff, and Temer, and a significant number of congresspersons and federal and state officials (Pearson and Magalhaes 2017). In addition, Joesley Batista confessed to paying bribes to these three presidents totaling more than 125 million USD over a fourteen-year period (Pearson and Magalhaes 2017). In return for this admission and payment of 3.4 billion USD to the government to be carried out by J&F Investimentos, the Batista brothers asked for immunity for these charges. Such an agreement between the Batista brothers and federal prosecutors was allegedly signed in May 2017 (Mano 2017). President Temer, as well as former Presidents Lula and Rouseff, denied these accusations (Runyon 2017). In February 2016, it was reported that JBS's acquisition of the Bertin Group involved fraud stemming from unpaid taxes associated with the undervaluing of the assets of the Bertin Group (Reuters Staff 2016).

The third type of corruption refers to the alleged bribing of health officials in charge of inspecting beef. In a strong anti-corruption operation known as "Weak Beef" (*Carne Fraca*), federal police raided a number of meat processors, including JBS, and discovered that they regularly paid meat inspectors to overlook safety violations (Runyon 2017). This wave of scandals prompted JBS to retain legal firms in Brazil and the United States. In addition, it affected the business side of JBS and prompted a restructuring of the company. As mentioned above, Joesley resigned as the company chairperson. Moreover, a number of assets in Brazil and also in the United States were placed on sale. According to some observations, this action was aimed at raising capital to pay for the mounting legal problems (Runyon 2017). Official press releases from JBS, however, contended that this restructuring would allow the company to focus on food processing and production and become more efficient (Runyon 2017). As net income reported, the end of the second quarter of 2017 showed a significant year-to-year decline and gross earnings increased as a result of the expansion of the beef sector in the United States (Runyon 2017). Arguably, the crisis engendered by the corruption charges will continue to affect the company for years to come, yet it is equally undeniable that the intervention of the Brazilian State created a very resilient large transnational corporation.

ANALYSIS

The research question proposed by this chapter refers to the issue of whether or not the new form of state capitalism experimented in Brazil leads to a type of emancipatory socio-economic development that benefits the working and middle classes and the poor. This type of emancipatory development is in line with the programmatic pronouncements of the PT and its recent leaders Lula and Dilma. The state support of JBS is employed as a case study to probe the nature of the new state capitalism. Given this research question, the analysis of the case study proposes three basic points that, however, cast doubt on the emancipatory character of state capitalism and stress its problematic nature. The adopted techniques of *analytic induction* and *negative cases* validate the analysis and its findings. Analytic induction refers to the acceptance of conclusions that logically fit the conditions that characterized the case. Simultaneously, it calls for the exclusion of pronouncements that are incompatible with the conditions determined by the events of the case study. Negative cases refer to the search for items with the case study that run counter to the hypothesized conclusions (Pascale 2011).

The first point consists of the fact that *the growth of JBS as a global company was possible because of the financial support that it received from BNDES*. For a number of years, JBS remained a regional company that prospered because of its geographical proximity with Brasilia. While this growth continued through the acquisition of a number of domestic companies, it, however, did not allow the company to transcend its national status. In the early 2000s, JBS planned to expand internationally. However, such an expansion involved exclusively the acquisition of a company in the neighboring country Argentina while additional steps did not materialize due to the lack of additional capital. In 2007, BENDES made this additional capital available as part of the Brazilian State strategy to foster development. Ultimately, this intervention led to the establishment of a transnational corporation as it permitted the transformation of JBS into a global leader in the agri-food sector.

The second point refers to the fact that while *BNDES' intervention to promote the global expansion of JBS was justified publically as part of the Lula Administration plan to promote socio-economic development, the primary result of this intervention was the expansion of JBS*. Almost since its inception, BNDES favored the financing of companies that were either already large and/or had plans to expand at the international level. While early on it supported infrastructure building that benefited an array of companies, BNDES rarely financed projects that involved small and medium enterprises. Additionally, its intervention has been concentrated in a handful of sectors that have significant influence at the political level. The support of companies with plans to expand globally continued under the PT administration that justified it through the argument that the State needs to assist these companies by compensating for the lack of private investment funds that characterize Brazil. Simultaneously, however, the Lula Administration subscribed to this strategy as a way to promote socio-economic development as it equated the support of large corporations with the creation of employment and local development. The Dilma Administration held the same position. While JBS expanded and validated the policy that state support can create transnational companies, development was confined to profit creation. The ways in which JBS operated domestically and internationally in terms of job creation, stable and justly remunerated employment, and the safeguard of the environment followed established corporate trends. These trends point out to the necessary insertion of the company into global circuits of production and consumption, the creation of precarious and poorly paid jobs, subcontracting, and limited respect for the protection of the environment. In essence, state capitalism favored the expansion of a global company with mostly negative consequences vis-a-vis employment, the overall economic conditions of the areas involved, and the protection of the environment.

The third and final point refers *to the lack of transparency that characterized the relationship between state intervention and JBS*. In particular and despite continuous pronouncements from the PT of greater government transparency and honesty, the relationship between BNDES and JBS emerged in an instance of widespread corruption. Lula has vigorously denied any wrongdoing and defined the admissions of guilt by the Batista brothers as a fabrication. Yet, the existence of bribes paid to officials of the State in a number of instances is undeniable. In essence, the policy of development based on state intervention has been impotent against corruption. As corruption per se is not a topic discussed in this chapter, it is relevant to point out that, in the case of Brazil, it continues to characterize the interaction between the polity and the economy. Additionally, the new phase of state capitalism has not been able to alter it, indicating the limits of the "alternative" stressed by pronouncements of the government and the PT.

CONCLUSIONS

The issue of state capitalism as an instrument for the achievement of substantive socio-economic development remains important. The analysis of the case of JBS and the support that it received from the Brazilian State elucidate at least three problematic aspects of this intervention. One of these aspects is economic, the second is ethical and political, while the third is strictly sociological. Economically, the intervention of the State created a large global company that pursued an ambitious expansionist strategy. It entered global circuits of production and employed established corporate strategies for the maximization of profit and the strengthening of its market share. These strategies involved global sourcing, capital hypermobility, subcontracting, and the acquisitions of companies weakened by negative economic outcomes. In this context, JBS operated as an efficient transnational corporation. However, it did little to act according to an agenda that would generate socio-economic development and contribute to the betterment of the conditions of the poor and the working and middle classes. At best, this posture followed the neoliberal theory of trickledown economics that contemplates the creation of profit that would eventually filter downward to the benefit of the lower classes. This outcome has rarely occurred historically as the growth of economic inequality is the most common result of its application (Langman and Smith 2018).

The State created an unscrupulous company that employed corruption as one of its most frequent tactics to achieve its strategic objectives. Accordingly, the State created an immoral company out of the investment of public money that was supposed to enhance the well-being of the Brazilian population. Additionally, rather than representing an alternative to past failed experiences of socio-economic development, it reproduced these experiences, despite the fact that this new type of intervention of the State was promoted by PT administrations that made the alternative to the status quo one of the most distinctive aspects of their programs. This specific outcome cast doubt on views that see programs of socio-economic development and ethical postures about the growth of society as political rather than structural matters.

Sociologically, state intervention has frequently been employed as a tool to maintain system stability. This has particularly been the case as system-destabilizing crises are either not corrected by the free functioning of the market or are expressions of the contradictions of the system itself. State intervention, in other words, is an instrument to avoid prolonged periods of socio-economic instability. The new type of state capitalism promoted by the Brazilian government is particularly problematic from the point of view of system stability because it adds economic, social, and political instability. It does not promote economic development relevant to the majority of the national population. It does not generate conditions that are conducive to social harmony. And it does not provide a model of social value that could enhance cohesiveness in society. In essence, it is a destabilizing factor.

The conclusion that is reached in response to this chapter's research question is that state capitalism as a tool to promote emancipatory socio-economic development is not effective. This conclusion, however, does not endorse free market approaches. This is a solution that existing research has demonstrated as being equally problematic. Conversely, it suggests that state intervention should be directed to objectives that are not simply related to the economic expansion of companies and their participation in global circuits of production. Following original pronouncements of the PT, it is in alternative patterns of development that emancipatory solutions to lack of development and crises can be found.

BIBLIOGRAPHY

ABC News. 2009. "Brazil's JBS Buys Majority Stake in Pilgrim's Pride for $800M." https://abcnews.go.com/Business/brazils-jbs-buys-majority-stake-pilgrims-pride-800m/story?id=8591393. Accessed October 10, 2009.

Aboites Manrique, Gilberto, Alessandro Bonanno, Douglas H. Constance, and Francisco Martinez Gomez. 2014. "Patrones de Organizacion Flexible: El Caso de la Avicultura." In David Castro Lugo and Reyna Elizabeth Rodriquez Perez (Eds.), *El Mercado Laboral Frente a las Transformaciones Economicas de Mexico* (pp. 47–70). Mexico City: Plaza y Valdes.

Aglietta, Michel. 1979. *A Theory of Capitalist Regulation: The US Experience*. London: Verso.

Agri-Pulse Staff. 2014. "Tyson Foods Sells Mexico, Brazil Units to JBS Subsidiaries." *Agri-Pulse*, July 28. https://www.agri-pulse.com/articles/4255-tyson-foods-sells-mexico-brazil-units-to-jbs-subsidiaries.

Amatori, Franco. 2017. "The Fascist Regime and Big Business: The Fiat and Montecatini Cases." In James Harold and Jakob Tanner (Eds.), *Enterprises in the Period of Fascist Europe* (pp. 62–77). New York: Routledge.

Arestis, Philip, and Alfred Saad-Filho (Eds.). 2008. *Political Economy of Brazil*. New York: Palgrave-Macmillan.

Associated Press. 2008. "Pilgrim's Pride Files for Bankruptcy." *The Street*, December 1. https://www.thestreet.com/story/10450631/1/pilgrims-pride-files-for-bankruptcy.html.

Baer, Werner. 2008. *The Brazilian Economy Growth and Development*. Knoxville: University of Tennessee Press.

Barreto, Elzio. 2007. "Brazil's JBS-Friboi to Buy Swift for US$ 225 mil." *Reuters*, May 29. https://www.reuters.com/article/us-swift-friboi-idUSN2930167420070529.

Bieber, Judy. 1999. *Power, Patronage, and Political Violence: State Building on a Brazilian Frontier, 1822–1889*. Lincoln: University of Nebraska Press.

Biller, David. 2017. "Brazil's Iron Lady Resigns as Head of BNDES Development Bank." https://www.bloomberg.com/news/articles/2017-05-26/brazil-s-iron-lady-resigns-as-head-of-bndes-development-bank. May 26.

Blankfeld, Keren. 2011. "JBS: The Sorry behind the World's Biggest Meat Producers." *Forbes*, April 21. https://www.forbes.com/sites/kerenblankfeld/2011/04/21/jbs-the-story-behind-the-worlds-biggest-meat-producer/#1077c6c47e82.

BNDES. 2017a. "Mission, Vision and Values." The Brazilian Development Bank. https://www.bndes.gov.br/SiteBNDES/bndes/bndes_en/Institucional/The_BNDES/mission.html. Accessed August 19, 2016.

BNDES. 2017b. "History." The Brazilian Development Bank. https://www.bndes.gov.br/SiteBNDES/bndes/bndes_en/Institucional/The_BNDES/history.html. Accessed August 19, 2016.

Bonanno, Alessandro. 2017. *The Legitimation Crisis of Neoliberalism*. New York: Palgrave-Macmillan.

Brandford, Sue. 2016. "BEDES Funded Belo Monte Dam—A Mega-Project with Mega-Problems." *Mongabay*, March 16. https://news.mongabay.com/2016/03/bndes-funded-belo-monte-dam-a-mega-project-with-mega-problems/.

Bremmer, Ian. 2010. *The End of the Free Market: Who Wins the War between States and Corporations?* New York: Penguin.

Cardim de Carvalho, Fernando J. 2013. "Public-Sector Bank Relative Insulation." January 23, Development and Cooperation. https://www.dandc.eu/en/article/brazils-state-owned-development-bank-bndes-probably-more-powerful-many-countrys-federal.

Carneiro does Reis, Márcio. 2018. "Reflecting on Counter-Hegemonic Strategies of Food and Nutritional Security: Notes on the Brazilian Case." In Alessandro Bonanno and Steven Wolf

(Eds.). *Resistance to the Neoliberal Agri-Food Regime: A Critical Analysis* (pp. 95–105). New York: Routledge.

Constance, Douglas H. 2016. "La Industria Avicola: Un Modelo de Globalacion, Neoliberalismo, y Acumulacion Flexible." In Lorenzo Alejandro Lopez y Francisco Martinez (Eds.), *Globalizacion y Agricultura: Neuvas Perspectivas en la Sociologia Rural* (pp. 41–48). Saltillo: D. R. Universidad Autonoma de Coahuila.

Constantino, Rodrigo. 2017. "Historiador Marco Antonio Villa Rebate Presidente do BNDES e Defende: Banco Merece una Auditoria Externa." July 15, Gazeta Do Povo. https://www.gazetadopovo.com.br/rodrigo-constantino/artigos/historiador-marco-antonio-villa-rebate-presidente-bndes-e-defende-banco-merece-uma-auditoria-externa/.

Crouch, Collin. 2011. *The Strange Non-Death of Neoliberalism*. Cambridge: Polity Press.

Fishlow, Albert. 2001. *Starting Over: Brazil since 1985*. Washington, DC: Brookings Institution Press.

Friedman, Milton. 1982 [1962]. *Capitalism and Freedom*. Chicago: University of Chicago Press.

Galeano, Eduardo. 1997. *Open Veins of Latin America: Five Centuries of the Pillage of a Continent*. New York: Monthly Review Press.

Gerschenkron, Alexander. 1962. Economic Backwardness in Historical Perspective. Cambridge, MA: Harvard University Press.

Gyton, Georgi. 2015. "Tyson de México Approved for Pilgrim's Pride Acquisition." June 2, *Global Meat*. https://www.globalmeatnews.com/Article/2015/06/02/Tyson-de-Mexico-approved-for-Pilgrim-s-Pride-acquisition.

Haddad, Monica. 2009. "A Spatial Analysis of 'Bolsa Familia' Is Allocation Targeting the Needy." In Joseph L. Love and Werner Baer (Eds.), *Brazil under Lula* (pp. 187–207). New York: Palgrave-Macmillan.

Harold, James, and Jakob Tanner (Eds.). 2017. *Enterprises in the Period of Fascist Europe*. New York: Routledge.

Harvey, David. 1990. *The Condition of Postmodernity*. New York: Blackwell.

JBS. 2017. "About JBS." JBS company website. http://jbs.com.br/sobre/. Accessed May 17, 2017.

J&F Investimentos. 2017. Company website. http://jfinvest.com.br/. Accessed May 17, 2017.

Kerr, Gordon. 2014. *A Short History of Brazil: From Colonial Peoples to the Modern Economy*. Harpenden: Oldcastle Books.

Kirkendall, Andrew. 2002. *Class Mates: Male Student Culture and the Making of a Political Class in Nineteenth-Century Brazil*. Lincoln: University of Nebraska Press.

Kurlantzick, Joshua. 2016. *State Capitalism: How the Return of Statism is Transforming the World*. Oxford: Oxford University Press.

Lazzarato, Maurizio. 2013. *Governing by Dept*. South Pasadena, CA: Semiotext(e).

Little, Walter, and Eduardo Posada-Carbó (Eds.). 1996. *Political Corruption in Europe and Latin America*. New York: Palgrave-Macmillan.

Langman, Lauren, and David A. Smith. 2018. *Twenty-First Century Inequality and Capitalism: Piketty, Marx, and Beyond*. Leiden and Boston: Brill.

Mano, Ana 2017. "JBS seeks U.S. Units IPO as Brazil Presses for CEO's Ouster." *Reuters* August 15, 2017. Online document retrieved at https://finance.yahoo.com/news/jbs-seeks-u-unit-ipo-001825012.html.

Martinez, Francisco, Douglas H. Constance, Gilberto Aboites Manrique, Cristina Sosa Zepeda, and Jonathan J. Almanza Hernandez. 2016. "El Sur va al Norte: La Expansion de las Empresas Avicolas de Paises Emergentes (Mexico y Brasil) hacia los Estados Unidos." In Luis Gutierrez Flores and Vicente German Soto (Eds.), *Perspectivas y Retors Actuales de la Innovacion en Mexico: Regiones, Sectores y Empresa* (pp. 215–254). Mexico City: Plaza y Valdez.

Mirowski, Philip. 2014. *Never Let a Serious Crisis Go to Waste*. London. Verso.

Mueller, Bernardo and André Rossi de Oliveira. 2009. "Regulation during the Lula Government." In Joseph Love and Werner Baer (Eds.), *Brazil under Lula* (pp. 93–114). New York: Palgrave-Macmillan.

Musacchio, Aldo, and Sergio G. Lazzarini. 2014. *Reinventing State Capitalism*. Cambridge, MA: Harvard University Press.

Nunes Costa Maria Alice, Licia Bravo, Elaine Borin, and José Eduardo Pereira Filho. 2017. "Corporate Social (Ir)responsibility in Brazil: Companies, Power and Ties Intertwined." In Lina M. Gómez, Lucely Vargas-Preciado, and David Growther (Eds.), *Corporate Social Responsibility and Corporate Governance. Concepts, Perspectives and Emerging Trends in Ibero-America* (pp. 297–316). Bingley, UK: Emerald.

Nylen, William. 2000. "The Making of a Loyal Opposition: The Workers' Party (PT) and the Consolidation of Democracy in Brazil." In Peter Kingstone and Timothy J. Power (Eds.), *Democratic Brazil: Actors, Institutions, and Processes* (pp. 126–143). Pittsburgh: University of Pittsburgh Press.

Pascale, Celine-Marie. 2011. *Cartographies of Knowledge*. Los Angeles: Sage.

Paulani, Leda Maria. 2008. "The Real Meaning of the Economic Policy of Lula's Government." In Philip Arestis and Alfred Saad-Filho (Eds.), *Political Economy of Brazil* (pp. 42–54). New York: Palgrave-Macmillan.

Pearson, Samantha, and Magalhaes, Luciana. 2017. "Brazilian Bribery Allegations Escalate Clash between Government, Business." May 22, *The Wall Street Journal* May 22. https://www.wsj.com/articles/brazilian-bribery-allegations-escalate-clash-between-government-businesses-1495404513.

Piketty, Thomas. 2014. *Capital in the Twenty-First Century*. Translated by Arthur Goldhammer. Cambridge, MA: The Belknap Press of Harvard University.

Polansek, Tom. 2017. "U.S. Bans Fresh Brazil Beef Imports Over Safety Concerns." June 22, *Reuters*. https://www.reuters.com/article/us-usa-brazil-beef-idUSKBN19D2VE.

Reuters Staff. 2016. "Brazil Tax Agency Alleges Fraud in 2009 JBS-Bertin Merger." February 28, *Reuters*. https://www.reuters.com/article/jbs-merger-investigation-idUSL2N1670H3.

Runyon Luke. 2017. "JBS, World's Largest Meat Company, Mired in Multiple Corruption Scandals in Brazil." August 3, *Harvest Public Media*. August 3. https://www.harvestpublicmedia.org/post/jbs-worlds-largest-meat-company-mired-multiple-corruption-scandals-brazil.

Ryan, Chloe. 2015. "JBS USA Completes Cargill Pork Purchase." November 5, *Global Meat*. https://www.globalmeatnews.com/Article/2015/11/05/JBS-USA-completes-Cargill-Pork-purchase.

Saad-Filho, Alfred. 2008. "Neoliberalism, Democracy and Economic Policy in Brazil." In Philip Arestis and Alfred Saad-Filho (Eds.), *Political Economy of Brazil* (pp. 7–23). New York: Palgrave-Macmillan.

Smithfield Foods. 2017. "Our Operations." Smithfield Foods company website. https://www.smithfieldfoods.com/about-smithfield/our-operations. Accessed June 12, 2017.

Streeck, Wolfgang. 2017. "The Return of the Repressed as the Beginning of the End of Neoliberal Capitalism." In Heinrich Geiselberger (Ed.), *The Great Regression* (pp. 157–172). Malden, MA: Polity Press.

———. 2014. *Buying Time*. London: Verso.

Tarrow, Sydney. 2011. *Power in Movement: Social Movements and Contentious Politics*. Cambridge: Cambridge University Press.

Tennesse Valley Authority (TVA). 2017. "The 1930s." Tennessee Valley Authority website. https://www.tva.gov/About-TVA/Our-History/The-1930s. Accessed May 6, 2017.

Topik, Steven. 1987. *The Political Economy of the Brazilian State*. Austin: The University of Texas Press.

Torres, Fernando and Francisco Góes. 2013. "BNDESPAR Concentrates 89% of Its Investments in Five Industries." March 3, *Direito e Infraestrutura*. http://direitoeinfraestrutura.blogspot.com/2013/03/infrastructure-bndes-concentrates-89-of.html.

Trevisani, Paulo. 2017. "Brazil's JBS Says Legal Issues May Delay IPO of International Unit." May 16, *The Wall Street Journal*. https://www.wsj.com/articles/brazils-jbs-says-legal-issues-may-delay-ipo-of-international-unit-1494953638.

Chapter Two

From the Neoliberal to the Developmental State?

The Ambiguous Political Paradigm Shift in Brazil

Paulo Niederle and Catia Grisa

Since the early years of the new century, the implementation of agricultural and rural developmental policies in Brazil has attracted the attention of a number of emerging countries as they aimed to adopt the concepts and instruments that characterized these policies. Despite this attention, however, results often missed declared goals as country specific state structures affected outcomes. Accordingly, it is important to understand the political-institutional factors that allowed Brazil to produce such policies. This is particularly important in order to avoid the misconception made by those public policy analysts that claim the (in)-effectiveness of policies without considering their place in relation to the institutional arrangements that frame state action. In essence, what we are proposing is that policy analysis must effectively "bring the State back in" (Evans, Rueschemeyer, and Skocpol 1985).

Following Pierson (2016), we define the State as the specific arrangement of institutional devices that organizes a broad set of social and economic relations. The construction of this arrangement responds to an intricate interplay of forces involving multiple actors (e.g., individuals, groups, classes, social coalitions, and bureaucracy). Nonetheless, once established, these devices become relatively autonomous and form organizational structures, such as ministries, departments, and public authorities, that take a relatively independent position vis-à-vis other actors. However limited, this autonomy allows the production of new devices (laws, administrative regulations, technical routines and public policy instruments) that—depending on both state capabilities and political and economic contexts—impact the distribution of resources, shape the ability to deploy power on the part of pertinent actors and, recursively, affect the restructuring of the State itself (Evans 1995).

As a result, understanding the construction, design, and effects of agricultural and rural development policies compels us to consider not only the policies themselves but also the complex set of interactions within the State, such as those involving conflicts among different actors and the coexistence of institutional mechanisms that are contradictory to the very actions of these state actors. Simultaneously, it is critical to identify whether or not and how the institutional arrangements specific to each policy or sector align with those that organize state action in other sectors and for other policies. In other words, it is critical to identify the extent to which agricultural and rural developmental policies are coherent between themselves and between them and the other policies (monetary, fiscal, educational, etc.) that characterize state action.

One way of carrying out this analysis is to identify the level of cohesion of different policies in relation to the "political paradigm" that guides state action. According to Hall (1993), this concept seeks to capture the ideas, interpretations, and representations of the world that define a specific way of analyzing the nature of public problems and, simultaneously, justifying the political-institutional choices to address them. We understand the concept of political paradigm as a "structure of meanings" that integrates and legitimizes state action. The support of this structure depends, on the one hand, on the resources that social actors utilize to implement their ideas. On the other hand, it depends on the capacity of these actors to legitimize and institutionalize these ideas using those among them that are compatible with the values of the society in question. However, actors also modify these ideas by relying on instruments such as economic means, coercion, the media, and academic knowledge (Babb 2012).

At least two problems make this type of analysis difficult. The first refers to the fact that, unlike in Kuhn's normal science, two or more political paradigms may coexist in constant opposition within the same State. However, apart from moments of paradigmatic crisis, one of them remains dominant guiding the production of institutional devices and public policies. In turn, it is up to alternative paradigms to try to delegitimize this process and find weak spots in the structure of the State where they can promote the production of specific devices and policies. The second problem consists of the fact that however great the stability of a paradigm, it is often a more transient and contingent situation than one can imagine (Mahoney and Thelen 2009). As we will illustrate later, this problem is particularly evident in the Brazilian case, where, over the last few decades, state action has generated a series of "anomalies" (Surel 1995). Heightened by political struggles among pertinent social actors, these anomalies demanded adjustments in the dominant paradigm that, when failed, led to its replacement with new institutional arrangements.

The objective of this chapter is to analyze how the paradigm shift that has guided the actions of the Brazilian State over the last three decades affected agriculture and rural developmental policies. The central question driving the analysis is to probe how these policies fit the transition from the neoliberal paradigm prevailing in the 1990s to the dominant neo-developmental paradigm in the 2000s. In order to do so, we initially analyzed the characteristics of the neoliberal paradigm that informed the actions of the Fernando Henrique Cardoso government (1995–2002) concerning both agribusiness and family farming policies. These two sociopolitical categories were part of different coalitions that competed for the control of the State. Next, we discuss the changes introduced in these policies and in these coalitions—due to the rise of the neo-developmental paradigm that guided the Workers' Party (PT) governments of Luis Inácio Lula da Silva (Lula) (2003–2010) and Dilma Rousseff (2011–2016).

The conclusions show that the "anomalies" that promoted the paradigmatic changes were amplified by economic crises that affected the distribution of resources among actors and by political crises that put in check the legitimacy of the strategies adopted by the dominant coalitions following dominant paradigms. Additionally, new public problems emerged for which the dominant paradigms did not have satisfactory answers. On the contrary and to a significant extent, these problems were produced by the supposed solutions that these paradigms pursued. Finally, we show that, despite the apparent rupture that replacing the neoliberal paradigm with neo-developmentalism may suggest, it may be more appropriate to think of this process in terms of evolution or transition. In many respects, the neo-developmental paradigm of the PT governments was more in line with its neoliberal predecessor than with the early "developmental approach" employed from the 1940s to the 1970s (Mahoney and Thelen 2009).

THE NEOLIBERAL PARADIGM: REACTIVE POLICIES TO "MARKET FAILURES"

In Brazil, the 1980s marked the end of twenty years of military dictatorship (1964–1984). This event was shaped by the rise of social movements that pursued the establishment of a people-oriented democratic society whose primary expression was the adoption of the Federal Constitution of 1988. The so-called "Citizen Constitution" proposed the decentralization of governmental actions that included greater power to states and municipalities; the expansion of social participation; the recognition of social rights for workers; restrictions on the inflow of foreign capital; and the granting of more space for state-owned enterprises (Sallum Junior 2003). However, the worsening of the economy and political reactions of the Brazilian elite—which never had democracy as an irrevocable principle (Souza 2017)—translated into a situation in which a number of the constitutional mandates were never implemented. In effect, the dismantling of the state apparatus and workers' rights characterized the years following the adoption of the Constitution.

In the "narrative" disputes (Jones and Mcbeth 2010) about the causes of the crisis, the Brazilian elite, aligned with the global neoliberal wave, managed to legitimize the idea that the crisis was the result of the excessive intervention of the State that prevented economic growth. In this process, in 1989, state intervention increased the national debt to 54 percent of GDP (compared to 15.7 percent in 1964) and generated an inflation of 1,972 percent a year in the "cursed inheritance of the prevailing developmental paradigm." Conversely, the proposed "solution" was a set of economic adjustment plans adopted as anti-inflationary and stagnation instruments. These plans involved the privatization and/or elimination of public companies and agencies; the prioritization of monetary policies over fiscal policies; the attraction of foreign direct investment, and the improvement of the balance of payments that implied greater trade liberalization, market deregulation, and rising interest rates.

To implement these measures, the business and financial elite joined a new political coalition led by Fernando Collor de Melo, a presidential candidate who, in 1989, defeated Lula—the major trade union leader in the country—in one of the most intense presidential elections the nation had ever experienced. However, amid corruption scandals, economic problems, stagnant employment, declining wages, and an intense political polarization that had existed since the elections, a scenario of strong political tension emerged creating conditions that led to the impeachment of Collor de Melo in October of 1992. From then on, it was incumbent upon the country's Vice President, Itamar Franco, to enact reforms and control the political crisis. To this end, a broad center-right coalition government was formed under which the Minister of Finance, Fernando Henrique Cardoso, began to coordinate a new economic stabilization plan.

Launched in 1994, the Real Plan consisted of a shock of economic orthodoxy that unified the Brazilian elite and appealed to international investors. Its success in stabilizing the economy ensured Cardoso's electoral victory to his first presidential term (1995–1998), even though it occurred at the cost of increasing social inequality, the implementation of a rentier pattern of growth, and the dismissal of a number of constitutional principles. Backed by the reorientation of a number of leftist activists and intellectuals toward the so-called "third way," Cardoso, once a leading proponent of Dependency Theory, defined his "historical task" as "to eliminate a piece of our past that still clutters the present and slows the advancement of society. I refer to the legacy of the Vargas era, its model of autarchic development and its interventionist state" (Bastos 2012: 780).

Following a fundamentalist neoliberal position (Cardinal and Sallum Junior 2003), Cardoso adopted new adjustment policies. They featured the sudden revaluation of the new currency (one Brazilian Real was equated to one US Dollar), the reduction of customs tariffs, bilateral free trade agreements, a semi-fixed and overvalued exchange rate policy, the ending of restrictions on foreign capital inflows, tax exemptions for the export of commodities from the primary sector, and a broad privatization program. The principal result of these measures was the control of inflation that fell from 631.54 percent per year at the outset of 1995 to 9.56 percent by the end of 1996. However, and despite its magnitude, this was only a relative control of inflation as it remained volatile and its reduction was only possible due to the increase of interest rates. In 1995, the basic interest rate reached 60 percent per year. Accordingly, while they satisfied financial and rentier groups, including those that profited from the existing public debt, the actions of the neoliberal government worsened the conditions of the economy by engendering economic stagnation, prompting the crisis of the domestic production and increasing unemployment. In addition, trade liberalization exposed domestic industries, including farming to cheaper foreign competition engendering the rapid worsening of the balance of trade in the late 1990s.

In 1999 as economic instability continued, the Brazilian Central Bank devalued the Real and abandoned the previous system of semi-fixed exchange rates in favor of a new regime of free exchange rates. This move paved the way for the acceleration of inflation, an increase in interest rates and more fiscal pressure that resulted in forceful attacks against the neoliberal paradigm. These conditions further favored the emergence of a minority developmental current within the political coalition of the Cardoso government. According to Bastos (2012), this current championed a competitive exchange rate able to reconcile the stability of current transactions with the promotion of industrial growth. Named by Sallum Junior (2003: 45) a "developmental liberal" current, it proposed "addressing the negative consequences of the liberal orthodoxy for specific sectors of the economy while promoting the growth of productive activities in the country."

Taking advantage of the devalued currency and the necessity to improve the balance of trade, the exporting segment of agribusiness became one of the most relevant sectors of the new economic policy (Delgado 2012). The State expanded incentives to agribusiness through export-oriented monetary and fiscal policies, as well as infrastructure and financing programs. Agricultural credit resources, for example, went from 11.3 billion of Reals in 2001–2002 to 21.7 billion of Reals in the following year. In terms of infrastructure, in 2000, the primary action was the creation of the *Modernization Program for the Fleet of Agricultural Tractors and Associated Implements for Harvesters* (Moderfrota). Added to this were normative changes to increase the participation of the financial sector in agriculture (Delgado 2012).

The exports of primary sector products (such as minerals, oil, soybeans, and meats) increased, positively affecting the balance of trade that showed a surplus of US $7.2 billion in 2002 from a deficit of US $11.6 billion in 1995. Accordingly, legitimated by its economic success and supported by the government coalition, agribusiness broke away from the old image of the "archaic latifundia" to propose the image of the most dynamic sector of the country. It further revived the old theses of "export vocation" and "comparative advantages" that have been so sharply criticized by the Developmental and Dependentist theorists since the 1940s (Furtado 1961). With broad state support, agribusiness increased agricultural productivity, colonized new regions such as the Amazon and the Cerrado, made Brazil the world's largest consumer of agrochemicals, and contributed to the "re-primarization" of the Brazilian economy (Nogueira 2017).

The rapid growth of agribusiness during the Cardoso administration paralleled the creation of institutional arrangements and policies in support of family farming (e.g., the National Program for Strengthening Family Agriculture [PRONAF]), the struggle against poverty (e.g., Solidary Community, School Fund), and land reform (e.g., Land Bank, Ticket to the Land). Although at first glance the creation of these policies may seem contradictory to the neoliberal paradigm, in reality, it was functional to it. In addition to reducing growing social tensions, these policies followed the neoliberal tenet that the State should act not only to improve market performance (Bonanno 2017) but also to correct its "failures" (Williamson 1985); that is, it should carry out activities that are attractive to private investors.

With regard to the land reform, its implementation was the result of the strong mobilization carried out by the Landless (Sem Terra) Movement, one of the principal anti-neoliberalism social forces. By the mid-1990s, this resistance gained further support due to the national and international high levels of visibility prompted by the many acts of violence against farmers. Two events assumed particular importance in putting the issues of land reform and social justice on the public agenda. The first was the Corumbiara massacre where, in August 1995, sixteen farmers were killed by a militia formed by police officers. The second was the massacre of El Dourado dos Carajás, where in April 1996, nineteen farmers were murdered by members of the military police. These events exacerbated social tension and made the land reform a legitimate public problem for the Brazilian society. Under these conditions, the State was forced to act.

In the 1990s, the State began the implementation of land expropriation programs. The execution of these programs was favored by a sharp decrease in the price of land to the point that even landowners viewed them as "good business." In effect, the difference between the market price and the compensations paid by the State gave landowners a de-facto financial grant that they used to buy cheaper land in other regions of the country, increasing land concentration. Over time, though, the land reform policy was adjusted to the neoliberal paradigm as the concept of the "land market reform" gained in popularity (Pereira and Sauer 2011). In 1996, influenced by the World Bank, the government created the Cédula da Terra (Ticket to the Land) Program and, in 1998, the Banco da Terra (Land Bank) Program. Both provided subsidized credit for farmers to purchase land. Under the justification of appeasing social conflict, reducing poverty and promoting access to land, these programs weakened the land reform process.

In essence, during the neoliberal government, the actions of the Brazilian State concerning agriculture can be summarized in six points. 1) The State promoted macroeconomic policy adjustments that favored the export of agricultural commodities. 2) It introduced institutional innovations that boosted trade liberalization and foreign capital inflows, including those pertaining to the market for agricultural inputs. 3) It created infrastructure and implemented credit programs that boosted the productivity of agri-food export companies. This was particularly the case for soybean production that jumped from twenty-five to fifty million metric tons between 1995 and 2005. 4) The State introduced agricultural credit programs (such as PRONAF) that allowed market access to the most affluent family farmers. 5) It enacted social policies that mitigated the effects of poverty and 6) it promoted land reform policies that contained the escalation of conflicts over the ownership of land.

THE NEO-DEVELOPMENTAL PARADIGM: ACTIVE MARKET-BUILDING POLICIES

Despite the containment of inflation and the improvement of the balance of trade, neoliberalism was unable to generate policies that would engender economic growth and job creation. One of the clearest symptoms of this crisis was the fact that in the 2002 elections "no presidential candidate defended [neo]liberal fundamentalism. [. . .] On the other hand, the members of the opposition were attuned to the liberal-developmental ideas, despite the exaggerated nationalist rhetoric that characterized some of them (Sallum Junior 2003: 49). As in the case of other countries, this made "the legitimation crisis of neoliberalism" explicit (Bonanno 2017) and paved the way for the electoral victory of the center-left coalition led by Lula.

The creation of a new political coalition notwithstanding, this new administration displayed a great deal of continuity with the previous government. Arguably, the most important aspect of this continuity consists of an economic policy aligned with the previous administration's macroeconomic program. According to Sallum Junior and Goulart (2016: 126), this continuity was made explicit by the Lula government's concern with "monetary stability as a structuring action of governability." In other words, the containment of inflation, the generation of a financial surplus, and a floating exchange rate were the new government's choices to appease the financial sector and commodity exporters (Toni and Cerqueira 2017). The two-term appointment (2003–2007 and 2008–2012) of the former Bank of Boston chairperson Henrique Meirelles to the presidency of the Central Bank is a case in point.[1] These are some of the reasons that led Ban (2012:1) to conclude that during the PT years, the socioeconomic regime "was neither a local replica of the Washington Consensus, nor a revolutionary departure from it. Instead, evidence suggests that it is a hybrid made out of economically liberal policy goals and instruments associated with the [Washington] Consensus and policy goals and instruments that can be traced to the developmental tradition."

Because of this hybridism, there is no consensus in the literature about the paradigm designation that prevailed in the first decade of the new century. Some theorists have attempted to formulate a concept that captures the strong influence of neoliberal ideas on the emerging new paradigm. This is the case of Ban (2012) and Sallun Junior (2003) who use the expression "liberal-neo-developmentalism." Others adopted the term "post-neoliberal" to stress the emergence of a different new paradigm (Sader 2013; Pochmann 2013). However, the definitions that prevailed were "neo-developmentalism" and "social-developmentalism" (Matei 2013; Bresser-Pereira 2016; Sicsú, Paula, and Michel 2007).

Regardless of the name employed, the new government adopted a posture that stressed a greater concern with the status of the internal market, the expansion of state investments in infrastructure, and the growth of state credit for private investments. It further pursued the capitalization and internationalization of the public oil company (Petrobras) and the support of industrial competitiveness through tax exemptions to capital. All of the above was accompanied by measures designed to abate poverty through the implementation of income transfer and housing and food programs, initiatives directed at the reduction of unemployment and the augmentation of the national minimum wage, and efforts to promote access to basic services such as education and health. Yet, these policies were implemented under the condition that they would not affect the export of basic commodities, the trade balance, and private sector profits. On the contrary, the State continued to act as the fiduciary of private capital, guaranteeing, above all, the expansion of the financial sector and agribusiness.

While the first Lula government (2003–2006) was mainly concerned with guaranteeing "governmentality," in its second term (2007–2010) domestic economic and political stability and an international market featuring higher prices for agricultural commodities allowed the strengthening of state intervention. Beginning with this second term, the new Ministry of Finance coordinated by Guido Mantega—a heterodox economist aligned with neo-developmentalism—intensified public investments in infrastructure, innovation, science and technology. The State further granted credit for the expansion of investments, stimulated domestic consumption, raised wages, and augmented income transfer programs such as Bolsa Familia (grants to aid poor families) and Fome Zero (a food assistance program for low-income families) (Toni and Cerqueira 2017). These policies resulted in an increase in economic growth rates, the reduction of poverty, the expansion of the middle class, and the lowering of inflation. In effect, during this time, inflation reached its lowest historical level despite the concomitant reduction of interest rates and the consequent expansion of consumption. As a result, the government won not only wide social approval, but also the support of the business class who profited from the expansion of the domestic market and, within it, the retail and construction sectors in particular (Neri 2010).

The policies of the Lula government promoted a greater presence of Brazilian commodities in the international market. This situation engendered a "perverse facet of this neo-developmentalist 'success.'" Critics point out that it legitimized *neo-extractivism* as the mode of accumulation (Sampaio Junior 2012, Acosta 2016). According to Gudynas (2012), a "balancing State" emerged that, on the one hand, promoted a capitalism of dispossession and, on the other hand, used the resources gained from this model for social policy spending. According to Milanez and Santos (2013), this was the trajectory of the Brazilian State between 2002 and 2013. During this time, state action involved three practices. The first refers to the expansion of oil and gas extraction capacity through the growth of investments by Petrobrás that jumped from $7.4 billion in 2003 to $45 billion in 2013. Second, there was the sharp increase of the public financing of companies in the extractive sector. Between 2003 and 2013, BNDES (the Brazilian State development bank) sharply increased its allocation of funds for projects of oil exploration, mining, and energy that went from 54 percent to 75 percent of its total investments. This percentage, however, reaches more than 89 percent if investments in paper-cellulose and food firms are included. Finally, the use of natural resources was deregulated and tax exemptions for companies exporting semi-finished products and products from the primary sector were preserved.

It is important to approach the association between neo-extractivism and the "developmental State" in relative terms. In effect, the strategy of accumulation through the export of commodities from the primary sector also guided the neoliberal policies of the 1990s. However, in that case it did not generate the same results because the boom in global commodity prices was a phenomenon of the 2000s. It is a shared understanding that, in the last two decades, the Brazilian State promoted a strategy of economic development centered on the intensification of the exploitation of natural resources and its insertion in international markets through the export of low technological content products. One of the principal examples of this pattern comes from the mining industry. Between 2003 and 2011, the export of extracted metals jumped from $3.4 to $44 billion, making it the primary reason for the trade balance surplus. Beginning in 2013, this role has been taken up by soybeans, which account for about 40 percent of Brazilian commodity exports from the primary sector. This demand is driven by China that imports 57 percent of the total value exported by Brazil.

The major beneficiary of this accumulation model was the export agribusiness sector that was considered a fundamental component for the preservation of economic and political stability in the Lula and Roussef governments. As a result, both administrations gave in to the interests of the major groups in this sector, avoiding, for example, substantial institutional changes in the Ministry of Agriculture (MAPA) and keeping ministers in line with the dominant agrarian-export strategy. Accordingly, the State broadened the supply of rural credit, facilitated repayment conditions, increased resources for productive infrastructure and marketing logistics, subsidized new private financing instruments, widened the opening of agricultural markets for foreign investments, and maintained intact exemption policies for the export of products from the primary sector (Delgado 2012).

The innovation of the Lula and Roussef governments was the strengthening of the Ministry of Agrarian Development (MDA) that had been created in 1999 by the Cardoso government with the objectives of alleviating social tensions, managing land reform, and promoting family farming. However, this strengthening has never allowed the MDA to challenge the hegemony of MAPA, "the agribusiness ministry." This was the case despite the fact that MDA acted in ways that created barriers and constraints to the neoliberal agenda, including actions in the sphere of international negotiations where the Brazilian government displayed contradictory positions. Moreover, despite managing public policies for 4.3 million family farmers (85 percent of all rural establishments), the MDA budget was never greater than one-fourth of the MAPA budget. Finally, the MDA has always remained an unstable institution, susceptible to the effective political pressure of agribusiness interests.

Despite the above-mentioned financial and institutional weaknesses, MDA built a broad set of policies that favored family farming. These include availability of credit, agricultural insurance, technical assistance, rural extension, marketing support, territorial development, rural housing, poverty reduction, food security and more (Grisa and Schneider 2015). In general, it can be said that these policies responded to strategies that were at times complementary and at times contradictory. On the one hand, they accentuated the modernization of the more capitalized family farms. One of the principal references in this sense was PRONAF, whose resources were concentrated in the monoculture of export commodities such as corn, soy, and coffee (Grisa, Wesz Junior, and Buchweitz 2014). On the other hand, these policies reduced rural poverty and food insecurity with programs such as the Bolsa Família and Brasil Sem Miséria (Brazil Without Poverty), and territorial development policies (France, Marques, and Del Grossi 2016).

Over time, however, existing contradictions became increasingly evident. The progress achieved through the implementation of pro-family farming policies was accompanied by setbacks due to the strong growth of agribusiness. As an example, the extractivist model engendered a significant growth of land acquisitions that resulted in increases in the price of land. In addition to augmenting the opportunity costs for small farmers and rendering land expropriation difficult for the land reform, this situation intensified the exploitation of natural resources and exacerbated conflicts over farm and environmental issues. The most affected social groups were indigenous peoples and traditional communities; that is, the same paradigm that legitimized pro-family farming policies produced effects that endangered this sector's existence.

NEO-DEVELOPMENTAL STATE: FROM THEORY TO POLICIES

Like in the case of neoliberalism (Thelen 2014), there are different types of the developmental State (Chang 2002). According to Bresser-Pereira (2010), the common denominator of all the types of "Brazilian neo-developmentalism" lies in the pursuit of a "Third Discourse" that, as indicated above, remains situated between the "old developmentalism" of the 1930s to 1970s and the "economic orthodoxy" of the 1980s and 1990s. The former was nationalist and industrialist in nature, promoted sectoral policies, maintained rigid monetary exchange rates, and was complacent with fiscal deficits and inflation. The latter was globalist and monetarist in nature. It favored the creation of free exchange rates, high interest rates, and fiscal adjustments that promoted growth through the export of goods from the primary sector and foreign direct investment. However, it also contemplated the control of inflation, wage growth, and public spending. In economic terms, the core of this third discourse is overcoming the traditional opposition between a strong State and the free market. In political terms, it proposes a new social pact among the government, the business elite, and labor.

Between 2003 and 2016, the behavior of the PT government was in line with this "Third Discourse." It promoted policies that reignited its ability to save and invest, gradually reduced interest rates, allowed the partial control of the fiscal deficit while tolerating some moderate indebtedness, and stimulated productive investment and domestic consumption. These policies further generated a stable exchange rate that increased the competitiveness of domestic enterprises but did not compromise exports. Inflation was controlled without subordinating the entire economy to austerity measures and the parallel growth of wages and productivity generated a strong internal demand and permitted the redistribution of wealth (Bresser-Pereira 2010; Mattei 2013; Sicsú, Paula, and Michel 2005).

The hybrid nature of the neo-developmental approach is exemplified by differences between the Cardoso and Lula/Rousseff administrations. The Cardoso administration defended the autonomy of the Central Bank and its fundamental objective of rising interest rates to avoid inflationary bubbles. The Lula and Rousseff governments, conversely, directed the Central Bank—which remained under the control of neoliberal economists—to promote growth policies and control inflation. The PT governments, however, also acted to stabilize the balance of payments, flexibly regulate capital inflows—limiting FDI in key sectors such as land acquisitions and oil exploration—and intervene to control the exchange rate to stimulate specific strategic sectors, such as agro-export. The creation of a strong internal market promoted through wage growth and fiscal subsidies was further employed as a tool to reduce the vulnerability of the domestic economy to the volatility of international markets.

Agricultural and rural developmental policies conformed to the new approach. In the case of policies for the exporting agribusiness, there were no substantial changes, but a process of deepening of the trajectory initiated in the late 1990s. This trajectory was characterized by two events. First, macroeconomic conditions further facilitated the competitiveness of Brazilian agricultural commodities in international markets. Second, the increase in state and private investments (including FDI) allowed Brazilian agri-food companies to lead important global commodity chains such as those of soybeans, meats, and mining. However, significant moves were also made concerning policies for family agriculture. As these policies promoted the expansion of food production, they also stimulated the growth of the domestic market for machinery and equipment, reduced unemployment, and curbed hunger and poverty. In essence, the outcomes of the implementation of these policies stressed the social and redistributive component of neo-developmentalism.

Here we should note important differences between the actions of the neo-developmental State and the neoliberal State. While neoliberalism employed social and land reform programs as palliative measures to alleviate the perverse effects of structural adjustments (especially in regard to unemployment and recession) and reduce social tensions, neo-developmentalism transformed social policies into instruments for the redistribution of income, reduction of inequality, and productive inclusion. Accordingly, these policies had important economic effects, as they increased domestic consumption and boosted local economies. As far as the land reform policy was concerned, however, their accomplishments were less impressive. The exponential increase in the price of land made the state policy of land expropriation unviable and the granting of credit to farmers for the purchase of land less effective. As the Lula and Rousseff governments avoided confronting agribusiness, the land reform policy primarily benefited existing settlements.

For more than a decade, neo-developmentalism managed to reconcile conflicting interests and promote a situation in which almost everyone profited. However, the fact that the financial and agrarian elites gained proportionately far more than workers, family farmers, and the rest of society widened the contradictions of this model. The situation became unsustainable with the international financial crisis of 2008. It engendered the reduction of the price of agri-food and other primary sector commodities, an increase of interest rates, inflation of production costs, and the reduction of FDI.[2] In order to mitigate the effects of this crisis and the widening domestic socio-political instability but also shore up positive results in the upcoming political elections, in 2009 the Lula government began to implement anticyclical policies centered on the expansion of credit and consumption. This move maintained public support and permitted the victory of the PT in the 2011 vote with the election of Dilma Rousseff as the president of the republic. However, it forced her new administration to implement a contradictory policy that featured cutting spending without reducing investment and income transfer measures (Bastos 2017).

The worsening of the international crisis reduced the state's ability to manage its contradictory policy. In an almost desperate attempt to reverse the economic crisis, the government implemented strong anti-inflationary measures aimed at stabilizing the exchange rate and energy and fuel prices. While these actions allowed for the re-election of Rousseff in 2014, they ended the governamentality that the center-left coalition had negotiated with financial and agrarian elites since the first Lula administration. State intervention sounded like a heresy to rentier groups that, gradually, began to break the "governance pact" and promoted anti-government movements. Neo-developmentalism was now equated with "state capitalism" or, according to the most vocal critics, with "Bolivarianism" (The Economist 2012).

Disappointed by the economic losses caused by the intervention of the State (of which the most symptomatic instance was the drop in value of the shares of Petrobrás generated by the state attempt to control fuel prices), a portion of the economic elite supported "the institutional coup d'état " perpetrated by a new neoliberal-conservative coalition (Jinkings, Doria, and Cleto 2017). In August 2016, Dilma Rousseff was relieved of her presidency in favor of a new government led by her vice-president, Michel Temer, who adopted a radically neoliberal stance. While it is perhaps too early to define this new variety of neoliberalism, its strong conservative and authoritarian character is quite clear when compared with "old neoliberalism" of the 1990s. An example of this is the end of support for family farming initiated by the Cardoso government. In addition to closing the MDA, the new government halted, reduced and/or altogether extinguished a broad set of policies in support of family agriculture (Niederle et al. 2018). Simultaneously, it issued new measures that facilitated the inflow of foreign capital, reduced the competitiveness of national industries, slowed domestic consumption, and increased levels of unemployment and poverty. These measures created new conditions that engendered strong social protest.

CONCLUSIONS

In Brazil, neo-developmentalism was born out of the crisis of neoliberalism, yet it ended up adopting a number of the very characteristics of neoliberalism. As a result, the contradictions arising from the hybrid and confused actions of the neo-developmental State generated the reproduction of radically asymmetric power relations (Morais and Saad-Filho 2011). While these actions promoted social and redistributive policies and opened spaces for the valorization of family agriculture, they also created macro-structural policies that benefited agribusiness, the export of commodities from the primary sectors that, among other things, jeopardized the well-being of family farmers, traditional communities and their social reproduction.

Would it have been possible for the governments of the PT to build another model and promote more substantial institutional ruptures? What would have happened if the international economic crisis had been abridged and its effects quickly overcome? This type of questioning only leads to unproductive conjectures in academic and political debates. In effect, over the last two decades, the contradictory agricultural and rural developmental policies that the Brazilian variety of developmental State has introduced have been exacerbated when it attempted to reconcile conflicting mechanisms of capitalist accumulation and the simultaneous defense of spaces for family agriculture and agribusiness. The economic and political limits of this coexistence have become flagrant over time, leading to the current context of paradigmatic crisis and uncertainties about the future.

NOTES

1. Meirelles was not included in the Roussef Government (2011–2016). During that period, he served as a consultant for private banks and as the chairperson of the board of directors of J&F Investimentos, a fund that controls JBS, the largest Brazilian agribusiness company (see Bonanno in this volume). After Roussef's departure in May 2016, and the establishment of a new neoliberal coalition, Meirelles assumed the post of Finance Minister under the government of Michel Temer. In the presidential elections of 2018, his candidacy in the governing coalition was justified in terms of defending neoliberal reforms.

2. Following a sustained growth between 2003 (US $10 billion) and 2011 (US $101 billion), FDI fell sharply in 2013 (US $69 billion). In turn, despite the increase in the volume of exports of primary sector products, the decline in international commodity prices caused the balance of trade to turn negative between 2011 (plus US $29 billion) and 2014 (minus US $4 billion).

BIBLIOGRAPHY

Acosta, Alberto. 2016. "Extrativismo e Neoextrativismo." In Gerhard Dilger, Miriam Lang, and Jorge Pereira Filho (Eds.), *Descolonizar o Imaginário: Debates sobre Pós-Extrativismo e Alternativas ao Desenvolvimento* (pp. 46–77). São Paulo: Fundação Rosa Luxemburgo.

Babb, Sarah. 2012. "The Washington Consensus as Transnational Policy Paradigm: Its Origins, Trajectory and Likely Successor." *Review of International Political Economy* 20(2): 268–297.

Ban, Cornel. 2012. "Brazil's Liberal Neo-Developmentalism: New Paradigm or Edited Orthodoxy?" *Review of International Political Economy* 20(2): 298–331.

Bastos, Pedro Paulo. 2012. "A Economia Política do Novo-Desenvolvimentismo e do Social Desenvolvimentismo." *Economia e Sociedade* 21: 779–810.

Bonanno, Alessandro. 2017. *The Legitimation Crisis of Neoliberalism*. New York: Palgrave-Macmillan.

Bresser-Pereira, Luis Carlos. 2016. "Reflexões Sobre o Novo Desenvolvimentismo e o Desenvolvimentismo Clássico." *Revista de Economia Política* 36(2): 237–265.

———. 2010. *Do Antigo ao Novo Desenvolvimentismo na América Latina*. São Paulo: FGV.

Chang, Ha-Joon. 2002. *Kicking Away the Ladder: Development Strategy in Historical Perspective*. London: Anthem Press.

Delgado, Guilherme. 2012. *Do Capital Financeiro na Agricultura à Economia do Agronegócio*. Porto Alegre: UFRGS.

Evans, Peter, Dietrich Rueschemeyer, and Theda Skocpol (Eds.). 1985. *Bringing the State Back In*. Cambridge: Cambridge University Press.

França, Caio, Vicente Marques, and Mauro del Grossi. 2016. *Superação da Fome e da Pobreza Rural*: Iniciativas Brasileiras. Brasília: FAO.

Grisa, Catia, and Sergio Schneider (Eds.). 2015. *Políticas Públicas de Desenvolvimento Rural no Brasil*. Porto Alegre: UFRGS.

Grisa, Catia, Valdemar João Wesz Junior, and Vitor Buchweitz. 2014. "Revisitando o Pronaf: Velhos Questionamentos, Novas Interpretações." *Revista de Economia e Sociologia Rural* 52(2): 323–346.

Gudynas, Eduardo. 2012. "Estado Compensador y Nuevos Extractivismos: las Ambivalencias del Progresismo Sudamericano." *Nueva Sociedad* 237: 128–146.

Hall, Peter. 1993. "Policy Paradigmes, Social Learning and the State." *Comparative Politics* 25(3): 275–296.

Jinkings, Ivana, Kim Doria, and Murilo Cleto (Eds.). 2017. *Porque Gritamos Golpe?* São Paulo: Boitempo.

Jones, Michael D., and Mark K. McBeth. 2010. "A Narrative Policy Framework: Clear Enough to Be Wrong?" *Policy Studies Journal* 38(2): 329–353.

Mahoney, James, and Katlen Thelen. 2009. "A Theory of Gradual Institutional Change." In James Mahoney and Katlen Thelen (Eds.), *Explaining Institutional Change: Ambiguity, Agency, and Power* (pp. 1–36). Cambridge: Cambridge University Press.

Mattei, Lauro. 2013. "Gênese e Agenda do Novo Desenvolvimentismo Brasileiro." *Revista de Economia Política* 33(1): 41–59.

Milanez, Bruno and Rodrigo Santos. 2013. "Neodesenvolvimentismo e Neoextrativismo: duas Faces da Mesma Moeda?" in *Proceedings of the Brazilian National Congress of Social Sciences*. Caxambu, MG: ANPOCS.

Morais, Lecio, and Alfredo Saad-Filho. 2011. "Da Economia Política à Política Econômica: o Novo-desenvolvimentismo e o Governo Lula." *Revista de Economia Política* 31(4): 507–527.

Neri, Marcelo. 2010. *A Nova Classe Média*. Rio de Janeiro: FGV.

Niederle, Paulo, Catia Grisa, Everton Picolotto, and Denis Soldera. 2017. "Narrative Disputes on Family Farming Public Policies in Brazil: Conservative Attacks and Civic Countermovements." In *Proceedings of the BRICS Initiative for Critical Agrarian Studies Conference*. Moscow: BICAS.

Nogueira, Rodrigo. 2017. "Desindustrialização Abismo Abaixo: Dependência Cambial e Abandono das Políticas de Competitividade no Brasil." Lacerda, Antonio (Ed.), *Desenvolvimento Brasileiro em Debate* (pp. 25–48). São Paulo: Blucher.

Novo-Desenvolvimentismo e o Governo Lula." *Revista de Economia Política* 31(4): 507–527.

Pereira, João, and Sergio Sauer. 2011. "A Reforma Agrária Assistida pelo Mercado do Banco Mundial no Brasil: Dimensões Políticas, Implantação e Resultados." *Sociedade e Estado* 26: 587–612.

Pierson, Paul. 2016. "Retornos Crescentes, Dependência da Trajetória (Path Dependence) e o Estudo da Política." *Ideias* 6(2): 335–392.

Pochmann, Marcio. 2013. "Políticas Públicas e Situação Social na Primeira Década do Século XXI." In Sader, Emir (Ed.), *10 Anos de Governos Pós-Neoliberais no Brasil* (pp. 145–156). Rio de Janeiro: FLACSO.

Sader, Emir. 2013. "A Construção da Hegemonia Pós-Neoliberal." In Sader, Emir. (Ed.), *10 Anos de Governos Pós-Neoliberais no Brasil*, (pp. 135–142). Rio de Janeiro: FLACSO.

Sallum Junior, Brasílio. 2003. "Metamorfoses do Estado brasileiro no Final do Século XX." *Revista Brasileira de Ciência Sociais* 18(52): 35–54.

Sallum Junior, Brasílio, and Jefferson Goulart. 2016. "O Estado Brasileiro Contemporâneo: Liberalização Econômica, Política e Sociedade nos Governos FHC e Lula." *Revista de Sociologia Política* 24(60): 115–135.

Sampaio Junior, Plinio. 2012. "Desenvolvimentismo e Neodesenvolvimentismo: Tragédia e Farsa." *Serviço Social & Sociedade* 112: 672–688.

Souza, Jessé. 2017. *A Elite do Atraso*: da Escravidão à Lava Jato. São Paulo: Leya.

Surel, Yvez. 1995. "Les Politiques Publiques comme Paradigmes." In Faure, Alain, Pollet Gilles and Philippe Warin (Eds.), *La Construction du sens dans les Politiques Publiques: Débats Autour de la Notion de Référentiel* (pp. 125–151). Paris: L'Harmattan.

The Economist, 2012. "The Rise of State Capitalism: The Spread of a New Sort of Business in the Emerging World Will Cause Increasing Problems." January 21, *The Economist*. https://www.economist.com/leaders/2012/01/21/the-rise-of-state-capitalism.

Thelen, Kathlen. 2014. *Varieties of Liberalization and the New Politics of Social Solidarity*. Cambridge: Cambridge University Press.

Toni, Jackson, and Kleber Cerqueira. 2017. "Da Esperança ao Desastre: Neodesenvolvimentismo e Crise Institucional na Experiência Brasileira Recente." In *Proceedings of the Latin-American Congress of Political Science*. Montevideo: ALACIP.

Williamson, Olivier. 1985. *The Economic Institutions of Capitalism*. New York: Free Press.

Chapter Three

March of the Daisies

Subject, Agriculture, and the State

Andrea Butto

Employing the history and social evolution of the women's organization "The March of the Daisies," this chapter probes the emancipatory role of the Brazilian State under the Workers' Party. The March of the Daisies is a network of movements that focus on the emancipation of rural women and, in particular, women who work in agriculture. It has been a fundamental force behind the struggle for land reform policies and the many initiatives that have democratized the rural space and agriculture in Brazil in recent decades. The Brazilian State under the administration of the PT acted as a positive agent in support of the March. However, some contradictions emerged as the State adopted a strategy that supported family farming and subordinate groups while also assisting large producers and agri-food corporations. In addition, the March struggled to oppose the male-dominated view that characterized the actions of many segments of the Brazilian society.

The chapter touches upon these themes by illustrating salient activities of the March beginning with its constitutions, early developments, and the organization of five Marches spanning from the year 2000, the year of the first March, to 2015, the year of the most recent March. These topics are discussed in the first section of the chapter. The second section focuses on the March's struggle for land, illustrating the many initiatives, claims, and gains that it obtained for rural women and the democratization of labor and social relations in agriculture. The third and fourth sections of the chapter discuss the topics of agroecology and water that, along with land, represent the three primary foci of the struggle of the March. The role of feminism in the actions of the March is briefly discussed in the fifth and the next to last section. It underscores the relevance that the diffusion of feminist ideas has had on the evolution of the March. The chapter concludes by stressing the problematic impact that the recent advent of conservative governments has had for the democratization of social relations in Brazilian rural life.

THE ORIGINS AND DEVELOPMENT OF THE MARCH OF THE DAISIES

The March of the Daisies is a network movement that connects autonomous social movements of rural and urban women as well as variegated social movements operating in the countryside (Scherer-Warren 2007). It maintains strong ties with trade unions linked to the National Confederation of Rural Workers and Family Farmers (or CONTAG) as "the Secretariat of the Women" of the CONTAG is responsible for the organization and administration of the March. As of 2019, there have been five editions of the March and there is an ongoing process of internationalization based on the establishment of the network "Daisies in a Network" (Butto 2017). In effect, the establishment of the March resulted from the actions of a number of groups. First, it originated from the work of an entire first generation of union militants and members of the Northeastern Rural Workers' Movement (or MMTR-NE). Second, it was also built on new interactions between the labor movement and women's movements in rural and urban areas. Finally, it found part of its roots in the discussions held at the First National Plenary of Rural Workers in 1997 and the actions leading to the claim of a minimum quota of 30 percent of women in the directive bodies of CONTAG.

This process emerged as a rich and revealing trajectory that stressed the great political courage of the feminist militants in CONTAG and their objective of gaining recognition and autonomy at the national level. Women in CONTAG no longer limited themselves to struggles for the rights to join the Union, self-organize as women, and claim representation. They wanted to add to these important achievements by moving forward and promoting mobilizations relevant to the entire society that included the support of, and alliances with, rural and urban feminist groups. Building on these actions, women also sought to deepen the democratization of gender relations within CONTAG through contributions to the debate on rural development and the conditions of women. These women claimed autonomy in the pursuit of their goals and planned to transcend the traditional objective of "Land Now" that had characterized the actions of CONTAG since the early 1990s. As CONTAG occasionally banned their flags from demonstrations, the women of the March offered a critique of CONTAG-supported programs such as the Alternative Sustainable Rural Development Project (PADRSS) that, they claimed, did not address issues fundamental for rural women. As they denounced PADRSS, they proposed an alternative model in which the role and future of women were central. In essence, the March wanted to be a space for women to express their struggles, training but also the formulation of proposals to rebuild and strengthen the trade union movement.

Initially, the March faced two important challenges. The first was to convince the leadership of CONTAG of the importance and viability of the March, while the second referred to building a set of alliances that could generate support within and outside the Union. The women leading the March acted on a program that made clear the specific situation of rural workers and the items that limited their full participation in CONTAG-organized national and local mobilizations. On its part, the leadership of CONTAG was concerned with the problems that the establishment of the March would engender in a context characterized by a difficult interaction between the government of Fernando Henrique Cardoso and rural social movements. In addition, CONTAG was aware that support for the March would constitute a financial challenge given the limited resources available.

Supported by the organizational work they performed within the Union and its state federations, women members of the March reinforced existing alliances with a variety of women's movements at different levels. This included alliances with the World March of Women that brought together urban and rural women, the trade union movement through the Single Workers Center or CUT, and the autonomous movement of rural women through MMTR-NE. After the first edition of the March, women gained greater legitimacy inside and outside CONTAG as resistance to the March's validity evaporated. In effect, the second edition of the March, in 2003, took place at a quite different political moment that coincided with the first year of the PT administration of Lula. Lula has always been a union man and assumed the presidency after working in the *Central Única dos Trabalhadores* (Workers' Center)—a trade union executive branch of which CONTAG remains a longstanding member and ally. In this context, the claims of the March began to be viewed in a new light, signaling a shift away from earlier opposition.

This change was symbolized by the land reform, one of the central components of the *Dignified Life in the Field Program* that the Lula government proposed and implemented. This program consisted of many of the claims originally put forward by rural social movements. As in the case of other Latin American and Caribbean countries, it originated from the mobilization of social movements and the redemocratization of the political and social spheres that it fostered. In this process, rural women emerged as legitimate protagonists of social change as their struggles and claims won the recognition of the Brazilian State (Heredia and Cintrão 2006). Ultimately, the intensity of these struggles and the actions of the federal government symbolized the "turn to the left" that occurred in Brazil after 2003 (Alvarez 2014).

The PT governments of Lula and Dilma Rousseff (2003–2016) promoted a democratic agenda for rural development. Established in a context of intense social dialogue, this agenda consisted of the implementation of a number of progressive public policies that included the land reform, measures in support of family agriculture, sustainable agri-food production, territorial development, and the equality and autonomy of rural women. In this context, the federal government further contributed to the implementation of this democratic agenda by creating new agencies with the purpose of supporting policies and programs for rural women. The results of all these activities included a novel political environment within the Brazilian State and the establishment of new spaces of political participation for women (Butto and Hora 2010). This emancipatory process/climate came to a crashing end with the 2016 forced removal of President Dilma Roussef from office and the establishment of a conservative government that initiated a process of dismantling of pro-rural women public policies.[1]

THE EDITIONS OF THE MARCH AND THEIR CLAIMS AND ACCOMPLISHMENTS

There have been five editions of the March in 2000, 2003, 2007, 2011, and 2015 respectively. Coordinated by CONTAG, they counted on the support of partner organizations that assisted in their preparations and executions. Additionally, this broader group counted on the participation of a number of social movements and organizations that jointly worked in the coordination of events and preparation of texts that promoted debates and the formulation of claims. This process was carried out by employing a participatory methodology that valued the formulation of policy agendas through the organization of events that, starting at the local level, reach the national level. This strategy proved to be highly effective in engaging women and strengthening alliances with partner organizations. Additionally, this effectiveness allowed the establishment of agendas whose contents reflected the reality of women from different social groups and regions and countered the tendency to shape policies and claims following established male-dominated views.

In the two most recent editions (2011 and 2015), the diversity of the March was more emphatically affirmed by changes in the expressions internally used to identify them. The 2011 March was referred to as the "March of Rural Women Workers." In 2015, this slogan was changed to the "March of Women of the Countryside, Forests, and Water" as a way to express not only unity but also differences in the social conditions of the women involved in the March of the Daisies. This change affected the content of the agenda and discussions along with the reflections contained in the texts produced and the claims generated (Aguiar 2015). For instance, claims and policy proposals of the 2015 March were organized and presented according to region and biome, reflecting changes not only in agri-food but also in the approach used to define the collective identity of the movement. Accordingly, these changes were not simply associated with the development of an internal identity that could preserve differences, but also referred to emerging relevant issues within agri-food in Brazil. It follows that concerns about the global nature of production, distribution and consumption, the strategies of adaptation and survival of small-scale producers, the expansion of the agricultural frontier, land concentration, biodiversity, and conservation assumed central importance (Van der Ploeg 2018).

Yet changes in agri-food and, in particular, the space that women occupy in this system are affected by a number of exogenous factors that include globalization, the power of transnational corporations, and global policies directed at the countries of the South (Cavalcanti 2014). In the Brazilian case and, as indicated above, during the Lula and Dilma governments, the federal government implemented important pro-family agriculture measures with special emphasis on poverty-stricken rural areas (Cavalcanti, Nierdele, Raynaut and Ferreira 2014). However, these efforts were limited by not only external forces but also internal contradictions. The transnational character of the agri-food system and its consequences for the country are key examples of external factors that impacted the effectiveness and results of domestic policies. Simultaneously, the federal government, while supporting family farming, also promoted a dualistic posture that consisted of support for the insertion of Brazilian agri-food companies into global circuits (Sabourin 2014). In this contradictory context and departing from the original demands put forward in 2007, the primary claims proposed by the March centered on the three fundamental components of the new model for agriculture: land, agroecology, and water (Silva 2008). These components were complemented by calls for the defense of a collective vision in the approach to land, labor, and natural resources and the proposal of a feminist approach in internal debates (Federici 2014). It is through an analysis of these three components that the evolution of the March will be further discussed.

LAND

The reference to Margarida Alves—a union leader murdered by large landowners in the 1980s—in the organization of the March is the best example of the centrality that the struggle for land ownership represented in these mobilizations. In the first edition of the March, and to ensure that the crime committed against this rural Union leader was not left unprosecuted, a significant mobilization took place (Butto 2017). In addition, the vigil organized during the trial and the intense mobilization that took place in all the participating states gave visibility to the call for the end of violence against women in rural regions. As this became one of the major struggles of the March, claims for the prevention of, and assistance for, violence against women ended up characterizing the history of the March. These actions also made it possible to associate support for the land reform with support for equality between men and women in land ownership and land access.

Land ownership has always been one of the primary claims in the agenda of the March of the Daisies. In its first 2000 edition, the main claim consisted of the request for the mandatory issuing of joint land titles. These titles had to certify that land ownership was awarded jointly to the members of a couple (or family), regardless of their marital status. This joint ownership provision was part of the new 1988 Constitution. Yet it was never implemented despite the fact that the government of Fernando Henrique Cardoso attempted to revise the rule of execution that regulated the selection of families benefitting from the land reform. This rule ensured that the names of the members of the family or couple, or the name of the woman in the event that she was single, were recorded on the deed. As this attempt did not come to fruition, in the 2003 edition of the March—taking place under the first Lula administration—the claim reappeared on the agenda and was successfully translated into legislation.

Additional claims associated with the rights to land and land access further characterized the actions of the March. In 2000, the March proposed training on gender and women's rights for all technicians assigned to provide technical assistance to land reform recipients. The theme of specific training and services for women reemerged in the fifth edition of the March where claims for technical assistance and rural extension that could enhance the qualifications of women in settlements were proposed. In 2003, the March requested a change in the functioning of the Agrarian Reform Program Information System (SIPRA) to allow the generation of data on women's access to land and the priority access to land by female heads of households.[2] This claim also resulted in new legislation (Butto and Hora 2010). In 2007, the issue of joint land titles reentered negotiations. This time, however, it was a claim for the universalization of all rights. In 2015, a new claim was introduced to review the titles issued in the period prior to the joint title ordinance. It referred to collective titles that required the inclusion of women as associates, and also individual titles where property record updates were necessary. The March struggled for the availability of credit for women, the creation of productive infrastructure, and housing in settlements. These struggles resulted in the establishment of specific credit programs for rural women such as "Assistance Mulher" (Assistance for Women) that was later renamed "Fomento Mulher" (Support for Women). As these claims began to be implemented, the March fought for dissemination, universalization, and the implementation of measures that promoted economic activities for women.

The struggle for the right to own land implied also the struggle against existing development projects. This situation resulted in the proposal of an amended version of PADRSS that contemplated the realization of broad land reform. Already in its first edition, the March denounced the agricultural policy contained in the "New Rural World Program" launched by the administration of Fernando Cardoso. This program rejected measures aimed at the fulfillment of the social function associated with family ownership of agricultural land and the expropriation of unproductive land. These measures were replaced by the sale of public land through market instruments and the implementation of the program "Cédula da Terra" (Ticket to the Land) that was developed in partnership with the World Bank. For the March, these policies benefited large landowners and promoted the marketization of land. Additionally, they restricted the rights of women by transferring not only state functions to the market but also to local states and municipalities that did not recognize the participation of women in land reform. The proposal of the March, conversely, supported the view that settlements should constitute democratic spaces of organization established in the respect of cultural, ethnic, gender, and generational diversities and that these spaces should be based on the participation of women in discussions and deliberations associated with political, social, and technical projects.

The 2007 third edition of the March marked a significant change in the discourse on land reform. It consisted of the resumption of the denunciation of the limits of the dominant model of development and land reform deemed too weak. It further contained the affirmation of the centrality of the democratization of the use of, and access to, land and water and the objective of ensuring the involvement of rural women workers in decision-making processes (Marcha das Margaridas 2007). This approach was reaffirmed in the 2011 edition through the further condemnation of the high growing levels of concentration of land ownership in Brazil. The increase in land concentration was due to the expansion of the world demand for food, agro-energy, and raw materials and the concomitant land grabbing phenomenon promoted by foreign investors (Marcha das Margaridas 2011). The March denounced the actions of members of the executive, legislative, and judicial branches that prevented the application of existing pro-land reform and pro-labor legislation. It further stressed claims regarding the maximum limit of the size of land ownership and the updating of productivity indexes (Marcha das Margaridas 2011).

The 2013 and 2015 editions of the March continued with its critique of the central aspects of the dominant model of development. This critique focused on the alliance between large landowners and dominant groups in the financial and industrial sectors, the commodification and exploitation of natural resources, the exploitation of labor, and the dependence on technology packages and their negative effects on the environment and human health. The phenomena of the expulsion of local populations from their land and violence in rural areas were also emphasized. More importantly, the March underscored that the struggle for the land was not simply about the democratization of socio-economic spaces, the strengthening of equal rights, and the opposition to agribusiness. It was about the affirmation that the struggle for land provides a new understanding of the importance of land and that this understanding should guide the implementation of a novel model for the development of agriculture. Following this approach, the redistribution of land should depart from views that center on individual interests and decisions. Conversely, it should be associated with collective views and processes whereby the struggle for land does not end with the creation of settlements but continues to include the sustainable and just use of natural and human resources and, more importantly, the possibility of finding collective solutions to existing problems. In this context, the struggle for land remains about the defense of local populations and their autonomy against large private corporate groups and their profit-driven plans.

These claims of the March were proposed in a context in which proposal for the land reform encountered opposition and problems. During the second term of Fernando Henrique Cardoso in the early 2000s, significant episodes of violence in rural areas accompanied a subpar implementation of the distribution of land that mostly referred to the recognition of rights of settlers and minorities. During this term, for instance, the entire budget devoted to land reform did not exceed 100 million reals (2012 value). This situation improved as the PT administration of Lula took office and this improvement continued throughout the years of the PT rule. For instance, by the time the Dilma Rousseff government ended, the amount spent on the land reform process totaled about 3.6 billion reals (2012 value). More importantly, the PT government proposed a policy that centered not only on the distribution of land but also on the implementation of policies aimed at the development of the settlements. During this period, more than half (54 percent) of all families historically involved in the land reform process received land (Brazil 2015). However, the pace of implementation of the land reform was not as rapid as expected by those who supported it, culminating in a clear reversal after the forced end of the Dilma Rousseff administration. Just in the last years after the ousting of Rousseff, for instance, the land reform budget was drastically cut to little more than one billion reals (Mattos 2017).

The reversal of trends associated with the end of the PT administration was not limited to the reduction of state investments. There have been important legislative initiatives that rolled back and/or eliminated pro-rural labor and land redistribution measures. The most relevant of them included the easing of anti-slave labor laws, the reduction of sanctions against deforestation, and legislative initiatives pertaining to land regulation. These new measures favored large landowners and agri-food corporations. Similarly, the advancement of equal rights in agriculture was halted as budget cuts restricted not only the implementation of the distribution of land but also the availability of resources for the improvement of the settlements. A relevant example is the case of the program "ATER for Women" that received 6.45 million reals in 2012, but was cut in 2017 (Brazil 2018). Importantly, these changes occurred as violence in the countryside increased, indicating an even more challenging scenario for the March of the Daisies than the other social movements operating in rural areas.

AGROECOLOGY

The second component of the new development model proposed by the March is agroecology. This has been an original and constant component of this movement as the formation of the March coincided with the establishment of an agro-ecological movement in the country and participation in early initiatives against the use of agrochemicals. To be sure, the agroecology movement grew out of previous efforts initiated by various organizations of rural women including the "National Coordination of Rural Women Workers" (ANMTR)[3] that in the 1990s was one of the first groups to recognize the importance of agroecology in the formulation of new approaches to the development of agriculture.

Earlier debates and claims on this issue that occurred prior to 2007 were associated more with the theme of the environment than agroecology. This agenda, however, already contained important claims, such as the request to ensure access to marketing services and sustainable technologies for women in farming, fishing, and extractive industries, and the denunciation of the negative consequences of the use of agrochemicals on the health of agricultural workers (Marcha das Margaridas 2007). Simultaneously, a number of the partner organizations of the March and NGOs were involved in the constitution of a national agroecology movement. Initiated in the 1980s with the creation of the first national network, this cooperation continued through the 1990s and further developed in the new century as symbolized by the establishment of the PTA (Project for Alternative Technology) network and the "National Coordination of Agroecology" or ANA in 2002. These organizations had counted on a significant participation of women since their beginnings (Siliprandi 2015).

Within the national PTA network, the Southeast PTA group counted on nine organizations and the support of the "Semper Viva Feminist Organization" or SOF. The women of the Southeast PTA Network promoted the exchange of experiences and reflections that supported a stronger participation of women in the "First National Meeting of Agroecology" or ENA in 2002. In this first ENA meeting, the women participants in the working group on gender challenged the focus of topics discussed in other working groups as they called for the inclusion of the gender issue in all the working groups constituting the meeting (Siliprandi 2015). Two years later, in a seminar of the Gender Working Group of the Southeast Forum of the PTA Network, the difficulties encountered for the inclusion of the issue of gender in the agendas of pertinent organizations were discussed. These discussions stressed the relevance of power differences as a source of problems for the emancipation of women along with problems concerning the limits of the approach to biodiversity proposed by ANA and the lack of depth in the discussion of issues related to food sovereignty in the defense of peasant agriculture. Moreover, the women gathered at this event requested the formalization of a permanent working group on gender relations. The Leadership of ANA accepted the proposal and deliberated that the number of delegates to the second ENA meeting were equally split between men and women. At that time, women members of ANA worked to the formulation of public policies that systematize the experiences of women and promoted policy formation based on feminism and agroecology (CONTAG 2004). SOF and the NGOs FASE (Federation of the Coordinations for Social and Educational Assistance) were instrumental in setting up the Gender Working Group, which later became GT Women. These organizations were already partner organizations of the March. Due to this initiative, in the second edition of the March held in 2003, women requested that agroecology be viewed as a fundamental component of PADRSS and that agroecology activities practiced by women be supported through the availability of credit, training, technology, and technical assistance (Marcha das Margaridas 2003).

In the 2007 third edition of the March and with the ANA Women's WG already in place, agroecology gained more visibility in the March agenda as it was recognized as a fundamental aspect of PADRSS. Additionally, the agroecological practices that women had implemented since the beginning of the new century became the source of claims that came to fruition in the proposal of the "National Program of Valorization and Improvement of the Production of Rural Women." This program was eventually included in the "Support Program for the Productive Organization of Rural Women" launched by the Ministry of Agrarian Development also as part of the Third March (Butto 2011).

In the 2011 March, agroecology was one of the instruments employed to construct a critique of the existing model of development. This critique stressed that this model emphasized mass production without considering a number of additional fundamental aspects. These aspects included: the respect of regional and cultural diversity, the promotion of the well-being of local communities, the support for the production and consumption of quality and healthy food, the implementation of sustainable agroecology systems, and the creation of conditions that would foster the implementation of this alternative model (Marcha das Margaridas 2011). In addition, the March emphasized the role of common goods as another important aspect to guide the debate about new forms of development, the economy, and the State. Simultaneously, the performances of women that used agroecology in the fields were employed as tools to demonstrate the role and importance of women in the construction of alternatives. Women's agroecological approach to the management of small plots, the care of plants and animals, the administration of self-consumption, and the conservation and productive use of native seeds were all presented as cases in point (Marcha das Margaridas 2011).

In 2012, the Federal government implemented the "National Policy on Agroecology and Organic Production." This program eventually evolved into a plan aimed at promoting the role of women in organic agroecology production as a way to strengthen their economic autonomy. The plan was announced by President Dilma Rousseff at the 2015 March of the Daisies. In this last edition of the March, three new issues emerged as pivotal in the overall discussion. They consisted of: gender conflict within the farm family about the agroecology practices adopted by women; the introduction of labor for self-consumption as part of the public policy agenda; and the inclusion in public policies of the issue of urban and semi-urban agriculture (Marcha das Margaridas 2015). Additionally, in this edition of the March, women requested measures in support of technical assistance and the implementation of rural extension programs, the establishment of training programs on feminism and agroecology for technicians, and the establishment of an award for women who generate agroecology-based innovations in family agriculture. In the important sphere of gender conflict within the farm family, claims were directed at empowering women in decision-making processes concerning agroecology by stressing the relationship between agroecology and feminism.

As formulated in the general discussion, agroecology was reaffirmed not only as a central component of the new model of development proposed by the March but also as a reason for the expanded role that women ought to perform in deliberations. For the March, the recognition of the unique relationship that women maintain with nature called for the preservation and valuation of practices that derived from this privileged relationship. This discussion echoed that which took place in the third meeting of ENA under the slogan "There is no Agroecology without Feminism." The conclusions reached in that meeting further underscored the importance of agroecology concerning ethical, social, and environmental justice. They also included related claims for the advancement of the conditions of women in farming such as the sharing of housework, the care and management of productive tasks, equality in social and political life, access to land, water, seeds and production conditions, and the rejection of violence (Contag 2014).

The debates on alternative agriculture and later on ecology showed the manner in which the social movements involved in the March had broadened the discussion on the sustainability of agriculture and its connection with pertinent issues. At the theoretical level, this debate was contextualized in that novel understanding of the role of women that stressed their engagement not only in the agroecology movement but also in the feminist movements of the global North and South (Guetat-Bernard 2014). This view further contemplated a systemic understanding of claims centered on moral changes and political transformations (Guetat-Bernard 2015).

The programmatic renewal associated with the emphasis on agroecology is relevant yet this area remains characterized by numerous challenges. For instance, national indicators of sustainable development show that in Brazil the use of agrochemicals more than doubled between 2005 and 2014 as it went from 3.2 kilos per hectare in 2005 to 6.7 kilos per hectare in 2014 (Brasil 2018). This is the result of the overall lack of enforcement of agribusiness regulations and, in particular, of the National Reduction Program of Agroxóticos or PRONARA (Schmitt, Niederle, Ávila, Sabourin, Pertersen, Silveira, Assis, Palm and Fernandes 2017). As solutions to these challenges continue to lack, the future does not look promising given the end of the PT administration and, more importantly, the 2018 electoral victory of the conservative ticket in Brazil.

WATER

As far as water is concerned, in the 2000 and first edition of the March, claims largely referred to access to water for residents of the semi-arid northeastern region. In this vein, additional claims involved proposals to build artesian wells in local rural communities. In the 2003 and second edition, this theme occupied a more central position in the agenda as indicated by one of the event's primary discussion documents entitled "Environment as a Focus in the Sustainability of Water Management and Agroecology" (Marcha das Margaridas 2003). In 2007, the March proposed an even greater emphasis on the struggle for water as it declared that water for human consumption and food production is a common good and should be defended accordingly. Its claims included the construction of cisterns, the use of technologies to capture and store water, the revitalization of water resources, and the implementation of participatory management of these resources (Marcha das Margaridas 2007). This approach contrasted the view that saw water as a market commodity whose best use was determined by its privatization and the capturing and redirecting of water basins according to commercial requirements. Fighting this corporate stance, the March extended its struggle for water from the semi-arid region to the entire country (Marcha das Margaridas 2007).

A significant portion of this change originated from initiatives of rural social movements. Particularly important was work of the "Coordination of the Brazilian Semi-Arid" (Articulação do Semiárido Brasileiro), an association that brought together more than three thousand organizations including NGOs and social movements. Its primary objective was to improve the living conditions in semi-arid regions in ten Brazilian states through a novel experience of rural extension based on enhanced participation and union activism (Amorim and Pirez 2010). Also important were initiatives of self-organization of women featuring the collective management of rainwater-storing technologies. In essence, in this third edition, the March sought to organize struggles that called for the implementation of measures that would ensure free access to water resources to local residents regardless of whether these resources were located on private land.

As the struggle for water escalated, the actions of the March were also directed at addressing the environmental problems generated by major developmental projects undertaken in previous decades, such as the construction of hydroelectric dams and irrigation projects and the expansion of agribusiness that included the implantation of large-scale monocultures such as those of eucalyptus, soybeans, and cotton.[4] These environmental problems included water and soil contamination, reduction of biodiversity, land degradation, and the resulting rural outmigration. These struggles were reaffirmed in the 2011 and fourth edition of the March. In addition, however, this March stressed the unique position and responsibilities of women in regard to the use and procurement of water for the family and the farm. In the vast majority of cases, women in the farm family are charged with the management of water for family use and the management of springs and wells for farm use. These responsibilities, the March stressed, require the empowerment of women in pertinent decision-making processes (Marcha das Margaridas 2011).

The claims of the 2015 March expressed great concern for the process of commodification of water and denounced the discriminatory practices of the Brazilian State in the concession of the use of water, its contamination due to the expansion of monocultures, and the restrictions of access to water created by the construction of dams on privately owned lands. In addition to these claims, the March joined the fight against the construction of irrigation projects on land controlled by agri-food companies and employed for the cultivation of irrigated fruit for export. In this context, the defense of water was linked not only to the ability of women to access it but also to the quality of this access. In particular, the March denounced the access restriction practices used by agri-food companies. Water, the March concluded, is a common good and a necessary condition for the autonomy of family agriculture in which women occupy a fundamental position.

The Brazilian State addressed many of the claims of the March as the PT government shared the March's view that access to water represents a fundamental dimension of human existence and food production. Specifically, it implemented the "National Program in Support of Rainwater Harvesting and Other Water Access Technologies" as well as the "Fresh Water Program" for the enhanced use of groundwater. Despite the long-term success of these programs, in recent years, the change in government resulted in their underfunding that de-facto halted their effectiveness. In 2017, for instance, the original budget called for the use of 249 million reals. However, the resources made available to the appropriate agencies did not reach 50 million reals. Moreover, in 2012, expenditures for access to water programs totaled almost 2 billion reals. In the 2018 budget, this sum was reduced to 212 million reals. This reduction is not simply statistics; it reflects the actual change that is occurring in the country and that largely defuses the actions of the March. It also leaves an important gap between the status of urban and rural areas as, for example, in 2016, according to national data, 93.9 percent of urban households had access to water through a public system as opposed to only 34.5 percent in rural areas (Brazil 2018).

FEMINISM OF THE RURAL SPACE AND THE MARCH

The struggles of rural women carried out through the March are rooted in the diffusion of feminism in the Brazilian rural space. Indeed, the diffusion of the ideas of, and debates about, feminism represent important instances of the effectiveness of the struggles undertaken by the March. To be sure, the relationship between feminism as a theory and practice and rural women is relatively new. In the recent past, women in rural areas hardly associated their struggles with the calls of feminism as they saw this theory/movement as somehow external to their experiences and something that was more amenable to urban, academic, and middle-class circles. In recent decades, however, this perception has changed as feminism ceased to be considered only a partial expression of knowledge and acquired a new political sense that permitted the reformulated expression of emancipatory practices and collective actions. Accordingly, feminism came to be perceived not only as the reconceptualization of inequality toward women and other social groups but also as a new way to conceptualize the role of women in private and public spaces and in the family and work. Women were recognized as a collective subject and as an integral part of a broader reconceptualization of people, society, and the rural.

In this context, rural feminism emerged as a construct built on different readings of lived practices and the space and time where they unfold. It implies an important reconceptualization of social relations that are recentered around the idea of greater proximity. In this construction, the public and private spaces are seen not only as unified, for the public is part of the private, but also different from the case of the urban space. In the urban space, private social relations materialize as generally restricted with a limited degree of sociability. In the rural space, conversely, neighbors tend to make their private life public, engendering patterns of greater sociability. The greater integration between the private and public spaces is expressed through a different practice of life and interaction with nature and the economy whereby there is no separation between productive and reproductive work. In essence, this view entails a deconstruction of the distinction between productive and reproductive work. It implies the appreciation of the work of women as an entity in which the notions of domestic family work and agricultural work merge and remain embodied in the activities of rural women (Paulilo 2004). Moreover, it overcomes the rigid sexual division of labor to claim the recognition of domestic work as a work for human reproduction that guarantees human life (Carrasco 2003).

CONCLUSIONS

Prior to the advent of the PT administrations of Lula and Dilma Rousseff, the political and economic gains of rural women were rather minimal. There was a limited structural and institutional framework to support women's claims along with limited spaces for dialogue and participative management. In this context, their demands were hardly addressed and this resulted in only marginal advancements with many already granted by the 1988 Constitution, such as social security rights and equal rights to land through the land reform. The change in government that occurred in 2003 opened up a new era for the struggle of rural women of which the March is the most explicit representation. The PT administration's most fundamental move was to recognize the March and its members as legitimate representatives of the struggle of rural women and, accordingly, to recognize their claims in the formulation of public policies for agri-food and natural resources/the environment. In addition, the State was very receptive in terms of recognizing the rights of women and fostering their implementation. This situation provided impetus within the movement of which the growth of the March is a case in point.

This favorable milieu notwithstanding, the struggle of the March remained difficult, as it had to face many challenges in building its organization and creating platforms of action. It also had to confront resistance within the Government and Union movement. This is a reason that further motivated the critical and successful posture of the March. Given these challenges, the adoption of feminist views and the consequent popularization of feminism among rural women constituted a significant step forward that fostered the power of the March. In regard to the research question of this volume on the emancipatory role of the actions of the PT, this experience of the March of the Daisies testifies to the important role that the PT-led Brazilian State played in fostering conditions amenable to the March's growth and the emancipation of rural women. This is particularly clear following the events that occurred after the forced end of the PT administration and the implementation of conservative governments. Under these new governments, many of the achievements of the March were rolled back or eliminated and others were targeted for elimination. While the gains achieved by rural women rested on the actions of social and political movements such as the March, the positive yet contradictory climate created by a progressive State constituted a fundamental condition for their success. This success is much more evident in light of the events that characterized the new conservative Brazilian administration.

NOTES

1. In 2016, the Brazilian parliament removed the president of the republic, Dilma Rousseff, by a majority of votes on charges of fiscal fraud. This accusation was based on alleged irregularities in budget matters and delays in providing public banks with financial resources necessary to guarantee the solvency of government programs. These practices, however, have been routinely employed by previous governments—as in the case of the government of Fernando Henrique Cardoso (PSDB)—and no charges were ever pressed against these administrations (Singer 2018).
2. Associating this claim with the struggles for recognition of the rights of women, they demanded the recognition of women as rural workers in the registration of settlements and in the declarations of the Rural Territorial Tax (ITR).
3. In the 1990s, ANMTR was the first instance of a network-based movement in Brazil. Its establishment initiated the process of transnationalization of the movement of rural women. CONTAG was part of it.
4. The 2007 agenda of the March also included support for the membership of women on environmental councils and river basin committees and on committees that addressed the formulation and management of policies for the sustainable management of water resources, the creation of environmental education policies, and policies on awareness about the adequate use of water (Marcha das Margaridas 2007).

BIBLIOGRAPHY

Aguiar, Vilênia Venâncio Porto. 2015. *Somos Todas Margaridas: Um Estudo Sobre o Processo de Constituição das Mulheres do Campo e da Floresta Como Sujeito Político*. Doctoral Thesis in Sociology. State University of Campinas. Campinas, São Paulo, Brazil.

Alvarez, Sonia. 2003. Um Outro Mundo (Também Feminista) é Possível: Construindo Espaços Transnacionais e Alternativas Globais a Partir dos Movimentos. *Estudos Feministas* 11 (2): 533–540.

Amorim, João Batista and Maria Luiza Pirez. 2010. "Associativismo em Rede e Desenvolvimento Local: o Programa Um Milhão de Cisternas no Município Alagoano de Olho D'Água do Casado". *Universidade Federal de Campina Grande* 30 (2): 100–110.

Brasil. 2018. *Câmara Interministerial de Segurança Alimentar e Nutricional. III Plano Nacional de Segurança Alimentar e Nutricional. Plansan 2016–2019. Balanço da Execução 2016/2017*. Brasilia: MDA.

———. 2015. *Ministério do Desenvolvimento Agrário. 12 Anos de Transformações, Lutas e Conquistas*. Brasilia: MDA.

Butto, Andrea. 2017. *Movimentos Sociais de Mulheres Rurais: A Construção do Sujeito Feminista.* Doctoral Thesis in Sociology. Federal University of Pernambuco. Recife, Pernambuco. Brazil.

Butto, Andrea and Karla Hora. 2010. "Mulheres e Reforma Agrária no Brasil." Pp. 19–38 in Adriana Lopes and Andrea Butto (Eds.) *Mulheres e Reforma Agrária: A Experiência Recente no Brasil.* Brasília: MDA.

———. 2011. "Políticas Para as Mulheres Rurais: Autonomia e Cidadania." Pp. 11–34 In: Andrea Butto and Isolda Dantas. (Eds.). *Autonomia e Cidadania: Políticas de Organização Produtivas Para as Mulheres no Meio Rural.* Brasília, MDA.

Carrasco, Cristina. 2013. "A Sustentabilidade da Vida Humana: Um Assunto de Mulheres." Pp. 12–47 in Nalu Faria and Miriam Nobre (Eds.). *A Produção do Viver: Ensaios de Economia Feminista.* São Paulo: SOF.

Cavalcanti, Josefa Salete Barbosa. 2014. "Globalização e Ruralidade" Pp. 17-32 in: Maria de Nazareth Baudel Wanderley (Ed.). *Globalização e Desenvolvimento Sustentável: Dinâmicas Sociais no Nordeste Brasileiro.* São Paulo: Polis; Campinas, SP: Ceres—Centro de Estudos Rurais—Unicamp.

Cavalcanti, Josefa Salete Barbosa, Paulo A. Nierdele, Claude Raynaut and Angela Duarte Demasceno Ferreira. 2014. Lá no Territorio: Un Olhar Cidadão Sobre o Programa Territórios da Citadania. Recife: Editora UFPE.

Contag. 2014. Secretaria de Mulheres Trabalhadoras Rurais da Contag. *Mulheres e Agroecologia.* Brasília.

Federici, Silvia. 2014. "O Feminismo e as Políticas do Comum em uma Era de Acumulação Primitiva" Pp. 145-158 in Renata Moreno (Ed.). *Feminismo, Economia e Política: Debates para a Construção da Igualdade e Autonomia das Mulheres.* São Paulo: SOF Sempre Viva Organização Feminista.

Guetat-Bernard, Hélène. 2014. "Agricultura Familiar: o Desafio do Gênero França-Brasil." Pp. 281-298 in Assis, Gláucoa de Olivera, Luzinete Somões Minella and Susana Bornéo Funck (Eds.). *Entrelugares e Mobilidade: Desafios Feministas.* Tubarão: Copiart.

———. 2015. "Travail, Famille et Agriculture. Enjeux de Genre et de Développement, Perspective Nord-Sud." Pp. 279-305 in Christine Verchuur, Isabelle Guérin and Hélène Guetat-Bernard (Eds.). *Sous le Développement, le Genre.* Marseille: IRD.

Heredia, Beatriz Maria Alásia and Rosângela Pezza Cintrão. 2006. "Gênero e Acesso a Políticas Públicas no Meio Rural Brasileiro" *Revista Nera* 9 (8): 1–28.

Marcha das Margaridas. 2015. *"Margaridas Seguem em Marcha por Desenvolvimento Sustentável com Democracia, Justiça, Autonomia, Igualdade e Liberdade—Cadernos de Textos Para Estudos e Debates."* Brasilia: CONTAG.

———. 2011. *Marcha das Margaridas 2011—Caderno de Textos Para Estudo e Debates.* Brasilia: CONTAG.

———. 2007. *Marcha das Margaridas 2007—Caderno de Textos Para Estudo e Debates.* Brasília: CONTAG.

———. 2003. "*Marcha das Margaridas 2003—Texto Base Para Debates*". Brasilia: CONTAG

Mattos, Luciano. 2017. Austeridade Fiscal e Desestruturação das Políticas Públicas Voltadas à Agricultura Familiar Brasileira. *Friedrich Ebert Stiftung Brasil* 39: 1-43. Online document retrieved at http://library.fes.de/pdf-files/bueros/brasilien/13933.pdf%20on%20November%2010, 2017.

Paulilo, Maria Ignez Silveira. 2004. "Trabalho Familiar: Uma Categoria Esquecida de Análise." *Estudos Feministas* 12 (1): 229–252.

Sabourin, Éric. 2014. " L'Agriculture Brésilienne en Débat : Évolutions Récentes, Controverses et Politiques Publiques." *Problèmes d'Amérique Latine* 4 (95): 33-55.

Scherer-Warren, Ilse. 2007. "A Política dos Movimentos Sociais Para o Mundo Rural." Paper Presented at the Confenrence "II Encontro da Rede de Estudos Rurais." Recife PE, Brazil, March 10–13.

Schmitt, Claudia, Paulo Niederle, Mario Ávila, Eric Sabourin, Paulo Pertersen, Luciano Silveira, William Assis, Juliano Palm and Gabriel B. Fernandes. 2017 "A Experiência Brasileira de Construção de Políticas Públicas em Favor da Agroecologia". Pp. 44–69 in Red Políticas

Públicas en América Latina y el Caribe (PP-AL) *Políticas Públicas a Favor de la Agroecología en América Latina y el Caribe*. Brasilia: PP-AL

Silipradi, Emma. 2015. *Mulheres e Agroecologia: Transformando o Campo, as Florestas e as Pessoas.* Rio de Janeiro: UFRJ.

Silva, Berenice Gomes. 2018. *A Marcha das Margaridas: Resistência e Permanências*. Doctoral Thesis in Sociology. Brasilia: University of Brasilia.

Singer, André. 2018. *O Lulismo em Crise: Um Quebra Cabeça do Período Dilma (2011–2018)*. São Paulo: Companhia das Letras.

Van der Ploeg, Jan Dauwe. 2018. *Camponeses e Impérios Alimentares: Lutas por Autonomia e Sustentabilidade na era da Globalização.* Porto Alegre: UFRGS.

Chapter Four

State Intervention in Agri-Food

From Implementation to Maintenance of Irrigated Fruit Production for Export in the San Francisco Valley

Cinthia Regina Nunes Reis and
Stéphane Gérard Emile Guéneau

INTRODUCTION

Brazil is the third largest producer of fruit in the world, but when it comes to exports, it ranks only 23rd globally (MAPA 2018). To correct this situation and optimize its productive potential, in 2018 and in collaboration with the private sector, the Brazilian State introduced the National Plan for the Development of Fruticulture (PNDF) involving the implementation of policies that could improve the quality of production and increase domestic consumption and exports. Central in this effort is the contribution of the San Francisco Valley. Comprised of municipalities in the states of Bahia (Juazeiro, Casa Nova, Sobradinho, Santo Sé, and Curaçá) and Pernambuco (Petrolina, Lagoa Grande, and Santa Maria da Boa Vista), it is responsible for more than 90 percent of Brazil's fruit exports, a status that it has maintained since the 1990s. To be sure, the development of the San Francisco Valley initiated in the 1960s through the adoption of a developmental model based on the modernization of farming. Continued through the end of the 1970s, this model contemplated the capitalist transformation of traditional farming whereby the construction of irrigation infrastructure and the mechanization of production emerged as fundamental aspects of the general transformation of this semi-arid region (Graziano Neto 1986). Known as "conservative modernization," this model saw the fundamental participation of the State that, through direct investment and other measures, permitted the inclusion of

Brazilian agri-food in global production circuits not only as a producer of fresh commodities and raw material for industrial processing but also as a consumer of industrial inputs and machinery (Sorj 1986). According to Cavalcanti and her associates (Cavalcanti, Mota and Gama 2002), in addition to granting credit and lands for the installation of irrigated settlements, state intervention consisted in the creation of public institutions, such as the Brazilian Agricultural Research Corporation (EMBRAPA) and the San Francisco and Parnaíba Valley Development Company (CODEVASF).

After this initial period of modernization, in the 1980s and 1990s public policies followed neoliberal postures. From 2002 to 2016, conversely, neo-developmentalism shaped them. Continuity, however, characterized both these periods as attempts to increase exports, expand market share, and effectively respond to the requirements of the global demand remained. Overall, these changes were driven by the process of globalization that, initiated in the early 1980s, featured the establishment of "production chains formed by multinational corporations that transcend national boundaries, identities and interests" (Castells 2000: 120) and the inclusion of the agri-food sector in global production and consumption networks (Bonanno 2003; Gereffi 1994; Santos 2011).

These food production and consumption networks function in accordance with the broadening of supply chains (Busch 2000). As fresh products reach distant and increasingly quality conscious consumers, new requirements emerge. They include the lengthening of the perishability period of fresh produce; greater differentiation of production; multiplication of market niches; greater specificity of consumer preferences; and the development of new products and markets with innovations in the areas of biology, communication, and transportation (Busch 2000). Additionally, the requirement to produce according to counter-seasonal windows generates new market outlets but also production constraints (Cavalcanti 1995). These constraints refer not only to the fact that production is limited to specific periods established by corporate retailers but also to the production requirements associated with quality certification whereby the sign of quality is awarded only if specific procedures are followed (Bendini and Murmis 2003; Belik 2001; Cavalcanti and Neiman 2005).

Initiated and carried out by corporate actors, this type of control is presented as a signal of the weakening of state regulation and power. Adopting a zero-sum form of reasoning, the expansion of the power of the private sector is associated with an equivalent decrease of state power and ability to intervene in the economy. However, this posture frequently overstates the actions of the private sector and, simultaneously, downplays the important role carried out by the State. More importantly, it pays limited attention to the intrinsic relationship that exists between corporate actors and the State, making it difficult to discern how the latter contributes to the growth of the former (Bonanno 2017). Cavalcanti and Dias (2015) address this problem by underscoring the importance of state intervention in the development of the San Francisco Valley. Analyzing EMBRAPA and CODEVASF, they illustrate the ways in which the Brazilian State promoted regional development projects that followed the requirements and needs of global markets and actors. Stressing the cases of the construction of rapid transportation infrastructure and media networks, they highlight the importance of the action of the Brazilian State in advancing corporate profit growth during the latter part of the twentieth century and the first decade of the twenty-first century.

Employing this view, dwelling on Michel Foucault's concept of governmentality (*gouvernementalité*) and contributing to this book's research question about the emancipatory role of the Brazilian State under the administration of the Worker's Party (PT), our intent in this chapter is to illustrate the role of the Brazilian State in the maintenance of the agro-export development model. We pursue this research objective through an analysis of the public policies that were implemented to ensure the viability of agribusiness in a context characterized by the importance of private certification systems and neoliberal globalization. Specifically, we focus on public policies that are defined either as directly—that is, interventionist economic policies—or indirectly—that is, social policies—supporting the agro-export development model. Overall, our objective is to show the complex and contradictory nature of state action. Organizationally, the remainder of the chapter is divided into three sections. The first briefly presents a review of pertinent literature and the theoretical dimension of our analytical approach based on the work of Foucault (2008). In the second section, we illustrate key aspects of the role of the State in the construction and maintenance of fruit production for export models of development adopted in Brazil. The third and final section provides a set of conclusions highlighting the contradictory role of the State.

STATE ACTIONS AND NEOLIBERAL GOVERNMENTALITY: CERTIFICATION AND PUBLIC POLICIES

Private certification systems understood as an instrument of regulation of production and marketing chains have been studied from various perspectives. In the economic literature, norms and standards are seen as instruments minimizing transaction costs in the so-called "long-distance chains" by homogenizing production processes. The quality and attributes of products are encapsulated and transmitted through certification labels or seals, reducing the asymmetry of information between producers and consumers and, therefore, facilitating the functioning of the market (Coase 1937; Williamson 1975). In the literature on global value chains, Gereffi (1994) analyzes the relationship between producers and buyers in the global market. He considers two forms of control of the chain. The first involves the control of producers who emerge as autonomous agents in decision-making concerning production processes and products. The second refers to control by buyers whereby these actors (e.g., large supermarket chains) shape production processes and product requirements. Considering the latter, certification develops an effective control system as buyers can purchase products endowed with the desired quality without investing in production processes and in often distant production sites.

Other theorists, such as Boltanski and Chiapello (1999), view certification as a mechanism that promotes socio-economic justice and fits the challenges associated with the social and environmental regulation of a global economy dominated by production chains. As this emerging system makes nation-state regulation increasingly difficult, certification, they continue, appears as an effective control formula whereby corporations extend these requirements to the entire production chain. Therefore, this ensures not only the credibility of their own business but also of their solutions to charges of exploitation of human and natural resources. In addition, these authors further contend that certification responds to the demands of niche markets. These are markets characterized by the demand for quality products in which quality is defined by the presence of items such as craft, traditional, organic, and agroecological production. Overall, these authors conclude, the search for certified quality products adds to the social critique of globalization and its standardization and artificialization of food production and consumption, and the equally relevant ethical and aesthetical critiques.

In a similar vein and adopting a political science approach, Guéneau, Lemeilleur, Verdier, Rivière and Leménager (2016) link the systems of certification to effective governance. Focusing on environmental governance, they contend that certification guides the behavior of stakeholders towards sustainable production filling the gap left by the withdrawal of the State in the context of economic globalization and the growing power of transnational corporations. Thus, private actors, such as private corporations and NGOs, they contend, effectively take on part of the functions of the public sector (Guéneau et al. 2016). To be sure, this view of the positive contribution of private certification disregards the fact that these forms of private regulation are part of the process of reconfiguration of public regulation rather than entities that are alternative to it. There is a growing participation of non-state actors in decision-making processes that indicates a strong interaction between private norms and instruments of public regulation (Lascoumes and Le Galés 2012; Fouilleux 2011; Guéneau et al. 2016). According to Guéneau (2018), the institutionalization of private initiatives requires a certain degree of public action, both in the phases of planning and implementation. These actions are based on ideas and values that influence the practices of the State vis-a-vis private initiatives.

It is in this perspective that Foucault's work on governmentality allows an analysis of the practices and motivations of the State to adopt certain representations of what society should be (Foucault 2008). Governmentality, in the broad sense, refers to a set of means that allow the imposition of patterns of behavior on individuals and groups. These patterns of behavior, however, do not necessarily require the spatial proximity of actors for they are applied from a distance. Social control, therefore, assumes a new and more pervasive form that centers on governmentality. Governmentality, or the "art of governing," is defined by Foucault (2008) as a particular way of exercising power that includes as one of its primary elements a specific political rationality, understood as a set of ideas, principles and knowledge that selects what should be the object of social concern for public action (Guéneau 2018). Foucault (2008) argues that competition, and therefore the market itself, can only occur if they are supported by active governance and are no longer viewed as the natural regulators of human interactions as occurred under liberalism. Accordingly, the neoliberal doctrine rescues the interventionist role of the State for the regulation of the economy since economic activity requires public legitimation (Foucault 2008). Therefore, the presence of the State is necessary since it is up to the State to guarantee and maintain the freedom of the market and competition. Foucault states:

> [. . .] it is possible that in this (neo) liberal policy the number of economic interventions is as great as in a planning system, but their nature is different (Foucault 2008: 184).

According to Foucault (2008), Neoliberalism is not synonymous with laissez-faire, but rather, it calls for vigilance and permanent state intervention. He stresses that for neoliberals, "market freedom needs an active and extremely vigilant policy"; therefore, in a neoliberal regime, the government is an active, interventionist government with a modus operandi that is in opposition to nineteenth-century liberalism. Accordingly, "the State is responsible for the result of economic activity." In this neoliberal context, state intervention differs from that of previous eras of the modern world as it specifically translates into techniques that impose patterns of behavior on individuals and groups. Their imposition from a distance signifies that individuals and groups are convinced of—i.e., they internalize—the necessity to adopt, and the desirability of, a certain mentality. This is the mentality of the free market (Pierre and Peters 2000). Foucault (2008), therefore, considers the State as one of the main actors of the art of governing individuals and groups.

This perspective helps us understand the performance of the State and its connections with the private sector in the context of a neoliberal governmentality represented by the certification system. This is understood as a standardization device that guides and controls productive behaviors at a distance. It imposes private definitions of quality standards that differentiate but also harmonize narratives of quality that—albeit private—need state action for the continuity of the process of capitalist accumulation. To analyze the role of the State, we review public policies seeking to understand their cognitive dimension and the reasons for their creation while conceiving of them as actions of one or more public or governmental authorities that might appear different but that display coherence, especially as regards the purpose and duration (Hassenteufel 2011).

In order to identify changes in the forms of public action along the process of creating and maintaining the agro-export development model of the San Francisco Valley, we sought to divide the institutional context into three different periods. The first is the *National-Developmentalist* period. This period spans from about 1960 to 1980 and features the industrialization of the country that was promoted through state programs supporting *import substitution* or the replacement of foreign imported products with domestic production. Specifically, import substitution refers to a growth strategy in which the expansion of the industrial sector is incentivized through the imposition of tariffs on imports and state subsidies to local firms. This developmentalist posture was applied to the agri-food sector along with measures for the modernization and industrialization of farming and food production (Graziano Neto 1986; Graziano da Silva 1999; Mattei 2014; Palmeira and Leite 1997; Sorj 1986).

The second is the period of *Neoliberalism*. This is to be understood as a phase of transition that began in the 1980s and continued through the beginning of the new century. Its central tenet was the reduction of state intervention that included the rolling back of state programs, deregulation of economic activities, privatization of state-owned companies, and liberalization of markets (Santos 2011; Sallum Jr. 2003; Grisa and Schneider 2014). As far as agri-food policies are concerned, the State followed a similar pattern whereby it reduced the financing of agricultural policies, increased the value of the domestic currency, making exports more difficult, reduced the number of institutions and quantity of funds dedicated to agriculture, and increased the irrigated productive area of San Francisco Valley (Martine 1991; Massuquetti 1998).

The third period is the *Neo-Developmentalist* period. Neo-developmentalism was introduced in the early 2000s with the establishment of the first Worker's Party Government in 2002. It centered on the cooperation between the State and private firms to promote the insertion of the latter into production and consumption circuits typical of globalization. In agri-food, globalization entailed the global circulation of products and the concomitant opening of markets. The ensuing enhanced competition was met by corporate calls for quality production. At the consumption levels, corporate retailers enticed consumers by promising quality products. At the production level, they required farmers to meet strict quality requirements for their commodities. The introduction of these requirements translated into the creation of certification programs that provided verification of the claimed quality of products (Cavalcanti 1995; Bendini and Murmis 2003; Belik 2001). From the point of view of social control, certification is an instance of control from a distance. Certification standards are determined in centralized corporate headquarters while execution is demanded at the local level. To meet certification standards, producers rely on direct and indirect state action. In the Brazilian case, this institutional context was marked by the adoption of public developmental policies that included previously excluded actors such as family farmers and traditional communities (Cavalcanti, Wanderley, and Niederle 2014; Grisa and Schneider 2014). Public policies, in turn, were divided into two groups: direct interventionist policies and policies based on indirect forms of intervention. Direct interventionist policies refer to economic policies and, in particular, those directed at the financing of the infrastructure and fiscal and financial subsidies. Indirect forms of intervention consist of social policies such as those that dealt with measures for the support of social need and labor mobilization.

THE STATE AND THE MODERNIZATION OF AGRICULTURE IN THE SAN FRANCISCO VALLEY

State intervention was fundamental in the processes of establishing and developing irrigated fruit production in the San Francisco Valley. It consisted of extended state intervention that promoted financial, technological, and human resources. In the national-developmentalist period, it included the building of infrastructure and the creation of a pool of labor following a Keynesian economic policy. This trend changed under Neoliberalism and involved a reduction of state direct intervention in favor of a process of privatization and the implementation of incentives to private actors. In the most recent Neo-Developmental period, state direct intervention resumed featuring a strong cooperation with the private sector.

The Construction of the San Francisco Valley under National-Developmentalism (1960–1980)

In 1945, the Brazilian State established the *Departamento Nacional de Obras Contra as Secas* (National Department of Works against the Drought or DNOCS) with the specific objective of creating the basic conditions for advanced production in the San Francisco Valley. Endowed with state funds, this institution invested in the building of infrastructures including dams, roads, bridges, ports, railways, hospitals, and landing fields. It also worked for the electrification of the area through the implementation of hydroelectric projects and the concomitant development of telecommunication networks. Important was the effort to make water available in this semi-arid region. Through irrigation, it acquired the necessary high productive capacity that fostered development. These investments were subsidized at the rate of 50 percent of the total value of the project in the case it involved private land. In the case of projects built by municipalities on public land, this percentage increased to 70 percent. Overall 75.2 percent of the water projects were located in private areas, making it difficult for small producers to access state-subsidized water resources (Paes 2009).

Federal public agencies acted effectively. Yet, this action often served the interests of a relatively small segment of the local population, making the unequal distribution of resources a characteristic of the type of developmental model applied in the region. Moreover, although DNOCS was designed to serve the entire Northeast, the states of Bahia and Pernambuco ended up attracting the vast majority of investments. The creation of the San Francisco Valley Commission in 1949, the Northeast Bank of Brazil in 1952, and CODEVASF in 1974 provided impetus to the financing of investments for irrigation projects and the availability of credit for agricultural producers (Moraes 2016). The implementation of the Second National Development Plan (PND 2) in 1974 defined the period's state action that established newly irrigated areas, promoted the expansion of fruit production, supported vocational training, and created the conditions for the proliferation of agri-business firms in the region. In essence, state direct intervention was instrumental for the growth of the local productive capacity. However, in so doing it also marked a policy shift that changed from the social goal of generating food security to the economic objective of creating an agro-industrial developmental pole based on irrigated agriculture (Silva 2012).

Neoliberalism and State Action in Support of Agri-Business in the Valley (1980–2002)

As indicated above, this period is characterized by a restructuring of state intervention featuring the reduction of subsidies and financing to producers, the reorientation of production toward global markets, reduced state participation in the management of the irrigated areas, and processes of privatization that emerged as state sponsorship declined. To be sure, in the 1980s, growers in the San Francisco Valley were not yet fully participating in the certification regulated global market. In effect, local production was still primarily oriented toward the domestic market while produce processing continued to be present. Promoted in the previous national-developmentalist period and heavily supported by the State, local processing firms, however, entered their final crisis in the 1980s. As state subsidies began to decline, these firms could not survive market fluctuations and global competition. By the end of the decade, both fruit processing and the once dominant vegetable production (i.e., tomatoes) de facto ceased to exist.

In agri-food, the 1990s saw the exponential growth of global competition with the enhanced process of concentration of capital. This rapid change was accompanied by the widespread adoption of neoliberal policies and the popularity of pronouncements in favor of the positive outcomes generated by the free functioning of the market. In this context, however, local producers became aware that it was extremely difficult to remain competitive without state support. Therefore, and against dominant political trends, they lamented the reduction of the intervention of the State. Their argument in favor of state intervention rested on the claim that the high levels of productivity, the efficient management of irrigated land, crop diversification and overall competitiveness could not be maintained without state support. Simultaneously, they rejected projects of privatization that called for producers to "emancipate" from state support (Estadão 2012a; 2012b). The outcome of this situation was that while the neoliberal Brazilian State promoted privatization and market liberalization, producers in the San Francisco Valley called for continuous support from the State.

The result of this contention consisted of the reduction of agricultural credit and tax incentives for producers that were consistent with the neoliberal policy that the government adopted at the time. Moreover, there was a significant reduction of technical assistance to local producers mitigated by the establishment of the Federal University of the San Francisco Valley (UNIVASF): an institution primarily devoted to the advancement of local agri-food. To be sure, while this project was formally launched in the mid-1990s, classes began in 2004 and campus construction was completed in 2008, six years after the Worker's Party government took office. Simultaneously, however, the opposition to privatization policies mounted by San Francisco Valley producers generated some results as the State continued to provide support for irrigation infrastructure and projects. Overall, this phase was characterized by a retraction of direct state support accompanied by a stagnation in the indirect actions and producers' requests for continuous state intervention.

State Intervention for the Development of Irrigated Fruit Production for Export under Neo-Developmentalism (2002–2015)

The 2002 election of Lula as President of Brazil and the associated political victory of the Workers' Party marked the beginning of the Neo-Developmentalist period. The political platform proposed by the victorious PT centered on a renewed wave of state intervention in the economy to promote growth directed at enhancing the well-being of the working class and the poor. Despite the pronouncements that illustrated this political project, the cognitive and practical dimensions that privileged agribusiness as the most desirable form of irrigated agriculture remained. They were also compatible with both Neoliberalism and the demand of the business community for state support of private investments. This State's posture represented the type of neoliberal governmentality experienced in the San Francisco Valley. Specifically and as far as direct intervention is concerned, the State invested important financial resources and provided subsidies for the development of infrastructure. An example of this direct state intervention consists of its actions to address the 2007–2010 water crisis in which CODEVASF invested resources in the order of more than 2.7 billion Reals between 2007 and 2010 and another 1.3 billion Reals between 2011 and 2014. Another instance is the "More Irrigation" Program that the Ministry of National Integration launched in 2012 with investments of more than 10 billion Reals. This program made the government responsible for the construction and maintenance of irrigation projects, infrastructure such as the expansion of the Petrolina airport, and financial programs such as the restructuring of credit for growers (Costa 2012).

Concerning indirect intervention, the State was instrumental for the training and mobilization of the labor supply necessary for agribusiness firms. However, and arguably more important, was the role of the State in the creation of social conditions that allowed workers to make themselves available for farm work. Instrumental for the success of this State's role and illustrative of the type of indirect intervention of the Brazilian State were the program "New Seed" and the establishment of the Municipal Environment Agency (AMMA).

The New Seed Program

During harvest (April to October), about 240,000 workers are employed in the San Francisco Valley. Some of the local commodities, such as grapes, required a significant number of specialized laborers. According to Lima and Miranda (2001), grape production requires, on average, 1,270 working days/hectare/year, mostly performed by female labor (80 percent of the labor force employed). Along with harvesting and packaging, particularly time-consuming is the manual pruning of grape bunches that provides the shape required by certification. Moreover, despite the fact that fruticulture occupies a large contingent of labor, jobs are seasonal. Accordingly, a significant number of local workers prefer employment in other sectors, such as construction. The net result is a shortage of seasonal workers for the harvest and other seasonal tasks such as pruning. As indicated above, there is a particular demand for female workers as they are paid less than men, do not enter alternative labor markets and are considered better suited for the work in fruit production (Cavalcanti and Bendini 2014; Cavalcanti et al. 2014). The New Seed program was part of the State's intervention to generate this supply of female labor for seasonal agricultural work.

Introduced in May 2010 by the city of Petrolina, this municipal program consisted of the overt objective of promoting a good early childhood for local children. Specifically, its stated objective aimed at the creation of conditions that would allow the full and balanced development of children residing in the communities of the metropolitan area. The text of the legislation states:

> [The objective of the program is] to promote, in collaboration with families and local communities, conditions that would favor the full development of the children of Petrolina in regard to their physical, psychological, intellectual and social aspects (Regimento Escolar do Programa Nova Semente. 2013 Art. 13:4).

Following this mandate, nurseries were established in rural areas adjacent to the city and, particularly, in locations close to irrigated fields. They operated during the normal hours of work in the fields of 6 a.m. to 6 p.m. Their proximity to the fields, however, was not simply a coincidence. It indicated the covert, and arguably more important, objective of this program: freeing local women from the duty of child-care and allowing them to be available for agricultural work. In effect, and since the implementation of this program, the supply of seasonal labor significantly improved in the region allowing agribusiness firms to count on a dependable yet relatively inexpensive labor. A member of the Secretariat of Economic and Agricultural Development of the municipality of Petrolina explains the situation accordingly:

> You may ask what has daycare to do with fruit export, right? And here comes the importance of the daycare centers established by New Seed. They open at five thirty or six o'clock in the morning and stay open until nightfall. They are available in the city, but above all, near the irrigated areas. We have data indicating that about 87 percent of women have now returned to work. Why is that? They got pregnant, had their children and then got stuck at home taking care of the babies. They could not work. Now we have the New Seed and all these women, that wanted to work and could not work, now have a job. There are more than 6,000 families participating in the program. It generates development because [. . .] we have 6,000 women who no longer stay at home but go to work (interview conducted on 6/26/2016).

The Municipal Environment Agency (AMMA)

Established in March 2011, AMMA is the environmental protection agency for the Petrolina metropolitan area. Its official goal is to "execute and enforce the policies and governmental directives regarding the environment within the municipal territory (Official Municipal Petrolina 2011). However, as in the case of New Seed, this overt function coexists with the covert function of meeting the demands of global corporate retailers. Specifically, large transnational supermarket chains employ certification to demonstrate the quality of their products to consumers. In this context, they require producers to meet specific standards including standards that specifically refer to the use of natural resources and the protection of the environment (Cavalcanti and Bendini 2014; Cavalcanti et al. 2014). An official of the city of Petrolina states:

> European importing companies stress the importance of socio-environmental sustainability. Therefore, because we have to comply with all these rules, the municipality created the Municipal Environment Agency. This was done exactly to expedite the process of certifications and environmental licenses that were previously issued by the State Environmental Agency (CPRH). This agency was slow and delays hurt our ability to export. We depend on the State and if it has a political crisis the society suffers, entrepreneurs and agribusiness suffer—all that depends on the State (interview conducted on 06/29/2016).

In essence, both the New Seed Program and the creation of the AMMA are parts of indirect state intervention in the economy. Legitimized through references to important social issues (i.e., early child development and environmental protection), they assisted agribusiness firms in their effort to maintain competitiveness in the global market.

CONCLUSIONS

In the San Francisco Valley, the State was and continues to be a central actor for the development models implemented in the region. In the national-developmental years, modernization mandated the implementation of strong direct intervention policies that, ultimately, characterized the period. Under the neoliberal period, the restructuring of state intervention centered on the reduction of subsidies and direct investment. However, it also involved support for firms in their effort to remain competitive in the global market. While advocates of the free-market, the neoliberal administrations did not hesitate to use state resources to assist local agri-food enterprises in their participation in global markets and competition.

In the Neo-developmentalist years, the State continued its significant role in the promotion of agri-food export-oriented policies. The declared objective of the PT administrations was to advance the cause of the working class and the poor. However, the form of governmentality employed during these years did not alter the asymmetric balance of power in the organization of local production processes. On the contrary, it incisively supported the same policy of agro-export that characterized the neoliberal period. The significant aspect of the role of the State in the Neo-developmentalist period was its dual dimension. On the one hand, it supported the aspirations of the local lower classes through specific policies and overt pronouncements. On the other hand, it generated significant support for agro-business through a number of measures that aimed at assisting private sector actors in their efforts to compete in the global market.

As far as the research question of this book is concerned, the analysis of the role of the State in the neo-developmentalist era speaks directly of the contradictory nature of the actions of the Brazilian State. Its contradiction is summarized by the dual nature of state intervention. In particular, it refers to the structural limits of actions that are intended to benefit actors with contrasting interests. The advancement of the conditions of labor in the San Francisco Valley remains problematic if it continues to be dependent on the increased competitiveness of agribusiness firms. This competitiveness, in turn, is affected by the overwhelming power of transnational corporate retailers that shape the production requirements in the region. While it is arguable that the ultimate objectives of the State under neo-developmentalism were emancipatory and responded to the legitimate interests of local stakeholders, the idea that the Brazilian State could simultaneously support labor and management emerge as seriously flawed. Finally, attempts to support the insertion of Brazilian producers in corporate-controlled global circuits underestimated the power that transnational corporations hold in contemporary society.

BIBLIOGRAPHY

Belik, Walter. 2001. *Muito Além da Porteira: Mudanças nas Formas de Coordenação da Cadeia Agroalimentar no Brasil*. Campinas: UNICAMP. IE.

Bendini, Monica and Miguel Murmis 2003. "Imágenes del Campo Latinoamericano en el Contexto de La Mundializácion." In Monica Bendini, Josefa Salete Cavalcanti, Migue Murmis, and Pedro Tsakoumagko (Eds.), *El Campo en la Sociologia Actual: Una Perspectiva Latino Americana* (pp. 5–15). Buenos Aires: Editorial La Colmena.

Boltanski, Luc, and Eve Chiapello. 1999. *Le Nouvel Esprit du Capitalismo*. Paris: Gallimard.

Bonanno, Alessandro. 2017. *The Legitimation Crisis of Neoliberalism*. New York: Palgrave-Macmillan.

———. 2003. "La Globalización Agro-Alimentaria: sus Características y Perspectivas Futuras." *Estudos de Sociologia* 9 (1): 31–53.

Busch, Lawrence. 2000. "The Moral Economy of Grades and Standards." *Journal of Rural Studies* 16: 273–283.

Castells, Manuel. 2000. *A Sociedade em Rede—A Era da Informação: Economia, Sociedade e Cultura*. São Paulo: Paz e Terra.

Cavalcanti, Josefa Salete Barbosa. 1995. "Globalização e Agricultura: Processos Sociais e Perspectivas Teóricas." *Estudos de Sociologia* 1 (2): 115–118.

Cavalcanti, Josefa Salete Barbosa, and Monica Isabel Bendini. 2014. "Globalization and Change in Labor Relations in Fruit Regions of Brazil and Argentina." In Alessandro Bonanno and Josefa Salete Barbosa Cavalcanti (Eds.), *Labor Relations in Globalized Food: Research in Rural Sociology and Development* (pp. 3–32). Bingley, UK: Emerald Group Publishing.

Cavalcanti, Josefa Salete Barbosa and Gustavo Dias 2015. "Cadeias Globais de Alimentos, Redes de Atores e Qualidades na Produção de Frutas para Exportação: elos entre Brasil e Alemanha." *Estudos de Sociologia* 2 (21): 279–310.

Cavalcanti, Josefa Salete Barbosa, Nazareth Wanderley, and Paulo Niederle (Eds.). 2014. *Participação Território e Cidadania: Um Olhar Sobre a Política de Desenvolvimento Territorial no Brasil*. Recife: Editora Universitária da UFPE.

Cavalcanti, Josefa Salete Barbosa, and Guillermo Neiman (Eds.). 2005. *Acerca de la Globalización en la Agricultura*. Buenos Aires: Ciccus.

Cavalcanti, Josefa Salete. Barbosa; Dalva Mota and Pedro Carlos Gama Da Silva. 2002 . "Mirando Hacia el Norte: Clase, Género y Etnicidad en los Espacios de Fruticultura del Nordeste de Brasil." *Áreas* 22: 161–181.

Coase, Ronald. H. 1937. "The Nature of the Firm." *Economica, New Series* 4 (16): 386–405.

Costa, Ecio de Farias. 2012. "Os Determinantes do Crédito na Fruticultura Irrigada no Vale do São Francisco." *BNDES WORKING PAPERS. Programa de Fomento à Pesquisa em Desenvolvimento Econômico*—PDE.

Diário Oficial Prefeitura Municipal de Petrolina. 2011. ano 1, n. 178, Pernambuco, 30 de março de 2011. http://pe.portaldatransparencia.com.br/prefeitura/petrolina/index.cfm?pagina=abreDocumento&arquivo=33E30A. Accessed February 7, 2017.

Estadão. 2012a. "Canal Exclusivo Leva Agua Até Fazenda de Irmão do Ministro. 2017. http://politica.estadao.com.br/noticias/eleicoes,canal-exclusivo-leva-agua-ate-fazenda-de-irmao-do-ministro-imp-,825706. Accessed January 5, 2017.

Estadão. 2012b. Obras de Irrigação Inacabadas no clã Coelho Põem em Xeque Parceria Público Privada. 2017. http://politica.estadao.com.br/noticias/eleicoes,obras-de-irrigacao-inacabadas-no-cla-coelho-poem-em-xeque-parceria-privada-imp-,825703. Accessed February 5, 2017.

Fouilleux, Eve. 2011. "Analisar a Mudança: Políticas Públicas e Debates num Sistema em Diferentes Níveis de Governança." *Estudos. Sociedade. e Agricultura* 19(1): 88–125.

Foucault, Michel. 2008. *Nascimento da Biopolítica*. São Paulo: Martins Fontes.

Gereffi, Gary. 1994. "Introduction: Global Commodity Chains." In Gary Gereffi and Miguel Korzeniewicz (Eds.), *Commodity Chains and Global Capitalism* (pp. 1–14). Westport & London: Praeger.

Graziano da Silva Jose. 1999. *O Novo Rural Brasileiro*. Campinas: Unicamp

Graziano Neto, Francisco. 1986. *Questão Agrária e Ecologia: Crítica da Agricultura Moderna*. São Paulo: Brasiliense.

Grisa, Catia, and Sergio Schneider. 2014. "Três Gerações de Políticas Públicas para a Agricultura Familiar e Formas de Interação entre Sociedade e Estado no Brasil." *Revista de Economi e Sociologia Rural* 52 (1): 125–146.

Guéneau, Stéphane. 2018. "La Gouvernance Privée de la Durabilité des Filières D'exportation Agroindustrielles Brésiliennes: Conséquences d'une Gouvernementalité Néolibérale." http://journals.openedition.org/bresils/2468; DOI: 10.4000/bresils.2468. Accessed December 7, 2018.

Guéneau, Stéphane, Sylvaine Lemeilleur, Anne-Gaëlle Verdier, Françoise Rivière and Thiphaine Leménager. 2016. *Le Développement des Dispositifs de Certification Environnementale dans les Outre-Mer. Quelles Perspectives pour la Préservation de la Biodiversité?* Paris: Etudes de l'AFD.

Hassenteufel, Patrick. 2011. *Sociologie Politique: L'action Publique*. Paris: Armand Colin.

Lascoumes, Pierre and Patrick Le Galès. 2012. "A Ação Pública Abordada pelos seus Instrumentos." *Revista Pós-Ciências Sociais* 9 (18): 19–43.

Lima, J. and E. Miranda. 2001. "Fruticultura Irrigada no Vale do São Francisco: Incorporação Tecnológica, Competitividade e Sustentabilidade." *Revista Econômica do Nordeste* 32 (Special Issue): 611–632.

MAPA. 2018. "Mapa Vai Lançar Plano para Aumentar Exportações de Frutas." http://www.agricultura.gov.br/noticias/mapa-vai-lancar-plano-para-aumentar-exportacoes-de-frutas. Accessed June 20, 2018.

Mattei, Lauro. 2014. "Considerações Acerca de Teses Recentes sobre o Mundo Rural Brasileiro." *Revista de Economia e Sociologia Rural* 52 (1): 105–124.

Martine, George. 1991. "A Trajetória da Modernização Agrícola: A Quem Beneficia?" *Lua Nova* 23 (9): 7–37.

Massuquetti, Angelica. 1998. *A Mudança no Padrão de Financiamento da Agricultura Brasileira no Período 1965–97*. PhD dissertation. Porto Alegre: College of Economic Sciences, Federal University of do Rio Grande do Sul.

Moraes, Alberto D. 2016. *Entre a Incerteza e a Confiança: Mercados e Relações Sociais de Troca Comercial dos Fruticultores no Polo Petrolina-Pe/ Juazeiro-BA*. PhD dissertation. Recife: Department of Sociology, Federa University of Pernambuco, CFCH, Programa de Pós-Graduação em Sociologia.

Paes, Reginaldo. 2009. *Alternativas para o Desenvolvimento Sustentável do Submédio São Francisco*. PhD Dissertation. Brasília: Center for Sustainable Development. University of Brasilia.

Palmeira, Moacir and Sergio Leite. 1997. "Debates Econômicos, Processos Sociais e Lutas Políticas: Reflexões Sobre a Questão Agrária." *Debates CPDA*. 1 September: 32–45.

Pierre, Jon and B. Guy Peters. 2000. *Governance, Politics and the State*. New York: St. Martin's Press.

Regimento Escolar do Programa Nova Semente. 2013. http://pe.portaldatransparencia.com.br/prefeitura/petrolina/index.cfm?pagina=abreDocumento&arquivo=33E30A59 Accessed March 5, 2017.

Sallum Jr. Brasilio. 2003. "Metamorfoses do Estado no final do século XX." *Revista Brasileira de Ciências Sociais* 18 (52): 35–55.

Santos, Rodrigo. 2011. "Redes de Produção Globais (RPGs): Contribuições Conceituais para a Pesquisa em Ciências Sociais." *Revista Pós Ciências Sociai* 8: 127–141.

Silva, P. C. G. 2012. *Projetos de Irrigação e o desenvolvimento do Submédio do Vale São Francisco*. Online document. https://ainfo.cnptia.embrapa.br/digital/bitstream/item/124737/1/Pedro.pdf. Accessed June 18, 2016.

Sorj, Bernardo. 1986. *Estado e Classes Sociais na Agricultura Brasileira*. Rio de Janeiro: Guanabara.

Williamson, Oliver. E. 1975. *Markets and Hierarchies: Analysis and Antitrust Implications*. New York: Free Press.

Chapter Five

Oil Palm Cultivation in the Brazilian Amazon

State Actions, Interest Groups, and Conflict

Dalva Maria da Mota, Moisés Mourão Júnior, and Heribert Schmitz

This chapter investigates the issue of the production of palm oil (*Elaeis guineenses*) in the Brazilian Amazon by focusing on the actions of the State, agri-food special interest groups, and the conflicts that the expansion of this cultivation in the Northeast of the state of Pará (NEP) generated. The growth of palm oil production is part of that international division of labor that assigns to selected regions in Asia, Africa, and Latin America the role of commodity producers for export to countries and regions such as India, China and the European Union. Criticisms and commentaries associated with this expansion engendered a heated debate on pertinent social, economic, and environmental issues that unfolded in various spheres, including academia, social movements, and research and development institutions. At the social level, this debate touched upon controversies such as the importance of the creation of new employment and more income versus the destruction of traditional ways of life or calls for the production of healthy food versus the deterioration of resources traditionally used by local populations. At the economic level, it contrasted ideas such as the desirability of limiting the negative effects of oil price fluctuations through the implementation of a plantation system versus the defense of small farm holders and the development of food security. At the environmental level, topics discussed included reforestation and the creation of alternative energy sources to curb gas emissions versus land grabbing and the reduction of biodiversity.

As in the cases of other commodities, opposing views notwithstanding, in Brazil, oil palm production is portrayed optimistically as an effective action of corporate agri-food (Veiga and Rodrigues 2016). Vieira, Ribeiro, and Fishlow (2017: 176) state that in the last decades, "[t]he Brazilian agricultural sector has performed a miracle in productive terms, despite the absence of incentives, limited planning and inadequate infrastructure." Leite and Wesz Junior (2016: 105–106) maintain a similar position in their analysis of the agri-food sector. They contend that it generated "a very positive performance in terms of production, productivity, export volume and trade balance. . . . [that is almost exclusively the outcome] . . . of private initiative and the entrepreneurship of agri-business leaders." Moreover, they add, this was achieved with the absence of or even despite the inefficiency of the State. Questioning these findings, Leite and his associates (2016) agree with the conclusion of Heredia, Palmeira, and Leite (2010: 165), who affirm, "[. . .] one cannot speak of agribusiness without thinking about the State and public policies that made possible not only its origins but also its expansion." They further add that:

> [O]ne of the elements to which the present text refers is the still important "role of the State" that, although minimized by the "interpreters" of trends in agribusiness, remains active either through sectorial policies related to the rural/agro-industrial environment, or through more global policies (such as infrastructure), or in the attempt to establish a regulatory framework in the fields of labor relations and the environment (Heredia et al. 2010: 173).

Considering this debate, the objective of the chapter is to analyze the actions of the State toward the expansion and strengthening of oil palm production, emphasizing the magnitude of these actions and the controversies regarding the role of the State. Invited "not to intervene" in the economy, the State becomes a central actor precisely because production turns viable due to state subsidies and intervention. As Bonanno indicates:

> [Under neoliberalism] any intervention of the State in the economy and society is considered negative unless it is directed at the creation of markets and the controlling of opposition. Therefore, while state intervention is condemned by neoliberals, it is also advocated when it establishes rules that favor the neoliberal view of society (Bonanno 2018: 39).

In the three governments of the Workers' Party (PT), the Brazilian State subscribed to a posture that made "poverty reduction and the achievement of equality long-term national objectives" (Singer 2010: no page). Singer (2010) contends that a convergence of interests between industrial capital and the emergent proletariat (the productive coalition) and financial capital and the traditional middle class (the financial coalition) emerged. This convergence of interests featured the fragility of, and antagonisms between, these fractions of capital. Concerning agriculture, we agree with Maluf (2017), who states that in actual terms "this antagonism was expressed especially in the granting of simultaneous, albeit unequal, support to different and conflicting agri-food production models. They were represented, at one extreme, by large-scale monoculture and, at the other, by family-based and diversified production" (Maluf 2017: 180).

According to Favareto (2017: 10), the international context imposed other aggravating factors because, in the case of the industrial sector, the space of the international insertion that Brazil sought from the time of the presidency of Getúlio Vargas to that of Lula was occupied by Asian countries. In the cases of the advanced tertiary and financial sectors, this space was occupied by North American and European countries. Consequently, Brazil and other countries in Latin America:

> [u]nderwent a process of re-primarization of their export patterns in spite of all developmental efforts of the last 80 or 90 years. This re-primarization of exports was accompanied by the outsourcing of the domestic economy that generated employment and income, especially in the commerce and services sectors (Favareto 2017: 10).

The implementation of the policy for oil palm production was part of this strategy, yet it occurred primarily after the financial crisis of 2007–2008 that put an end to the ability of the PT to finance its social democratic model. Moreover, the Dilma administration (2011–2016) implemented policies based on the concept of "one agriculture," eliminating differences in the treatment of family farming and corporate agriculture (Favareto 2010: 8). All farms became part of "agribusiness," making membership in this category problematic and difficult to discern. In effect, this was a return to the vision that prevailed during the military dictatorship of the 1960s whereby all farmers were considered rural producers regardless of the size of their operations and income. Simultaneously, it erased all the gains obtained by the pro-family farming political movement that pressed the Fernando Henrique Cardoso government first and the Lula administration later to enact specific policies such as the National Program for Strengthening Family Agriculture or PRONAF. The elimination of the Ministry of Agrarian Development (MDA) under the Temer administration completed the process of ending specific policies for small-scale agriculture.

THE PRODUCTION OF OIL PALMS IN THE STATE OF PARÁ

Regardless of its use, production volume and environmental and social impact, the cultivation of oil palms attracts worldwide attention. Oil palms account for 20 percent of the world's permanent cropping areas with a two-to-threefold increase forecasted by 2050. According to data from the US Department of Agriculture, production estimates for 2018 are 65,320 tons for Asia, 4,463,000 tons for the Americas and 2,796,000 tons for Africa (United States Department of Agriculture 2018). Agri-food corporations dominate the production chain and control large portions of land often used for monoculture. Corporate production coexists with medium and small-scale producers that operate by employing different systems of production and production contracts.

In the state of Pará, the industrial cultivation oil palms initiated in the 1940s and, currently, accounts for almost 90 percent of the entire production of Brazil—equal to 300 thousand tons of palm oil (Homma 2016). Despite official pronouncements about its use as biofuel, Pará palm oil is predominantly employed by the food and pharmaceutical sectors as Brazil imports about 90 percent of its vegetable oil (Bentes and Homma 2016). In recent years, palm oil imports far outstripped exports. According to calculations from Bentes and Homma (2016), in the 2010–2015 five-year period, Brazil imported 1,899,891 metric tons of palm oil for a total of US $1,981,840,000. However, the monetary ratio of exports over imports increased steadily from 5.35 percent in 2010 to 23.63 percent in 2014. By 2015, this ratio jumped to 34.48 percent due to the strong exchange rate with the dollar.

Even though it is considered to be underestimated, the palm oil production data set generated by the *Brazilian Institute of Geography and Statistics* (IBGE 2017) is the only national source that—featuring a 1988 to 2015 historical series—allows estimates of the planted area, production, and municipalities involved. Reflecting on this data set, we identify three production phases. The first, or "initial," phase spanned from 1988 to 1994. It consisted of the implantation of the palm oil fields in the Amazon region promoted by economic development institutions such as the Superintendência do Desenvolvimento da Amazônia (Superintendency for Development of the Amazon) or SUDAM. This action was accompanied by the establishment of the first private firms that operated over a planted area of about 107,000 hectares. Planting took the form of a double concentration with palms grown near the metropolitan area of Belém and in the vicinities of the municipalities of Tailândia and Moju. To be sure, cultivation also expanded closer to a smaller but growing number of additional municipalities. It was a phase of fundamental experimentation and productivity was low at about twelve tons per hectare.

A second, or "strengthening," phase took place from 1995 to 2009 and showed a marked geographic change. In this phase, the production area extended towards the NEP, reaching a total of about 171,500 hectares. Most of this production took place in the municipalities of the "initial" phase and in the municipalities of the microregion Tomé-Açu. This micro region was particularly suitable for cultivation due to the ease of access to land and abundant rainfall. In this phase, the number of municipalities involved in production remained largely constant with some variations indicating a concentration in the main production poles, particularly in the municipality of Tailândia. Productivity increased to about eighteen tons per hectare.

The third and contemporary phase, or "expansion," began in 2010. It is characterized by the strong intervention of the State, particularly through its support of pertinent scientific research under the leadership of the Brazilian Agricultural Research Corporation (Empresa Brasileira de Pesquisa Agropecuária) or EMBRAPA. In this expansion phase alone, this research and extension agency of the Brazilian State published 419 scientific works on palm oil culture, of which, however, only 14 percent dealt with socioeconomic issues (BDPA 2018). Additionally, this phase featured an increase in the areas planted that reached about 273,000 hectares concentrated in the NEP (IBGE 2017). This mesoregion contains 95 percent of the state production while the metropolitan area of Belém holds only 5 percent of production (Mourão Júnior 2017). In the expansion phase and throughout Brazil, public policies were specifically implemented to support raw material producing regions that featured the cultivation of oil palms, castor beans, and jatropha for biofuels. According to official pronouncements, the aim of this initiative was to diversify energy sources and reduce the national dependence on imported fossil fuels. It also intended to represent a paradigmatic shift that centered on the establishment of an innovative model with the support of the State and the involvement of the sector corporations, unions, and family farmers.

In the case of oil palms, this initiative involved a set of actions that promoted the concentration of land, extensive homogeneous planting, the creation of industrial plants, and links with international markets (Silva, Magalhães and Farias 2016). They served the interests of established economic groups, segments of social movements and of middle and small farmers who produced for agroindustries (Abramovay and Magalhães 2007). These actions, however, negatively affected traditional communities whose ways of life included different conceptions of time and space, independence from modern markets, and a benign interaction with the environment (MP-PA 2014). Estimates for oil palm cultivation in Pará indicate an area of more than 244,000 hectares distributed in thirty-one municipalities (Brandão and Schoneveld 2015). According to the data, about 90 percent of the total land is controlled by nine agribusiness firms while the remaining 10 percent belongs to 1,240 farmers that operate family farms under contract with agribusiness firms (Abrapalma 2014). These farms devote at least ten hectares of land and the appropriate farm family labor force to oil palm cultivation.

The expansion of oil palm cultivation is a highly concentrated process with strong support from the State. Problems associated with this expansion are interpreted in different ways. According to the president of the Brazilian Association of Palm Oil Producers (ABRAPALMA):

> [T]he greatest challenge of any producer in Pará is land tenure. If Pará wants to grow in the agricultural area, it will have to solve this. No one is investing because of the lack of land regulation" (Diário do Pará on line 2017).

According to Wilkinson (2017: 18), the issues are different and more specific:

> After the global financial crisis of 2007/2008, the discovery of the pre-salt oil reserve, shrinking expectations about the global ethanol market and the campaign against land grabbing itself, concerns about land and foreign investment in Brazil became more explicit.

Admittedly, there has been a decrease in the expansion of oil palm cultivation due to some of the aforementioned reasons along with the existence of requests for public policies that promote the creation of jobs and income while protecting the environment, notably in regard to climate change, and decrease land grabbing (Backhouse 2013).

PUBLIC POLICIES: INSTRUMENTS FOR THE PRODUCTION OF PALM OIL

As illustrated earlier, the expansion phase of palm oil production in Pará has been characterized by the fundamental support of a number of public policy initiatives. Notable among them are: the *Programa Nacional de Produção de Biocombustível* (National Biofuel Production Program) or PNPB, the *Programa de Produção Sustentável de Palma de Óleo* (Sustainable Palm Oil Production Program) or PSOP and *the Zoneamento Agroecológico* (Agroecological Zoning) or ZAE-PALMA. Simultaneously, interest groups organized to promote this model of expansion.

The Programs of Public Policies and Other Federal Initiatives

In 2005, during a visit to a palm oil company in the state of Pará, the then President Lula announced the approval of a project by Congress to:

> transform palm oil into biofuel to be a substitute for the diesel oil used in tractor, truck and bus engines for the entirety of Brazil. This means that, over

time, Brazil can become the first country in the world to have such a strong policy of biofuel production and the production of biodiesel from oil palms, castor beans, soybeans, sunflowers and so many other things that can allow us to become a great country. Brazil will use oil to export and replace diesel with biodiesel that generates many more jobs, much less polluting, and can transform Brazil into a much more independent country (Presidência da República, Secretaria de Imprensa e Divulgação 2005).

The project Lula referred to is the PNPB. Launched in 2004 by the federal government, it combined support for the production of palm seeds with initiatives for the development of family agriculture, forest conservation, and the decrease of the country's dependence on imported fossil fuels. This policy focused on the accumulated experience of the production of alternative bio-energy that saw in the *Proálcool* program of the 1970s a more relevant example. These positive views were contrasted by critical analyses. One critic observed that "[the call for] ecologically sustainable developmental projects in already anthropogenic areas . . . crossed the public debate practically without being questioned" (Backhouse 2013: 6). In addition, when reviewing the phenomenon of extractivism in Brazil, another scholar stated:

While the Andean nations dissected the economic and political components of progressive extractivism, in Brazil neither the major NGOs nor many academics achieved the necessary independence from the governments of the Workers' Party (PT) to contribute to that critique (Gudynas 2017: 120).

Overall, studies that document the ways in which monocultures generate the disruption of traditional ways of life (Nahum and Santos, 2013), land concentration (Silva, Magalhães and Assunçao de Farias 2016) and biodiversity loss abound, making PNPB a symbol of the contradictory nature of the strategy of the Lula government (Butler and Laurance 2009; Lees, Moura, de Almeida, and Vieira 2015).

The contradictory nature of the PNPB is further illustrated by its Social Fuel Seal (SCS). This is an important initiative of PNPB designed to bestow upon pertinent actors the politically relevant status of promoters of social inclusion.[1] Social inclusion is a critical issue concerning the production of global commodities that is viewed as a progressive step in response to charges of exploitation of natural resources and indigenous peoples leveled against corporate plans to exploit natural resources. As part of a public policy coordinated by the MDA[2] under the Lula Government, this initiative was supported by corporate representatives and segments of social movements alike. These groups publicized it among farmers and associated it with alternative forms of production. Incentives—at the least in its first formulation—included technical support and credit designed to increase farmers' income. Among the conditions that biofuel companies had to meet to secure SCS was that they needed to train family farmers in the production of palm oil and that this training had to be compatible with food security and the generation of income (MDA 2017). Additionally, and for the case of the state of Pará in particular, companies could secure financial and operational advantages if they acquired 15 percent of raw materials from family farms. These rules are still in effect at the time of this writing in mid-2018. Similar conclusions apply for the case of the state of Pará. As in the rest of the country, despite these incentives, SCS did not have the expected impact in the state. Data from the Secretaria Especial de Agricultura Familiar e do Desenvolvimento Agrário (Special Secretariat for Family Agriculture and Agrarian Development) show that in 2017, less than 1 percent of palm oil production was transformed into biodiesel and that there was only one company that owned a SCS in the state (SEAD 2018).

Overall, evaluation studies show that the success of PNPB remains limited as the number of family farmers involved falls below expectations (Pires 2015). Explaining the PNPB limited impact, the president of the Câmara Setorial da Cadeia Produtiva da Palma de Óleo (Sector Chamber of the Palm Oil Production Chain), contends that the primary reason for the lack of local production of biofuel is the absence of a processing plant in the state as the nearest plant is located in the state of Bahia (Abrapalma 2017a). Additionally, he stresses structural and political impediments by arguing that:

> We lack public policies for the production of biodiesel in Pará that would allow us to meet future national demand levels. In order to achieve this goal, we would have to expand the planted area to 300,000 hectares and prices would have to be higher and subsidized (Abrapalma 2017a: 8).

Additionally, pertinent studies conclude that the PNPB idealized the production of palm oil for biofuel but its incentives missed the proposed goal. Paradoxically, however, this promoted other productions as palm seed acquisitions by the transformation industry occurred primarily in established crops, such as soybeans, rather than oil palms (Castro 2011; Silva 2013).

Launched by President Lula in 2010 and identifying Pará as the primary production area (90 percent of the entire domestic oil palm crop is generated by this state), the PSOP is designed to promote and regulate the expansion of palm oil production through the availability of credit for different types of producers and the implementation of agro-ecological zoning. In the case of the availability of credit, this effort includes three types of financing implemented through the Bank of Brazil and the Bank of Amazon. These are the Pronaf Eco Dendê (for family farmers) and the Propflora and the Produsa (both for rural producers and cooperatives). Beginning in 2010, among these programs, Pronaf Eco Dendê alone paid about 72 percent of the 93 million reals disbursed for Pará (Banco da Amazônia 2016).

Academic studies on the PSOP attempt to regulate the expansion of oil palms in the Amazon through agro-ecological zoning and indicate that the Zondendê Agroecological (Zoning Program), or ZONDENDÊ, represents a fundamental component of this effort. Launched by EMBRAPA in 2010, it has identified 13.6 percent of the Amazon region, or 31.8 million hectares equal to 3.7 percent of the total size of Brazil, as suitable for palm oil production. Plantations, however, are restricted to areas that have been deforested before 2007. This is considered a reference year in the mapping of the Amazon by Programa de Monitoramento da Floresta Amazônica Brasileira por Satélite (PRODES) (Amazonian Forest Monitoring Program by Satellite) of the Instituto Nacional de Pesquisa Espacial (INPE) (National Institute of Space Research).

In addition, PSOP wants to silence critics that stress the negative consequences of palm oil production. Often referring to the cases of Malaysia and Indonesia, these critics show that these two major palm oil-producing countries suffer serious consequences from oil palm cultivation, such as the destruction of native forests, expropriation of native peoples, and declining food security (White 2012; Norwana, Kunjappan, Chin, Schoneveld, Potter, and Rubeta 2011). To counter these criticisms and avoid repeating errors, PSOP has promoted planting restrictions and instituted controls in areas considered "altered" or "degraded." Even with these restrictions and controls in place, uncertainties concerning some areas remain, resulting in environmental conflicts with indigenous peoples (Turé-Mariquita) and quilombolas (Silva, Silva, and Macedo 2016; Ribeiro 2017). In addition, small landowners sell their land as prices increase, hoping to obtain wage labor (Backhouse 2013; Silva, Magalhães, and de Farias 2016). This choice is motivated by their desire to have a regular income in light of the crisis of the traditional cutting and burning agriculture and the concomitant depletion of natural resources. They also see it as a move to enhance employment opportunities for younger family members. In a survey of 346 Amazon villages, 75 percent of respondents stated that the main expectation in relation to oil palm cultivation is that a family member could obtain employment as a wage worker.

At the local level, financial support for firms that operate under the supervision of SUDAM takes two forms. The first, and most common, refers to fiscal incentives that reduce the corporate tax by up to 75 percent. They are granted to legal entities that hold projects to implement, modernize, expand, or diversify productive firms. Beneficiaries of this type of incentives include Palmasa S/A (Igarapé-Açu), CRA (Agropalma-Belém), Marborges (Moju), and Mejer (Bonito). The second form consists of support generated through the "Fundos de Desenvolvimento da Amazônia" or FDA (Amazon Development Funds). It also concerns legal entities that carry out projects for the implementation, modernization, expansion, or diversification of productive initiatives and consists of the financing of private infrastructure projects, technological innovations, and services. Key benefits include special grace periods, semiannual repayments of payments and interest, financing up to twenty years, attractive fixed interest rates, or financing from the Development Fund itself. Benefits have only been accessed by Belém Bioenergia Brasil S/A (Tailândia, Tomé-Açu, Mãe do Rio). However, this company left the project after paying off its debt in a single installment.

The Sector Chamber

The Sector Chamber (Câmara Setorial) of the Oil Palm Productive Chain is one of the initiatives of the PSOP. In general, sector chambers were established in the late 1980s and "were an attempt to generate analyses on the sector competitiveness that would identify the causes of existing economic problems and indicate the strategies of actions to address them" (Estival, Gomes, Teixeira, Teotonio, Correa 2014: 44). Gonçalves Júnior and his associates (Gonçalves Júnior, Alves, Shikida, Staduto, and de Rocha Júnior 2009: 185) trace the history of the sector chambers, stressing the crises and difficulties from the point of view of efficiency. According to these authors:

> the State created spaces for the private sector to manage sector policies but continues to participate in decision-making, given the "tripartite" character of the Chambers (State, companies, labor) (Gonçalves Júnior et al. 2009: 185).

Scholars agree that the chambers were initially very focused on monetary stability (i.e., controlling inflation) and it was only in 1991 that their purposes were broadened. Founded in 2008:

> The Sector Chambers of Agribusiness are the result of the organizational technological evolution of the sector as they establish priority actions, discuss issues related to the supply of products or inputs in quantity and quality, and establish prices that remunerate all stakeholders while encouraging farmers to remain in activity. In addition to private interests, public interests are also addressed within the Chambers, such as guaranteeing the supply of goods and services and the sustained growth of the production chain, increasing income, employment and the generation of economic multipliers within the chain (Gonçalves Júnior et al. 2009: 185–186).

The functioning of the chambers is criticized from a number of viewpoints. They include the disproportion that exists among the representatives of the segments that compose them, the distorted identification of priorities, the inadequate location of meetings (Brasilia) that hinders the participation of less affluent actors, the difficulty to deal with conflicting issues, and the lack of universality in the establishment of social priorities that engenders less equity in the agenda. Gonçalves Júnior and his associates indicate that: "workers did not have many issues to discuss within this chamber as its agenda and composition was dominated primarily by representatives of employers and public administrators" (Gonçalves Júnior et al. 2009: 205). Additionally, these authors found that in the chambers there is a persistent conflict between representatives of the productive sector who wish to reduce taxes and representatives of the public sector who seek to increase tax revenue for the State (Gonçalves Júnior et al. 2009: 206).

The Sector Chamber of the Oil Palm Productive Chain was founded in August 2011, under the coordination of the Ministry of Agriculture, Livestock, and Food Supply (MAPA), and meets bimonthly with representatives of the Federal Government and representatives of palm oil producers, workers, and consumers in Brasilia. "The sector and thematic chambers propose, support, and accompany actions for the development of the activities of the Brazilian agribusiness productive chains" (MAPA 2018). In 2017, there were twelve meetings among the twenty members and two permanent guests with representatives of the Federal Government (MAPA) with industrial and producer associations constituting the majority of the attendees. The smallest participation was from representatives of labor (CONTAG) and the Ministry of Agricultural Development that attended only once.

Veiga and Rodrigues (2016: 2) analyzed the influence of the private sector on domestic public policies through a study of the corporate strategy of a company in the Sector Chamber of Palm Oil. They state that:

> The collective action about oil palms is provided by the government and non-state actors that created the dialogue space within the bargaining arena represented by the Sector Chamber.

Similar to observations by other authors regarding power relations, Veiga and Rodrigues (2016) further contend that one of the members (a leading company) of the Chamber "was able to influence the agenda and priorities of the public policy" (Veiga and Rodrigues 2016: 11). They add that "in all meetings of the chamber, the company operated as a strategic actor and, in collaboration with governmental authorities, built the public policy for palm oil in Brazil" (Veiga and Rodrigues 2016: 12).

LOCAL ACTIONS FOR THE IMPLEMENTATION OF THE MODEL

Local Incentives and the Parliamentary Front of the Palma

Incentives for the strengthening of oil palm cultivation are part of the state intervention in the sector. Two recent examples are illustrative of the nature of these state actions. The first refers to 95 percent tax exemption for fifteen years that the Commission of Incentives of the Government of the State of

Pará granted to a company plan to establish a plant to refine palm oil in Tome-Açu (PARÁ 2030). The second is about the Decree No. 2004 of March 7, 2018, of the Government of the State of Pará that grants companies funds equal to 20 percent of the value of projects that involve productive investments in the areas identified as priority areas by the Pará 2030 Program. This Program includes oil palm cultivation.

As part of the public initiatives in support of the strengthening of palm oil production, the Parliamentary Front of the Palma (FPP) was created in the State Assembly of Pará in 2017. This is a supra-party organization that, theoretically, should not follow ideological grouping as it has frequently occurred in the Brazilian State assemblies in recent years (Coradini 2010: 241). Coradini states that de facto, "there is a strong association between the distribution of members of parliament in parliamentary fronts and the political alignments and party affiliation" (Coradini 2010: 254). He also notes that the participation of parliamentarians depends "directly on their level of association with interest groups and the conditions and their positions in the social space" (Coradini 2010: 255).

In the case under analysis, the relationship between the FPP and the dominant interest group (entrepreneurs of palm oil production), is made explicit by Abrapalma:

> The FPP was created to promote the culture of oil palms as an essential activity for the socioeconomic development of Pará and improve the quality of life of the local population. Among its objectives is the promotion of partnerships between the public and the private sector, with a view to developing joint actions aimed at sustainable development (Abrapalma 2017b: 4).

In the words of FPP leader, Congressman Iran Lima:

> From the moment a Congressperson has to discuss pertinent issues, he has an obligation to become an expert in these subjects and this is the expectation of voters. This approach to the palm oil production chain, one of the most important in our state, is healthy and relevant (Abrapalma, 2017b: 5).

There is a demand to promote an organizational model based on the partnership between the public and private that is supported by producers and recognized by members of congress that stresses the importance of this productive chain. Accordingly, they mediate contacts and posture themselves in a way that symbolically confers prestige to the activity and garners commitment from authorities. Three examples mark the performance of FPP. The first was a meeting among representatives of FPP, Abrapalma, mayors from the palm oil-producing region, and the Secretary of Public Security of the State of Pará. The objective was to discuss the difficulties caused by the constant climate of violence in the municipalities of the oil palm producing region

(Abrapalma, 2017a). The second refers to a meeting among FPP, Abrapalma, and mayors with the President of the Legislative Assembly of Pará (Alepa). On the agenda, there was the review of the sector and complaints related to the use of the off-limits areas of the Legal Reserve and Palmar. The meeting included discussions with the Commander-in-Chief of the Military Police, the President of the State Court of Justice, and the President of the Land Institute of Pará (ITERPA). A third meeting took place between the Secretary of Transportation of the State of Pará and mayors to discuss infrastructure bottlenecks in areas planted with oil palms (Abrapalma 2017a).

SOCIAL AND ENVIRONMENTAL PROTOCOL

The State Public Ministry proposed a Conduct Adjustment Agreement (TAC) between companies that produce palm oil. The proposal was eventually rejected on the grounds that each company had different characteristics that would have been difficult to be summarized in one single TAC. In response, in 2014, the state government through its institutions, Abrapalma, the Federation of Agriculture and Livestock of the State of Pará (FAEPA), banking institutions, and service providers signed a Protocol of Socio-Environmental Actions for the Cultivation of Palms with the purpose of:

> establishing an institutional partnership between the public and the private sectors, aimed at creating conditions that would enable the implementation of joint actions aimed at the sustainable development of the production chain of palm oil in an objective and transparent manner. Special importance is given to the integrated production of small family producers (PARÁ 2014: 3).

Among the actions planned were those associated with the generation of jobs, technical assistance to family farmers involved in the cultivation of oil palms; support for production, maintenance, and marketing of subsistence crops; support for the marketing of farmers' associations or cooperatives; training of farmers; and support for educational initiatives and farmers' quality of life with emphasis on housing, health, public safety, leisure, culture, basic sanitation, roads, and access to the electricity grid (PARÁ 2014).

The protocol of intent was signed by only eight signatories. This document already demonstrated the recognition of the precarious quality of life of the inhabitants, as also explained by the Bujaruense Association of Farmers (ABAA) in a letter to President Lula and the then Governor at the launch of the PSOP in 2010:

> Family farming throughout the Northeast of Pará, particularly in the municipalities of Bujaru, Concordia, Acará, and Tomé Açu, is caught in an obsolete production system of cutting and burning that is harmful to the environment and unable to produce food and income so desperately needed by small farm-

> ers. Due to the almost total absence and ineffectiveness of government agencies in charge of training our farmers and the lack of human resources, structures, and equipment, our region's family agriculture has not been able to overcome the level of subsistence. Accordingly, it is unable to face the challenges of the market economy and the opportunities generated by federal programs (Acevedo Marin, and Backhouse 2014: 19).

In 2017 and in regard to the precariousness of services in general, one farmer stated that:

> But as for the other things, of the state government and the mayor, all is bad. Look, this road over there, every two years they try to fix it with a machine that only scrapes the ground. It does not build the road; it simply scrapes the ground. Then you go to the doctor's station right there—it's even worse—they don't even have medicine for a stomachache. There's only one guy there, and if you get cut, he stitches you and gives you some disinfectant—that's all he has. Often even the thread for the stitches is missing (a fifty-year-old farmer).

Previously, the content of the protocol was part of the efforts of palm oil companies to promote contract farming among family producers. Following this effort and related promises, local residents developed expectations about improved infrastructure and economic well-being. A local promoter describes the interaction with farmers about growing palms thusly:

> Yes, we promised roads, even better education, schools, infrastructure and such. During the first period this was only implicitly suggested to farmers. But all changed during the second phase, when we went to visit the homes of farmers individually (personal communication with a farming technician 2018).

Even if the protocol received limited formal support, local mayors promoted initiatives in favor of the expansion of oil palm cultivation (Abrapalma 2017a). In 2002, the municipality of Moju in partnership with a company and other institutions selected farmers for new projects (Cruz 2006: 125). In January 2011, the Municipality of São Domingos do Capim signed a technical cooperation agreement with the Technical Assistance and Rural Extension Company (Emater), with the purpose of strengthening the execution of technical assistance activities for approximately eight hundred family farmers who were estimated to participate in the PNBP (Gomes and Magalhães 2016). The Prefecture of Irituia publicized the advantages of oil palm cultivation. However, segments of the Catholic Church carried out systematic opposition work including sermons during masses. More recently, in 2017, the city of Garrafão do Norte supported a company with the provision of earthmoving machinery deployed on a site where a processing industry is scheduled to be built—a great hope of the local population in terms of job creation.

In general and in the different scales, there was support to the proposal of adoption of palm oil production as an important developmental tool for the agriculture of Pará, even if signs of distrust were wide spread:

> Back in 2007, even when it was the government's proposal, that in the case it was Lula who brought this proposal in Tomé Açu, we felt some of the politicians behind us. They came here with us, they talked, they argued for us and after 2012, we did not have this support anymore (JC, farmer and union leader).

This understanding is shared by other actors. In this sense, we agree with Borges (2010: 145) who contends that "the ruling elites, collectively, were interested in the implementation of public policies capable of promoting the economic and social development of the state, and thus increasing the capacity for revenue extraction on the part of the government." Borges also acknowledges that in the long term, the positive effects of economic growth on voters' income translate into higher levels of political support, such as the case of the Bolsa Família Program in the North and Northeast of Brazil for the Lula Government.

CONCLUSIONS

The expansion and strengthening of oil palm production in the Brazilian Amazon is part of that broader process of creating new productive spaces engendered by the 2007–2008 global crisis. This event generated a significant increase in the prices of agricultural commodities and encouraged massive investments in land in Africa, Asia, and Latin America (Wilkinson 2017). In this chapter, we illustrated how the expansion of palm oil production was advanced through an alliance between the State, local, and global companies. They jointly worked for the construction of a new production model legitimized by calls about its social and environmental desirability (Cavalcanti and Bendini 2014). It involved the implementation of public policies that gave strength to the concept of the centrality of the primary sector (agriculture and natural resources) and advocated the expansion of commodity production for global markets (Castro 2012).

In this context, the State played a central role in the three phases that characterized the expansion of oil palm cultivation in the Brazilian Amazon. It provided scientific and technical support and created favorable economic conditions that benefitted the interests of corporate groups. The PNPB was fundamental in this expansion in Pará as it was a central component of a strategy that used State instruments to leverage growth. Business interest groups contributed to this initiative as well by promoting a discourse that stressed the importance of international competition, sustainability, energy diversification, and social inclusion. Despite critical voices that denounced the perils of the monoculture of oil palms, little resistance actually materialized. This situation was partially the result of growing popular expectations about job growth fueled by corporate promises about increased productive investment, infrastructure building (schools, roads, etc.), and lucrative contracts for family farmers. Contracts appeared a suitable solution to the difficulties that farmers had experienced about selling their crops, receiving technical assistance, meeting phytosanitary requirements, and introducing alternative crops.

The expansion of oil palm production was further promoted by the then President Lula, who broke down resistance from social movements and supported a tripartite coalition that included the State, companies, and farmers. Such a coalition was viewed with optimism. However, its functioning did not meet the expectations of farmers that turned out to be quite advantageous for corporations and politicians at the local, state, and national levels. Central in the advancement of the interests of corporate groups was the role of the Sector Chambers. The virtually nonexistent participation of representatives of family farmers left these institutions under the full control of corporate groups. At the local level, Parliamentary Fronts and the cooperation between companies and local political leaders further supported corporate groups. In these terms, the commitment to implement a policy that promoted the interests of companies included the joint effort of federal, state, and municipal governments. Overall, the disproportional power available to companies hampered the development of local territories and the advancement of the interests of stakeholders (i.e., farmers and local residents).

NOTES

1. According to the MDA (2018): "The Social Fuel Seal is an identification component created by the Decree No. 5,297 of December 6, 2004 and granted by the MDA to those biodiesel producers that meet the criteria described in Administrative Rule 512 of 5 September 2017. Following Pronaf, the Seal confers on its possessor the character of promoter of social inclusion of family farmers." The holders of the Social Fuel Stamp have access to State financial incentives.

2. A ministry exclusively devoted to issues associated with family agriculture that existed between 2003 and 2016. Its establishment was one of the results of the struggle of rural social movements.

BIBLIOGRAPHY

Abramovay, Ricardo and Reginaldo Magalhães. 2007. *Access of Family Farmers to Biodiesel Markets: Partnership between Large Companies and Social Movements*. São Paulo: Universidade de São Paulo. http://citeseerx.ist.psu.edu/viewdoc/download?doi=10.1.1.568.9041&rep=rep1&type=pdf. Accessed May 13, 2018.

Abrapalma. 2014. *Planilha de Mapeamento da Palma de Oleo no Brasil*. Belém: Associação Brasileira de Produtores de Óleo de Palma.

———. 2017a. *Mais um Ano Juntos: Abrapalma Relatório*. Belém: Associação Brasileira de Produtores de Óleo de Palma.

———. 2017b. *Release visita Abrapalma*. Belém: Associação Brasileira de Produtores de Óleo de Palma. http://www.abrapalma.org/pt/wp-content/uploads/2017/05/Release_visita_Agropalma_maio_17.pdf. Accessed April 10, 2018.

Acevedo Marin, Rosa E. and Maria Backhouse. 2014. *Guerra do Dendê: Quilombolas Atingidas pela Expansão do Dendê no Pará*. Manaus: UEA Edições.

Backhouse, Maria. 2013. *A Desapropriação Sustentável da Amazônia: o Caso dos Investimentos em Dendê no Pará*. Berlin: Freie Universität Berlin.

BDPA. 2018. *Base de Dados da Pesquisa Agropecuária*. Brasília: Embrapa Informática Agropecuária. http://www.bdpa.cnptia.embrapa.br. Accessed June 4, 2018.

Banco da Amazônia 2016. Recursos Pronaf e Pronaf Eco Dendê Agricultura Familiar 2002–2016. Belém: Banco da Amazônia S/A.

Bentes, Elisabeth dos Santos and Alfredo Kingo Oyama Homma. 2016. *Importação e Exportação de Oleo e Palmiste de Dendezeiro no Brasil (2010–2015)*. Belém: Embrapa Amazônia Oriental.

Bonanno, Alessandro. 2018. "Best Practices: The Artificial Negativity of Agri-Food." In Alessandro Bonanno and Steven A. Wolf (Eds.), *Resistance to the Neoliberal* (pp. 35–49). New York: Routledge.

Borges, André. 2010. "Federalismo, Dinâmica Eleitoral e Políticas Públicas no Brasil: uma Tipologia e Algumas hipóteses." *Sociologias* 12 (24): 120–157. (May/August).

Brandão, Frederico and George Schoneveld. 2015. *The State of Oil Palm Development in the Brazilian Amazon: Trends, Value Chain Dynamics, and Business Models*. Bogor, Indonesia: CIFOR.

Butler, Rhett A. and William F. Laurance. 2009. "Is Oil Palm the Next Threat to the Amazon?" *Tropical Conservation Science* 2 (1):1–10.

Castro, César Nunes de. 2011. *O Programa Nacional de Produção e Uso do Biodiesel (PNPB) e a rodução de maMtéria-Prima de Oleo Vegetal no Norte e no Nordeste*. Brasília, DF: IPEA.

Castro, Edna. 2012. "Expansão da Fronteira, Mega Projetos de Infraestrutura e Integração Sul-Americana." *Caderno CRH* 25 (64): 45–61. (January/April).

Cavalcanti, Josefa Salete Barbosa and Mónica Isabel Bendini. 2014. "Globalization and Change in Labor Relations in Fruit Regions of Brazil and Argentina." In Alessandro Bonanno and Josefa Salete Barbosa Cavalcanti (Eds.), *Labor Relations in Globalized Food* (pp. 3–32). Bingley: Emerald Group Publishing.

Coradini, Odaci Luiz. 2010. "Frentes Parlamentares, Representação de Interesses e Alinhamentos Políticos." *Revista Sociologia e Política* 18 (36): 241–256.

Cruz, Benedito Ely Valente. 2006. *Territorialização e Organização Espacial do Grupo Agropalma*. Master Thesis in Geography. Belém: Universidade Federal do Pará.

Diário do Pará on line. 2017. *Problemas Fundiários Atrapalham Produção de Oleo*. http://www.diarioonline.com.br/noticias/para/noticia-418820-problemas-fundiarios-atrapalham-producao-de-oleo.html. Accessed April 10, 2018.

Estival, Katianny Gomes Santana, Luiza Reis Teixeira, Arise Natiana Araujo Teotonio and Solange Rodrigues Santos Correa. 2014. "Política dos Coronéis do Cacau aos Espaços de Participação Política: Estudo de Caso da Câmara Setorial do Cacau no Brasil." *Revista de Ciências Gerenciais* 18 (27): 43–52.

Favareto, Arilson. 2017. "Concepções de Desenvolvimento e de Intervenção Pública no Brasil Rural sob o Governo Temer e Além." *Revista Raízes* 37 (2): 7–26.

Gomes, Lucinaldo Soares and Sônia Barbosa Magalhães. 2016. Agricultores Integrados do Dendê e Questões Relativas ao Sistema de Produção no PA, Terra Nova. *EcoDebate*. https://www.ecodebate.com.br/2016/05/30/agricultores-integrados-do-dende-e-questoes-relativas-ao-sistema-de-producao-no-pa-terra-nova-por-lucinaldo-soares-gomes-e-sonia-barbosa-magalhaes/. Accessed January 31, 2017.

Gonçalves Júnior, Carlos Alberto, Yony Brugnolo Alves, Pery Francisco Assis Shikida, Jefferson Andronio Ramundo Staduto and Weimar Freire da Rocha Júnior. 2009. "Um Estudo das

Deliberações da Câmara Setorial do Açúcar e do Álcool, Usando Análise de Correspondência." *Revista de Economia e Sociologia Rural* 47 (1): 183–210.

Gudynas, Eduardo. 2017. "Los Ambientalismos Frente a los Extractivismos." *Nueva Sociedad*, (268): 110–121. (March-April).

Heredia, Beatriz; Moacir Palmeira and Sérgio Pereira Leite. 2010. "Sociedade e Economia do 'Agronegócio' no Brasil." *Revista Brasileira de Ciências Sociais* 25 (74): 159–176.

Homma, Alfredo Kingo Oyama. 2016. *Cronologia do Cultivo do Dendezeiro na Amazônia*. Belém: Embrapa Amazônia Oriental.

IBGE. 2017. *Base de Dados SIDRA*. Rio de Janeiro: Instituto Brasileiro de Geografia e Estatística. http://www.sidra.ibge.gov.br/. Accessed May 13, 2018.

Lees, Alexander C., Nárgila G Moura, Arlete Silva de Almeida and Ima C. G. Vieira. 2015. "Poor Prospects for Avian Biodiversity in Amazonian Oil Palm." *PLoS ONE* 10 (5): 1–17.

Leite, Sergio Pereira and Valdemar João Wesz Junior,. 2014. "Estado, políticas públicas e agronegócio no Brasil: Revisitando o papel do crédito rural." *Revista Pós Ciências Sociais* 11 (22): 83–108.

Maluf, Renato. 2017. "Abastecimento Alimentar, Inflação de Alimentos e o Contexto Urbano no Brasil." In Renato S. Maluf and Georges Flexor (Eds.), *Questões Agrárias, Agrícolas e Rurais: Conjunturas e Políticas Públicas* (pp. 179–193). Rio de Janeiro: E-Papers.

MAPA. 2018. Câmaras Setoriais: Palma de Óleo. Brasília: Ministério da Agricultura, Pecuária e Abastecimento. http://www.agricultura.gov.br/assuntos/camaras-setoriais-tematicas/camaras-setoriais-1/palma-de-oleo. Accessed May 13, 2018.

MDA. 2017. O Selo Combustível Social. Brasília: Ministério de Desenvolvimento Agrário. http://www.mda.gov.br/sitemda/secretaria/saf-biodiesel/o-selo-combust percentC3 percentADvel-social. Accessed April 3, 2018.

Mourão Júnior, Moisés. 2017. *Modelização Espacial de Territorialidades no Estado do Pará: Entre a Amazônia dos Rios e das Estradas*. Doctoral thesis in geography and urban planning. Paris: Université Sorbonne Nouvelle.

MP-PA. 2014. Instituto Evandro Chagas Detecta Contaminação por Agrotóxicos na Região de Expansão do Dendê. Belém: Ministério Público do Estado do Pará. http://www.mppa.mp.br/index.php?action=Menu.interna&id=4380&class=N. Accessed May 13, 2018.

Nahum, João Santos and Bastos dos Cleison Santos. 2013. "Impactos Socioambientais da Dendeícultura em Comunidades Tradicionais na Amazônia Paraense." *ACTA Geográfica* (Ed. Especial, Geografia Agrária): 63–80.

Norwana, Awan Ali Bema Dayang, Rejani Kunjappan, Melissa Chin, George Schoneveld, Lesley Potter, and Andriani Rubeta. 2011. *The Local Impacts of Oil Palm Expansion in Malaysia: an Assessment Based on a Case Study in Sabah State*. Bogor, Indonesia: CIFOR.

PARÁ. 2014. *Protocolo de Intenções socioambiental da Palma de Oleo*. http://www.abrapalma.org/downloads/Protocolo_Palma.pdf. Accessed April 13, 2018.

PARÁ 2030. 2018. *Açaí e Palma Ganham Novas Indústrias*. Belém: Secretaria de Estado de Desenvolvimento Econômico, Mineração e Energia. http://para2030.com.br/acai-e-palma-ganham-novas-industrias/. Accessed April 10, 2018.

Pires, Vivian Beatriz Lopes. 2015. *Impacto Social do Programa Nacional de Produção e Uso de Biodiesel (PNPB) no Nordeste: 2008/2013*. Master thesis in agrobusiness. Brasília: Universidade de Brasília.

Presidência da República. 2005. *Discurso do Presidente da República, Luiz Inácio Lula da Silva, por ocasião da visita à Fazenda Agropalma*. Brasília: Presidência da Repúblic, Secretaria de Imprensa e Divulgação. http://www.biblioteca.presidencia.gov.br/presidencia/ex-presidentes/luiz-inacio-lula-da-silva/discursos/1o-mandato/2005. Accessed June 26. 2018.

Ribeiro, Lissandra Cordeiro. 2017. *"Mesmo com Essas Coisas Ruins Que o Dendê Trouxe, eu Não Saio Daqui": Resistência à Agroindústria do Dendê na Comunidade do Castanhalzinho em Concórdia do Pará*. Master thesis in peasant agriculture and sustainable development. Belém: Universidade Federal do Pará.

SEAD. 2018. *Selo Combustível Social*. Brasília: SEAD, Coordenação Geral de Energias Renováveis (CGAER). http://www.agricultura.gov.br/assuntos/camaras-setoriais-tematicas/documentos/camaras-setoriais/palma-de-oleo/2018/26aro/selo-combustivel-social.pdf. Accessed May 13, 2018.

Silva, Elielson Pereira da, Sônia Barbosa Magalhães and André Luís Assunção de Farias. 2016. "Monocultivos de Dendezeiros, Capital Transnacional e Concentração de Terras na Amazônia Paraense." *Campo-Território* 11 (23): 165–195.

Silva, Fabiana Carneiro, Jamilli Medeiros de Oliveira Silva and Cátia Oliveira Macedo. 2016. "Quilombolas e Agronegócio do Dendê em Disputa pelo Território no Alto Acará-PA." In Cátia Oliveira Macedo, Fabiano de Oliveira Bringel, Rafael Benevides de Sousa, and Rosiete Marcos Santana (Eds.), *Os "Nós" da Questão Agrária na Amazônia* (pp. 169–189). Belém: Editora Açaí.

Silva, José Alderir da. 2013. "Avaliação do Programa Nacional de Produção e Uso do Biodiesel no Brasil—PNPB." *Revista de Política Agrícola* 22 (3): 18–31.

Singer, Andre. 2010. "O Lulismo e seu Futuro." *Piauí*. Rio de Janeiro: Alvinegra 49 (October). http://piaui.folha.uol.com.br/materia/o-lulismo-e-seu-futuro/. Accessed June 20, 2018.

United States Department of Agriculture. 2018. *Palm Oil Production by Country in 1000 MT*. https://www.indexmundi.com/agriculture/?commodity=palm-oil. Accessed June 17, 2018.

Veiga, João Paulo Cândia and Pietro Carlos Rodrigues, 2016. "Arenas Transnacionais, Políticas Públicas e Meio Ambiente: o Caso da Palma na Amazônia." *Ambiente & Sociedade* 19 (4): 1–22.

Vieira Filho, José Eustáquio Ribeiro and Albert Fishlow. 2017. *Agricultura e Indústria no Brasil:Iinovação e Competitividade*. Brasília: Ipea.

White, Julia, and Ben White. 2012. "Gendered Experiences of Dispossession: Oil Palm Expansion in a Dayak Hibun Community in West Kalimantan." *Peasant Studies* 39 (3–4): 995–1016.

Wilkinson, John. 2017. "Land Grabbing e Estrangeirização de Terras no Brasil." In Renato Maluf and Georges Flexor (Eds.), *Questoes Agrárias, Agrícolas e Rurais: Conjunturas e Políticas Públicas* (pp. 12–19). Rio de Janeiro: E-Papers.

Chapter Six

State Intervention and Irrigated Agriculture in the San Francisco Valley, Brazil

Productive Transformations and New Organizations of Work

Guilherme J. Mota Silva

Employing a perspective that focuses on the global transformations that affected agriculture in recent decades, this chapter analyzes the role of the State in the development of irrigated fruit production in the San Francisco Valley of Brazil. This approach stresses the connections between transformations at the local levels and domestic and global processes. In effect, changes that have occurred in the region since the second half of the twentieth century have been sharply influenced by global trends that include the production, commercialization, and consumption of agri-food items and by changes in the country's economic policy. In this context, the State played a fundamental role as it contributed to the insertion of the San Francisco Valley into global agri-food circuits of production and consumption.

The chapter discusses changes in the irrigated fruit-growing areas that include the regions of Petrolina in the state of Pernambuco and Juazeiro in the state of Bahia. With a population of 742,759 in an area of 35,436,857 km^2, this overall region is known as the Sub-region of the San Francisco River basin in the Northeastern semi-arid region of Brazil. Its soil is arid and, accordingly, its rainfall is scarce, totaling on average 350 mm per year. Due to its irrigation infrastructure, however, it has emerged as one of the largest domestic producers of fresh fruit for export, accounting for almost 5 percent of the total value of Brazilian fruit production. The crops cultivated locally include coconuts, melons, acerola, bananas, guava, mangos, and table grapes with about 15 percent of mangos and grapes destined for export. In 2018, this region accounted for 69 percent and 90 percent of domestic exports of mango and grape respectively, mostly servicing the European and US markets. The European Union alone absorbs 80 percent of the grapes and 65 percent of the mangos exported while the US imports 15 percent of the grapes and 30 percent of the mangos. The remaining 5 percent of exports go to a number of countries and regions including Canada, Asia, South America, and the Middle East.

Following this introduction, the chapter continues with a section that briefly describes key periods that characterized the creation of advanced irrigated agriculture in the Valley. Attention is placed on the years that cover the post-World War II decades up to the 1990s. This period is discussed in the third section. It stresses the modernization posture taken by the State and its important economic intervention for the creation of the irrigation infrastructure that permitted the growth of quality fruit production in the region. The social dimension that this original plan included is underscored along with the authoritarian character of the time patterns of development informed by the military dictatorship that governed Brazil. The neoliberal period of the 1990s is analyzed in the fourth section. It underscores the consequences of the withdrawal of state support to local fruit producers proposed under the discourse of "emancipation from state support." As family farmers could not adequately compete without technical and financial assistance from the State, emancipation translated into the virtual end of the social project originally associated with the creation of irrigated agriculture.

In the next-to-last section of this chapter, the further growth of the San Francisco Valley during the years of the PT administrations is reviewed. The PT initiated policies aimed at improving the conditions and remuneration of labor. While this objective was partially achieved, the expansion of fruit production in the region is based on its insertion in global circuits defined by quality certification. The certification of fruit quality is necessary to satisfy the requirements of global corporate supermarket chains. However, the section stresses that certification involves processes that increase workloads, feminize labor, and ultimately increase the exploitation of workers. Dwelling on the contradictions that emerged from the Neo-developmentalist policy adopted by the PT, the chapter concludes by stressing the limits associated with the emancipatory project of state capitalism in Brazil.

THE TRANSFORMATIONS OF THE SAN FRANCISCO VALLEY AND THE CHANGES IN CAPITALIST AGRICULTURE

Despite the often-mentioned natural benefits associated with the presence of the San Francisco River, the development of this region is not primarily due to its abundant natural resources. As indicated by a wealth of research, its growth is socially created and, in fact, reflects the implementation of a specific set of developmental models centered on the intervention of the Brazilian State (Cavalcanti 1997; Cavalcanti and Neiman 2005; Silva 2001). Following existing literature, the agri-food productive growth of the San Francisco Valley can be divided into three periods. The first and longer period goes from the colonization of the region until the middle of the twentieth century. In this period, the area remained relatively underdeveloped as it was characterized by quite dispersed agricultural operations consisting of traditional farms practicing subsistence agriculture.

Spanning from the 1950s to the end of the 1980s, the second period was marked by the beginning of planned state intervention in the region. During this time and following the then-dominant theory of the modernization of the economy and society, the San Francisco Valley received strong financial and institutional support from the State. The fundamental view adopted by the State was that socio-economic development should be achieved through planned State investment and institutional support designed to stimulate economic activities and create the human resources necessary to support them. In this context, the Brazilian State distributed land to settlers and established infrastructure for the development of irrigated agriculture. Accordingly, along with the canalization of the waters of the San Francisco River, the State executed works that improved transportation, communication, and production. Ultimately, it was instrumental in the creation of the San Francisco Valley agro-industrial pole of development.

The third period began in the 1990s and coincided with the end of the implementation of modernization policies. It further consisted of new forms of state support of irrigated fruit production and the expansion of the associated labor market. This third period can be further divided into two—yet very important—sub-periods. The first sub-period refers to the neoliberal years of the 1990s. During this time, the administrations of Fernando Collor de Mello and Fernando Henrique Cardoso promoted market-oriented policies that fostered the deregulation and financialization of the economy. The second sub-period corresponds to the administrations of the Workers' Party (PT) that began in 2002 and ended in 2016. Under the PT's public policies, especially for rural areas, the government adopted a more inclusive posture that aimed at addressing ethnic and gender inequalities and focused on the needs and development of family farming. To be sure, these three periods roughly coincide with the stages of development of the capitalist system often identified in the pertinent literature. In the case of agri-food, these stages are associated with corresponding agri-food regimes. As theorized by Friedmann and McMichael (1989), the early "colonial regime" was followed by the "mercantile-industrial regime" of the second part of the twentieth century and the contemporary "corporate regime" of the neoliberal globalization era.

As for the rest of the country, the Brazilian State played a major role in the economic and social transformations of the San Francisco Valley (Araújo 2002; Cavalcanti 1999; Silva 2001). Its actions included direct public investment, measures to attract capital from other regions of the nation and other countries, and the implementation of public policies that ensured the maintenance and availability of labor for irrigated agriculture. In the first post-World War II decades, most of these policies were guided by a rather authoritarian conception of development based on a very centralized authority, lack of dialogue with local stakeholders, and the absence of concerns about the social, economic, and political inclusion of marginal groups and the poor. Moreover, these were measures that favored a type of productive unit and required a type of labor force that differed from those locally available. As a result, the social configuration of the region involved not only a set of diverse groups of individuals that moved to the region attracted by the opportunities offered by the expansion of agriculture but also social movements that persistently struggled for land, water and, above all, the recognition of the rights of their members. The latter comprised quilombolas, native tribes, the movement of landless rural workers, and the movement of groups displaced by the construction of dams (Cavalcanti, Wanderley and Niederle 2014).

EARLY STATE INTERVENTION AND THE GROWTH OF THE AGRO-INDUSTRIAL COMPLEX IN THE SAN FRANCISCO VALLEY

From the imperial period until the middle of the twentieth century, the domestic policy concerning the San Francisco Valley was limited to issues related to the regularization of the navigation of the river. Beginning in 1946 and following the promulgation of the new Federal Constitution, the role of the Brazilian State changed considerably as its intervention became part of the planned regulation of economic activities. In effect, state intervention in the San Francisco Valley was specifically mentioned in the Constitution with plans to devote at least 1 percent of the total national revenue to this region's socio-economic development. The text of Article 29 of the Constitution reads:

> The Federal Government shall be obliged, within a period of twenty years from the date of the promulgation of this Constitution, to draw up and execute a plan for the full exploitation of the economic possibilities of the San Francis-

> co River and its tributaries. This plan shall be financed through no less than one percent of the country's tax revenue (Brazil 1946: Article 29).

Following this constitutional norm, in 1948, the State created the Commission of the Valley of San Francisco (*Comissão do Vale do São Francisco* or CVSF). Included among the agencies of the federal government, the CVSF's primary mission was to develop a general plan for the use of the water and other resources of the San Francisco River and submit it for approval to the Brazilian Congress. In the plan, CVSF was required to specify items such as measures for the regulation of the course of the river, the distribution of its waters, the development of hydroelectric energy, the modernization of the transportation grid, and strategies for the overall appropriate and efficient exploitation of the resources of the river and the valley. Among these tasks, the promotion of, and planning for, the growth of agriculture and irrigation assumed particular importance. Additionally, through the work of the CVSF, feasibility studies and research projects for the construction of publicly funded and managed irrigation areas along the river were initiated in conjunction with initiatives of technical support for local producers.

From its inception, the CVSF aimed at the establishment of modernized agricultural operations based on the availability of irrigation infrastructure, the introduction of agrochemicals, and a rationalized use of human and natural resources. To this end, CVSF created and maintained extension and experiment stations that included advisement programs, initiatives for the dissemination of new farming techniques, and demonstrations of the viability of irrigated agriculture. CVSF further recognized the job creation potentials associated with the development of irrigation. As such, irrigated agriculture was considered a tool that could counter the migratory flows that pushed Northeastern rural residents to the metropolitan areas of the Southeast of the country. Despite these initiatives, commitment and the significantly large quantity of financial resources that it invested, CVSF was not very successful in expanding irrigated agriculture in the region. It also failed to generate increases in productivity and crop diversification as local farming remained largely unchanged. Overall, the performance of the CVSF is representative of the first efforts of the Brazilian State to intervene in a planned manner in the region. At the same time, though, the nineteen years of operation of CVSF were essential for creating the conditions for the future development of the region (Damiani 2003).

In 1967, the CVSF was replaced by the San Francisco Valley Superintendence (*Superintendência do Vale do São Francisco* or SUVALE). SUVALE initiated significant work with the Superintendence for Development of the Northeast (*Superintendência para Desenvolvimento do Nordeste* or SUDENE) to develop irrigated agriculture in the Petrolina and Juazeiro region. Specifically, SUDENE implemented plans that contemplated the growth of agricultural production and the minimization of the negative consequences of droughts. Affected by the political changes that resulted in the military dictatorship following the 1964 coup d'état, these projects evolved, however, into initiatives that promoted the almost exclusive creation of large agri-business firms. Preceding the creation of SUDENE, the 1959 study of the Working Group for the Development of the Northeast (GTDN), "A Development Policy for the Northeast" stressed that irrigated agriculture ought to be understood in terms of its social function. It should be "destined to a social purpose, that is, to give stability to food production" (Furtado 1959a:37) and to promote the end of subsistence farming and the development of a commercial form of agriculture based on monetary exchange.

> Food production is the most fragile element of the economy of the semi-arid region. It may seem that the problem lies in creating a stable supply of food, whether based on irrigation or based on the opening of new wetlands on the periphery of the region. However, the issue is not limited to the instability of the food supply. Its most important aspect is that most of the food production is not integrated into the market. In order for the population to be able to buy food from irrigated areas or from other sources, it will be necessary first to have the necessary purchasing power, that is, a monetary income (Furtado 1959b: 71).

Conceived in this way, state intervention promised to be not only a mere attempt to modernize the productive forces but also to address the social question. This objective, however, was not achieved during this period.

To a significant extent, the situation described above was the result of the actions of the Brazilian State under the military dictatorship. Already evident in the 1960s, the pro-agri-business approach of the State became more pronounced in the 1970s. Implemented by the government of General Ernesto Geisel, the 1975–1979 Second National Development Plan (II PND), promoted a pro-business view of agricultural modernization. It indicated that agriculture should play a new role by "stressing Brazil's vocation as a world supplier of food, agricultural raw materials, and industrialized agricultural products" (II PND 1974:26). The plan involved a strategy for the country's socio-economic growth in which the development of the agricultural sector translated into measures that would promote the creation and growth of large agricultural firms. This process would count on the financial and fiscal support of the State, the increased use of modern inputs, the diffusion of new technologies, and the development of public agricultural research programs implemented through federal agencies such as EMBRAPA (II PND 1974).

In this context, a number of programs were created to promote agricultural modernization in the Northeast, in general, and the San Francisco Valley, in particular. Notable among them were the Northeastern Irrigation Program (NIP), the Special Program for the Valley of San Francisco (PROVALE), and the Program for the Development of Agroindustry in the Northeast (PDAN). These and other initiatives involved the allocation of resources not only for the modernization of agriculture but also for the creation and improvement of infrastructure. However, the 1974 establishment of the San Francisco Valley Development Company (*Companhia de Desenvolvimento do Vale do São Francisco* or CODEVASF) illustrates the type of modernization of agriculture that the military government proposed for Brazil. CODEVASF was created as a public company. Yet the vision that informed its actions centered on the idea that the exploitation of the natural resources of the Valley of the San Francisco River should be carried out through the generation of private profit via private, large, agri-business firms. In this new context, the social goals associated with the promotion of irrigated agriculture were de facto eliminated as the logic that supported local residents' access to land, water, and food security contrasted projects and the rationality that promoted the expansion of agri-business.

Beginning in the mid-1970s, a developmental model based on the production of high-value crops was implemented in the irrigated region. Additionally, this model contemplated the intervention of the State to stimulate the growth of an agro-industrial complex (CAI) that would use local agricultural products as inputs for an equally local processing industry. Conceived in this way, state financial intervention in the San Francisco Valley aimed at the strengthening of a CAI that linked an input producing sector (agriculture) with processing and other relevant industries that benefitted from the availability of agricultural products. Importantly, rather than being a regional developmental policy, it was elevated to a model to be adopted for the entire domestic agriculture.

> The formation of agro-industrial complexes (CAIs) in the 1970s was based on the inter-sectorial integration of three basic elements: the industries that produce for agriculture, (modern) agriculture, and agro-processing industries. All of them are supported by strong government incentives (funds for agro-industrial activities, support programs for agricultural products, loans for the purchase of machines, modern equipment and inputs, and more) (Graziano da Silva 1993: 2).

The Northeastern Investment Fund (FINOR) played a leading role in attracting capital for the industrialization of the region. Through FINOR, the largest tomato processing companies in Brazil were established in the San Francisco Valley. They include the Companhia Industrial de Conservas Alimentarias, and Companhia Industrial e Mercantil Paoletti. Additionally, AGROVALE, a major company that produces sugar and ethanol, was also established locally. This wave of investments, however, was halted by the fiscal crisis of the Brazilian State that, initiated in the mid-1980s, continued through the first half of the 1990s.

THE NEOLIBERAL AGENDA AND CREATION OF IRRIGATED FRUIT PRODUCTION

Following this crisis, the adoption of neoliberalism as the guiding economic doctrine by the Brazilian government generated a restructuring of the intervention of the State. While neoliberalism contemplates the reduction of the direct intervention of the State in the management of the economy and, therefore, in the direct support of agricultural production, the end of the old form of State intervention was followed by the adoption of a new form of intervention. This form of intervention was based on the creation of conditions that would favor the growth of large corporations. This policy was deemed appropriate to address the crises that affected agriculture and the country.

> During the 1980s and 1990s, emerging economies—such as Brazil—experienced serious crises that motivated international financial institutions—such as the IMF and the World Bank—to require the implementation of restructuring plans. [. . .] In this context, multinational institutions, the financial class and the officialdom of the State acted to impose the implementation of neoliberal policies to emerging economies. One result was the consolidation of the position of global corporations as privatizations of domestic assets and the opening of domestic markets contributed to the reduction of wages and the weakening of the power of national states (Bonanno 1999: 50).

In the San Francisco Valley, the implementation of the neoliberal agenda translated into the end of direct support for local farms and processing firms. This move particularly affected the production and processing of tomatoes that, once dominant in the region, virtually disappeared in the space of a few years. In addition, the State withdrew support for the irrigation of farmland. Known as the "policy of emancipation," it shifted the costs of irrigation from the public sphere to private initiatives. Encouraged by the State and faced with increasing costs of production, local producers initiated the cultivation of high-value fruit for export in the global market (Silva 2009). Supported by neoliberal pronouncements, this increased reliance on the open market, however, penalized family farmers but allowed large agri-business companies to take advantage of existing infrastructure and the productive potentials of the region. Accordingly, a number of large agri-food corporations invested in the region and implanted operations locally. Instrumental in this process was CODEVASF that through a variety of initiatives gave impetus to the implantation of fruit production for export.

The national irrigation policy underwent change beginning in the mid-1980s. This change involved the implementation of programs such as the National Irrigation Program (PRONI) and the Northeast Irrigation Program (PROINE) that redefined the previously agreed upon public and private responsibilities concerning irrigation. Under the new policy, public intervention was limited only to the execution of major works and the building of infrastructure. In addition, the revised irrigation policy contemplated the expansion of irrigated areas. However, following the privatization of farming programs and the concomitant reduction of state spending, the implementation of this objective centered on the establishment of private associations of family farmers and agri-food companies.

This change negatively affected local family farmers in at least three different ways. First, they joined the above-mentioned private associations lacking organizational experience and, more importantly, organizations that could represent their collective interests. As a result, large producers gained control of these organizations. Second, the increases in production costs and in irrigation maintenance fees along with reduced technical assistance generated by the withdrawal of state support created economic hardship for family operations. Many of these small farmers left the sector. Third, the technical and economic requirements for the implementation of irrigated fruit production also contributed to the marginalization of family farmers. This situation further translated into the concentration of land in the hands of those producers with greater financial and technical means (Cavalcanti 1999).

> The consequences of the crisis are different in the cases of family farmers and agri-business producers. While short-cycle agriculture experienced a significant crisis in the irrigated areas, fruit production rapidly expanded. This transition is marked by an intense process of exclusion of family farmers that takes place through the concentration of land ownership. The result of this process completely altered the profile of existing producers that are now those endowed with advanced technical means and capital (Silva 2001: 92).

In the following years and in partnership with other federal agencies, CODEVASF built twelve public irrigation areas in the San Francisco Valley. These publicly-created spaces covered 59,259 hectares and generated 50,992 direct jobs and 76,745 indirect jobs (CODEVASF 2019). Of these twelve areas, seven were located in the Petrolina-Juazeiro complex, corresponding to an irrigated area of 48,605 hectares. Importantly, almost 70 percent of this area was occupied by large agri-business companies indicating the difficulties that family operations continued to have in entering this highly competitive market (CODEVASF 2019). In effect, after the initial period of construction of the irrigated areas, little attention was paid to local family farms. After receiving land and irrigation equipment, they were left without virtually any technical and financial assistance. As a result, local family farms became quickly unprofitable (Britto 1995; Cavalcanti 1997; Graziano da Silva 1989). The State legitimized this situation through pronouncements associating the difficulties of family farms with a market-generated "natural selection" whereby only the most competent, trained, or dedicated producers could remain in business.

> In the irrigated areas, the increased sale of parcels of land is viewed as a process of "natural selection," that eliminates inefficient operations. This view dismisses other reasons that lead farmers to sell their lots such as difficulties in the commercialization of their products or unrepaid loans. Those who purchase these parcels need to prove financial solvency. Yet, they do not have to show that they can work the land, have no other property and all the other requirements that were originally requested of local settlers. . . . This is a distortion of the original objective of the irrigated settlement projects. The result is a movement of land concentration disguised as a "natural" occurrence (Bloch 1996: 32).

The model of development of the irrigated areas adopted by CODEVASF is representative of the new neoliberal posture adopted by the State. It required profitability at all costs and placed it above any other aspects of farming life. In this sense, the selection of the cultivation of fruit for export, the emphasis on agri-business operations and the privatization of technical support conforms to neoliberal policy requirements.

> From the perspective of neoliberalism, farmers and their families have to become producers who must adopt the logic of market rationality and abandon those other forms of rationality that have historically formed part of family and peasant agriculture or that have inspired alternative visions of economic action. At the same time, the land is not only a factor of production but, above all, a market asset whose financial dimension constitutes its fundamental aspect (Bonanno 2016: 111).

Yet in spite of reference to the neoliberal discourse as a way to legitimate changes in state action, large agri-businesses continued to request state support that they received in terms of assistance provided by federal agencies and technical support that was originally designed to assist family farms. The State, in other words, was de facto transformed into an agency for the expansion of agri-business. FINOR was instrumental in attracting capital to the region. Stressing the favorable natural conditions, the irrigation infrastructure, and existing state incentive, FINOR supported investments of a number of domestic and international groups that established operations in the San Francisco Valley.

> Cheap land, new fruit varieties and the expansion of Petrolina airport are making the San Francisco Valley more attractive in the eyes of global agri-food corporations. The region, which is endowed with a dry climate, good quality water, deep and fertile soil, has been attracting investors from many parts of the world. . . . The French group Carrefour invested 25 million reals in the region, and in October it will inaugurate its third agricultural operation in

> the San Francisco Valley: the "Organic Farm of the Valley." This farm is located in Petrolina. This is a municipality that counts on another enterprise of the group: the farm "Valley of the Grapes." The third farm is "Labrunier" that is located in locality Casa Nova on the Bahia side of the Valley. . . . The group Silvio Santos is another corporation that showed interest in the region. Through FINOR which is managed by SUDENE, the group invested 18 percent of its taxable revenue—about 3 million reals—in the enterprise "Frutivita" which is owned by businessman Eduardo Maciel. In return, Silvio Santos receives 100 percent of the preferred shares of Frutivita. Frutivita, in turn, has already invested 10 million reals and is expected to harvest a thousand metric tons of mangos and grapes in the year 2000. "With the expansion of the airport runway, our products will arrive fresh in England, Germany, Holland, Scandinavia, and France," says Maciel (Gazeta Mercantil 1999: B20).

The economic crisis that affected the country was employed to justify the "policy of emancipation" and the associated reduction of state support for family farms. However, the State's discourse was not employed in the case of corporate agriculture that continued to be supported. An article that appeared in the specialized newspaper *Jornal do Commércio* entitled "Incentives Enable Irrigated Fruit Production in the San Francisco Valley" illustrates how corporations benefited from public funding throughout the mid-1980s and 1990s. A passage from that article states:

> The economic expansion of fruit production in the San Francisco Valley—which already occupies 100,000 irrigated hectares—attracts an increasing number of companies to the Region. Most of these projects receive direct or indirect incentives from SUDENE. In the past 15 years, the State has financed a number of fruit and wine corporations in the municipalities of Petrolina, Santa Maria da Boa Vista and Lagoa Grande with more investments expected for the coming years. State intervention privileged firms that combine advanced productive capacity and research techniques. At least three farms created with incentives from FINOR are exemplary of this trend: Guararapes Agrícola Agropecuária, Timbaúba Agrícola S.A. and the Organic Valley. Owned by the Queiroz Galvão group, the first two have been active for more than five years, with an estimated annual production of 3,500 metric tons of mangoes and 1,700 metric tons of grapes. Together, they received 7.9 million reals from FINOR (Jornal do Commércio 2000:1B).

It is evident, therefore, how the elimination of the social objectives originally set for irrigated agriculture was not simply an economic issue but a political one that, driven by the neoliberal orientation of the government, marginalized the local family farm population. Cavalcanti (1999) observes:

> Despite the fact that originally settlers from the Sertão region established family farms on awarded plots at the beginning of the colonization of the Valley, many of them were unable to remain in production and became hired laborers for other producers (Cavalcanti 1999: 163).

Since then, the implementation of advanced techniques of production and investments allowed producers in the San Francisco Valley to increase their market share. Along with the financial and technical components, however, producers took advantage of two additional market-driven dimensions. The first refers to the targeting of production to specific time periods. These are counter-seasonal market windows that allow fresh fruit from the San Francisco Valley to enter global circuits of commercialization in periods when the production from other world regions stagnates. The second refers to the exponential growth of the demand for quality, exotic, fresh fruit. Based on a new culture of healthy food consumption that emerged in the global North at the end of the twentieth century, this trend indicates a significant shift in the type of fresh food demanded on the global market. It centers on the certification of quality and the establishment of new standards for taste, esthetic, and labor (Bonanno and Cavalcanti 2014).

THE GROWTH OF FRUIT PRODUCTION FOR EXPORT AND CHANGES IN LABOR RELATIONS UNDER THE NEO-DEVELOPMENTALIST PERIOD

In 2003, with the establishment of the first government of the PT under the presidency of Lula (2003–2011), Brazil inaugurated a new economic policy. Proclaiming the end of neoliberalism, it adopted a program of economic growth based on increased state spending, planning, and regulation along with income distribution measures. However, despite the adoption of these Keynesian moves, the country's Neo-Developmentalist program did not completely break with the neoliberal ideology (Boito Jr. 2012). In effect, it included a variety of actions that followed the tenets of Neoliberalism. These actions included fostering the insertion of Brazilian companies in the global market through enhanced competitiveness, tying state spending to fiscal responsibility, controlling inflation through the regulation of monetary liquidity, and maintaining a relatively low exchange rate for the national currency, the Real. This new economic policy was implemented through a new and broad social pact that, while it could count on the participation of a variety of class fractions of the Brazilian society, was ultimately directed by the domestic bourgeoisie (Bresser Pereira 2013). Accordingly, as the local bourgeoisie was allowed to pursue its interests, agribusiness continued to occupy a leadership position in the definition of the domestic agri-food policy.

As mentioned, one of the primary characteristics of the economic policy of the Lula government was the establishment of a favorable exchange rate. It differed from the policy adopted in the 1990s by the administrations of presidents Collor de Melo (1990–1992) and Fernando Enrique Cardoso (1995–2002). Under these administrations, much of the economic policy centered on the neoliberal tenet of maintaining high interest rates that, while controlling inflation, hurt the growth of exports and the balance of trade because it overvalued the Real against other currencies, including the dollar (Bresser Pereira 2013). Under the Lula government, conversely, the lower value of the Real promoted the growth of exports and created a surplus in the balance of trade that kept increasing throughout the years of the PT administration (BACEN 2019).

The export of global commodities such as minerals and agri-food products was fundamental for the maintenance of this positive balance of trade. In the case of agriculture, the expansion of fruit production also counted on the establishment of a number of specialized institutions, such as PRODEFRUTA (or Program for the Development of Fruit Production). Created in 2003 and financed by the National Bank for Economic and Social Development (BNDES), PRODEFRUTA was established with the objective of promoting fruit production for the global market through measures that would make credit accessible to producers and ensure their competitiveness in the market. In this context, exports from the São Francisco Valley increased considerably. From 2005 to 2017, more than 20 percent of the total value of fruit exported from Brazil was produced in the San Francisco Valley while, also in 2017, the value of mango and grape exports represented 26 percent of the total Brazilian fruit exports.

The global financial crisis of 2008, however, engendered a crisis of fruit exports. The prices of the commodities produced in the San Francisco Valley dropped sharply with negative consequences on profitability. The effects of the crisis were particularly acute in 2009 when the total value exported decreased by more than 30 percent from the previous year. This situation led to "conditions of uncertainty regarding the destinations of production, job preservation and the economic solvency of local producers" (Pires and Cavalcanti 2012: 277). However, growers' organizational capacity and appropriate state intervention mitigated these negative effects. In this context, the role of the State was essential, above all, due to the implementation of credit and debt renegotiations carried out by state-owned banks and the reorientation of production toward the domestic market (Pires and Cavalcanti 2012). By 2010, exports of mangos and grapes resumed their growth.

Given the magnitude of the expansion of fruit production for export that took place in the 2000s, it is not surprising that it engendered significant economic and social change in the San Francisco Valley. According to data from the Brazilian Institute of Geography and Statistics (IBGE), in 1990, there were only 2,029 hectares planted with mangos and grapes in this Petrolina, Juazeiro region that grew to 14,847 and 30,721 hectares in 2000 and 2010 respectively. This expansion continued in the following years, albeit at a reduced rate, as 2017 data indicate that 32,286 hectares were occupied by these cultures. Growth also involved the introduction of quality production regulated by international quality standards. As indicated above, these standards cover not only production techniques but also labor relations and labor use.

> These export-oriented sectors tend to respond well to special requirements associated with the implementation of quality standards about phytosanitary conditions and product presentation. This situation often implies new types of labor relations and new forms of labor management that emerge as prerequisites for the achievement of global competitiveness under the current market conditions. Accordingly, this redefinition of labor relations mandates new types of duties for workers and advanced forms of coordination of the various components of the production process that include work time, know-how, technology and human resources (Cavalcanti 1997: 85).

Quality standards were introduced and enforced through third-party product certification whereby agri-food corporations employ certification firms to legitimize their claims about product quality, the respect of the safety of workers, and the protection of the environment.

> The control over products materializes through certification that acts as a pass for the recognition of the quality of products or, in case of rejection, for their exclusion from global supermarket chains. The quality standards necessary to obtain the appropriate certification label vary according to the buyers, agreements, and audits. Accordingly, producers often need to have a good prior knowledge of the place, buyer, distributor, and retailer of his/her products (Cavalcanti and Dias 2015: 283).

In this context, certification imposes a new logic of control over the production and commercialization of fruit. Now control is established not only through existing legal norms, but also, and more importantly, through private international certification firms. Periodically, these firms carry out audits on the farm to ensure compliance with standards and, as a result, this new form of validation of quality reaches consumers under the shape of the certification label attached to the product.

In terms of labor relations, fruit for export requires the achievement of new tasks that cover not only the management of labor but also its uses. Constant inspection of labor use and labor tasks implies an increase in the labor time employed to produce a given unit of product. Given the fact that labor is paid by the unit of product (box of grapes or mangoes), this situation results in an increase of the relative exploitation of labor. Moreover, as certification requirements pertain to a variety of facets of the production process, workers are required to learn new techniques of production that are considered pre-requisites for employment. In essence, therefore, while quality products are heralded as environmental and labor-friendly, in the case of the San Francisco Valley, their production conceals new forms of labor exploitation (Bonanno and Cavalcanti 2012).

Despite these conditions, a positive by-product of the expansion of production in the San Francisco Valley was the increase in farm jobs. In 1990, there were only 2,606 area workers employed in farming. By the end of 2017, this number expanded to 29,456 jobs. Simultaneously, however, the availability of jobs did not translate into a reduction of the poor conditions of labor in the region and the high levels of inequality that characterized it. This situation emerged despite the actions of organized labor that, through the local Farm Workers' Unions (*Sindicatos de Trabalhadores Rurais* or SRT), supported wage-workers' claims for better working conditions and remunerations (Souto Jr., Silva and Lima 2012). The State significantly contributed to the regulation of labor relations. It mediated between management and labor and introduced labor policies that contributed to the maintenance of relatively low labor costs. Beginning in 1994, representatives of agribusinesses and trade unions met annually to negotiate wage levels and labor issues (Souto Jr. 2013). In this context, the State, through the relevant participation of the Ministry of Labor and Employment, was instrumental in the implementation of the "Collective Labor Convention (CCT)" that represented a significant mechanism for building agreement between management and labor (Silva 2016; Silva 2016).

Under these conditions, the push for lower labor costs remained a constant feature of the actions of agri-businesses in fruit production. Firms pursue labor cost containment through three fundamental strategies. First, they implement short term contracts whereby workers are hired for relatively short periods and their rehiring depends not only on their performance in the fields but also on their behavior. Second, as mentioned above, the implementation of certification strategies served as a mechanism to increase not only labor productivity but also the absolute number of hours worked. Finally, there has been an intense process of feminization of labor as female workers are hired instead of their male counterparts. While the skills associated with the work of women are heralded as superior to those of men, the higher vulnerability of women in the labor market and their greater willingness to accept lower wages and higher workloads are factors that largely explain the behavior of firms (Bonanno and Cavalcanti 2014; 2012; Silva 2016; Silva 2016).

Labor unions have opposed these practices and, particularly under the PT administrations, promoted strikes and demonstrations that, claiming better wages and working conditions, impacted the actions of agri-food companies in the region. As a result, wage levels have improved yet this improvement has remained marginal. Since the mid-1990s, on average, the daily wage collectively negotiated for the region-hired workers has exceeded the national minimum wage level by about 16.00 reals (3.4 US dollars). To this end, instrumental has been the role of the PT administrations that maintained increases in the minimum wage above the rate of inflation between 2004 and 2016. Prior to 2004, wage growth did not necessarily represent an increase in real wages (wage levels minus the rate of inflation) as increases did always match the annual inflation rates. Ultimately, state measures functioned as important forms of income distribution, increasing the consumption capacity of the lower income families (Carvalho 2018).

The reduction of social inequality was one of the primary objectives of the Workers' Party as it took control of the government in 2003. Arguably, one of the most important of these interventions in the region is the program *Bolsa Família*, the largest income transfer program ever implemented in Brazil. According to data from the Ministry of Social Development (MDS) in 2018, more than 87 thousand families benefited from this program in the San Francisco Valley. In some municipalities, such as Santa Maria da Boa Vista, located in the Petrolina metropolitan areas, the program covered more than 56 percent of the total population (MDS 2018). In the case of programs specifically directed to family farming, the Food Acquisition Program (*Program de Aquisição de Alimentos* or PAA), and the National School Feeding Program (*Programa Nacional de Alimentação Escolar* or PNAE) are noteworthy. Both programs are designed to facilitate the State's purchase of agricultural products from family farms. According to data from the Department of Social Development and Citizenship of Petrolina (SEDESC)—the agency responsible for implementing the programs—in 2016, 3.7 million Reals went to farmers involved in PAA and PNAE.

These and an additional number of other state policies aimed at the redistribution of wealth and social inclusion speak to the meaning of the Neo-developmentalist model adopted by the Workers' Party. It presupposed a social pact that contemplated different forms of intervention for different social classes. As indicated above, in the case of the working class, the State attempted to address poverty and socio-economic inequality through income redistribution. In the case of the domestic bourgeoisie, the State fostered this class's interests through expanded public financing and planning. To be sure, this period's Neo-developmentalist model characteristics also represent its most important contradictions. Its income distribution policy increased access to consumption but did not break with the structural conditions that give rise to social inequalities. Its support of the local bourgeoisie underestimated the difficulties of competing with transnational corporations at the global level. In the case of agri-food, these contradictions are exemplified by the government's inability to implement an effective policy of land reform and the failure of a number of important state-sponsored corporate projects (see Bonanno in this volume).

Since the 2016 impeachment of President Dilma Rousseff, Brazil has reintroduced a more orthodox neoliberal agenda centered on the reduction of state spending and the deregulation of pro-labor legislation. The enacting of legislation that supports labor outsourcing and deregulates labor relations engendered the precarization of labor that involves new forms of hiring, labor flexibilization, decreasing wages, the reduction of health and safety standards, the weakening of trade unions' power, and limited access to labor justice. This agenda strengthened with the 2018 election of Jair Bolsonaro to the Presidency.

CONCLUSIONS

The intervention of the Brazilian State in the San Francisco Valley was fundamental for the growth but also significant transformation of the entire productive structure and social and economic relations in the San Francisco Valley. It favored economic actors from other and more affluent regions of the country, such as the South and Southeast regions of Brazil, along with international groups that received privileged treatment to the detriment of the local groups. Predominantly financed by the State, the creation of the irrigated areas led to processes of social exclusion as it fostered the development of an agriculture based on business models that excluded local family farmers' access to land and water. The Neo-developmentalist model adopted by the PT governments mitigated social inequality through income redistribution policies and by augmenting the consumption power of the working and lower classes. However, and despite these results including a reduction of poverty in Brazil, this policy has not been able to overcome the structural conditions that engendered the sharp inequality that characterizes the country. In addition, large international corporations and sectors of the national bourgeoisie linked to agribusiness have continued to control investments and affect state policies.

The research question of this book probes the emancipatory power of the Brazilian case of state capitalism. The contradictory outcomes illustrated in this chapter speak to the problematic nature of reintroducing Keynesian based, Neo-developmentalist economic policies in an economy that is global and dominated by powerful transnational corporations. The most fundamental of these contradictions rests on the difficulty of reconciling wealth redistribution and social justice policies with the corporate requirement of generating high rates of profit. In addition, corporate defined profitability frequently clashes with the implementation of pro-labor and pro-environment measures. Opposition to the PT program and the recent election of a conservative and pro-market president and government further indicate the fragility of a social democratic approach that tries to unify a push for socio-economic equality with corporate demands. Perhaps state capitalism is the best and more practical solution available to progressive forces in Brazil as well as other parts of the world. But different to the high days of planned and socially oriented capitalism of the first post-World War II decades, contemporary global capitalism cannot count on the presence of a strong and organized labor movement. As the threat of strong labor-led struggles is marginal at best, experiments such as that of the PT in Brazil are ultimately controlled by corporate and conservative forces. This is the ultimate message that emerges from the analysis presented in these pages.

BIBLIOGRAPHY

Araújo, Tânia Bacelar. 2002. "Nordestes: que Nordeste?" http://www.fundaj.gov.br/index.php?option=com_content&view=article&id=470&Itemid=414/obte013.doc. Accessed January 6, 2019.

BACEM. 2019. "Brazilian Balance of Trade." https://tradingeconomics.com/brazil/balance-of-trade. Accessed February 7, 2017.

Bloch, Didier. 2008. *Agroecologia e Acesso a Mercados. Três Esperiências na Agricultuar Familiar da Regia Noreste do Brazil*. São Paulo: Oxfarm.

Boito Jr., Armando. 2012. "As Bases Políticas do Neodesenvolvimentismo." Paper presented at the 9th Fórum de Economia da Fundação Getúlio Vargas. São Paulo, June 22–25.

Bonanno, Alessandro. 2016. "Tierra, Capital y Trabajo en el Proceso de Reestructuración Neoliberal de la Agricultura." http://www.upa.es/upa/_depot/_uploadImagenes00/Tierra percent20capital percent20y percent20trabajo.pdf. Accessed February 7, 2018.

———. 1999. "A Globalização da Economia e da Sociedade: Fordismo e Pós-Fordismo no Setor Agroalimentar." In Josefa Salete Barbosa Cavalcanti (Ed.), *Globalização, Trabalho, Meio Ambiente. Mudanças Socioeconômicas em Regiões Frutícolas para Exportação* (pp. 47–94). Recife: Editora Universitaria.

Bonanno, Alessandro, and Josefa Salete Barbosa Cavalcanti (Eds.). 2014. *Labor Relations in Globalized Food*. Bingley, UK: Emerald Publishing.

———. 2012. "Globalization, Food Quality and Labor: The Case of Grape Production in Northeastern Brazil." *International Journal of Sociology of Agriculture and Food* 19 (1): 37–55.

Bresser Pereira, Luiz Carlos. 2013. *O Que Esperar do Brasil?* Rio de Janeiro: FVG.

———. 2009. *Globalização e Competição por Que Alguns Países Emergentes Têm Sucesso*. São Paulo: Campus.

Britto, Maria Creusa de Sá y Petrolina. 1995. *Origem, Fatos, Vida, Uma História (do Desbravamento do Município a 1992)*. Tribuna do Sertão Jornal e Gráfica, Petrolina-PE.

Brazil. 1946. *Constituição de 1946*. Brasilia: Republica Federativa do Brasil. Article 29.

———. 1999. "Desigualdades Sociais e Identidades em Construção na Agricultura de Exportação." *Revista Latino-Americana de Estudos do Trabalho* 5 (9): 75–102.

———. 1997. "Frutas Para o Mercado Global." *Estudos Avançados* 11 (29): 79–93.

Carvalho, Laura. 2018. *Valsa Brasileira: Do Boom ao Caos Econômico*. São Paulo: Editora Todavia.

Cavalcanti, Josefa Salete Barbosa, and Gustavo Dias. 2015. "Cadeias Globais de Alimentos, Redes de Atores e Qualidades na Produção de Frutas para Exportação: elos entre Brasil e Alemanha." *Estudos de Sociologia* 2 (21): 279–310.

Cavalcanti, Josefa Salete Barbosa, Nazareth Wanderley, and Paulo Niederle (Eds.). 2014. *Participação Território e Cidadania: Um Olhar Sobre a Política de Desenvolvimento Territorial no Brasil*. Recife: Editora Universitária da UFPE.

Cavalcanti, Josefa Salete Barbosa, and Guillermo Neiman. 2005. (Eds.). *Acerca de la Globalizaciónen la Agricultura*. Buenos Aires, Ciccus.

CODEVASF 2019. "Companhia de Desenvolvimento dos Vales do São Francisco e do Parnaíba." https://www.bnamericas.com/company-profile/en/companhia-de-

desenvolvimento-dos-vales-do-sao-francisco-e-do-parnaiba-codevasf. Accessed January 23, 2019.

Damiani, Octavio. 2003. "Diversificação Agrícola e Redução de Pobreza: A Introdução no Nordeste Brasileiro de Produtos Agrícolas Não-Tradicionais de Alto Valor e Seus Efeitos sobre Pequenos Produtores e Trabalhadores Rurais Assalariados." *Revista Econômica do Nordeste* 34 (1): 42–84.

Friedmann, Harriet, and Philip McMichael. 1989. "Agriculture and the State System: the Rise and Decline of National Agricultures, 1870 to the Present." *Sociologica Ruralis* 29 (2): 93–117.

Furtado, Celso. 1959a. *Orientação da Economia do Nordeste*. Rio de Janeiro: Confederação.

———. 1959b. Operação Nordeste. Rio de Janeiro: Ministério da Educação e Cultura, Instituto Superior de Estudos Brasileiros.

Gazeta Mercantil. 1999. "Fruticultura Atrai Investidores para o Semi-Aárido." June 8: B20.

Graziano da Silva, José. 1993. "A Industrialização e a Urbanização da Agricultura Brasileira." *Revista São Paulo em Perspectiva* 7 (3): 2–10.

———. 1989. *A Irrigação e a Problemática Fundiária do Nordeste*. Campinas, SP: Instituto de Economia da Unicamp/PRONI.

II PND. 1974. II Plano Nacional de Desenvolvimento: 1975–1979. http://bibspi.planejamento.gov.br/handle/iditem/492. Accessed February 20, 2018.

Jornal do Commercio. 2000. "Incentivos Viabilizam a Fruticultura Irrigada no Vale do São Francisco." *Jornal do Commercio*, April 27: 1B.

MDS (Ministério do Desenvolvimento Social). 2018. Relatório Bolsa Família. https://aplicacoes.mds.gov.br/sagi/RIv3/geral/index.php?relatorio=153&file=entrada#. Accessed February 12, 2019.

Pires, Maria Luisa, and Josefa Salete Barbosa Cavalcanti. 2012. "Imagens da fruticultura do Vale do São Francisco: Cooperativa, Reinvenção de Estratégias e Criação de Oportunidades em Tempos de Enfrentamentos da Crise Global." In Carla Craviotti (Ed.), *Tramas Productivas y Agentes Sociales en la Fruticultura Globalizada* (pp. 223–246). Buenos Aires: Editora Miño y Dávila.

Silva, Camilla de Almeida. 2016. *"O Que A Gente Quer Pra Um, A Gente Quer Pro Outro": Uma Análise Sobre as Questões de Gênero e a Agenda Política dos Sindicatos de Trabalhadores e Trabalhadoras Rurais na Fruticultura Irrigada do Polo Petrolina/PE-Juazeiro/BA*. Campina Grande: UFCG.

Silva, Guilherme J. Mota. 2016. *Os Frutos Da Resitência: Sindicalismo e Luta dos Assalariados da Fruticultura Irrigada no Submédio São Francisco*. Campina Grande: UFCG.

Silva, Pedro C. 2009. "Dinâmica e Crise da Fruticultura Irrigada no Vale do São Francisco." In Aldenôr Gomes da Silva, Josefa Salete Barbosa Cavalcanti and Maria de Nazareth B. Wanderley (Eds.), *Diversificação dos Espaços Rurais e Dinâmicas Territoriais no Nordeste do Brasil* (pp. 69–95). João Pessoa: Zarinha Centro de Cultura.

———. 2001. *Articulação dos Interesses Públicos e Privados no Pólo Petrolina-PE/Juazeiro-BA: em Busca de Espaço no Mercado Globalizado de Frutas Frescas*. Campinas/SP: UNICAMP.

Souto Jr., José Fernando. 2013. "Se Parar, a Fruta Apodrece: Fordismo e Sindicatos no Vale do São Francisco." *Revista Espaço de Diálogo e Desconexão* 7 (1): 2–22.

Souto Jr., José Fernando, Guilherme J. Mota Silva, Sara C. Lima. 2012. "O Lugar da Ausência: Luta de Cclasses e Direitos na Fruticultura Irrigada do São Francisco." In Regina Celeste de Almeida Souza, Carolina de Andrade Spínola, and Elvina Perpétua Ramos Almeida (Eds.), *Rio São Francisco: Ocupação Territorial: Problemas Socioambientais: Desafios e Possibilidades* (pp. 77–90). Salvador: UNIFACS.

Chapter Seven

Family Farmers Besieged between Neo-Developmentalism and Neoliberalism

The Role of the State in Agriculture and the Contradictions of the Present Time

Beatriz Medeiros de Melo

Focusing on agri-food and the conditions of family farmers, this chapter offers some reflections on the role that the Brazilian State played in the socio-economic development of agri-food in Brazil in the last three decades. These considerations are based on the results of theoretical reflections and empirical investigations that this author carried out over the last 6 years in different parts of Brazil. These regions include the territory of the Northeast—home of the largest proportion of family farmers in the country (49.7 percent)—and the state of San Paulo, in the Southeast—an area that features a rather limited presence of family farmers but a high level of integration into the market economy. Following this introduction, the first section of the chapter discusses the implementation of neoliberal policies that occurred in the decade of the 1990s. It further reviews policies in support of family farming also introduced at the time.

The second section analyzes salient events that characterized the first two decades of the new century, stressing the problematic nature of the policies that have been implemented by the administrations (Presidents Lula and Dilma Rousseff) of the Workers' Party (PT) since it took office in 2003. The problematic nature of the government policy rests on the fact that it pursued contradictory objectives. On the one hand, the government openly supported corporate agri-food through the implementation of a combination of established and new strategies that allowed the further integration of Brazilian agri-food companies into the global market as well as the global exploitation of Brazilian natural resources. On the other hand, the government followed its declared objective of strengthening family agriculture through a set of income redistribution policies and measures aimed at combating poverty and family farmers' limited access to land and productive resources. This second section also points out the change in policy direction represented by the end of the PT's regime and the appointment of the administration of Michel Temer. In the third section of the chapter, recent actions of the State are analyzed focusing on the continuities and ruptures with the past. The question that is ultimately addressed concerns the level of sovereignty that the Neo-developmentalist policies of the PT government engendered. This analysis of the problematic nature of PT policies connects with the research question of this edited book about the emancipatory power of state capitalism.

THE STATE AND THE REPRODUCTION OF SOCIAL RELATIONS IN FARMING IN BRAZIL: NEOLIBERALISM IN THE 1990s

In the 1980s and 1990s, Brazil experienced a severe economic recession that ended the developmentalist policies of the previous decades. To address the crisis, the State contracted private loans with international financial institutions that eroded the solvency of the country, initiated a period of high inflation and promoted a fiscal crisis of the State. The increased indebtedness and its servicing required a restructuring of domestic spending that involved a sharp decrease in public investment in all economic sectors and social spheres. In the case of farming, existing programs in support of farm credit and price support programs were rolled back. Simultaneously, a rigid monetary policy, implemented to combat inflation, strengthened the value of the domestic currency with negative consequences on the ability of local producers to compete in international markets. In this context, the State contributed to the consolidation of the sector that was a strategic objective of government policies (Delgado 2012; Leite 2005).

In the late 1980s and 1990s, neoliberalism was identified as the ideal policy to promote economic growth. Fostered by the popularity of the period's Washington Consensus, it contemplated deregulation through the reduced intervention of the State in the control of the economy and the opening of local markets to international competition. Heralded by the Clinton Administration as the most effective political recipe for success, the US and international financial institutions—such as the International Monetary Funds and the World Bank—recommended the adoption of Neoliberalism to a great number of countries of the South, including Brazil. The reduced intervention of the State in the economy translated into the privatization of public assets that, however, resulted in de-industrialization, the growth of unemployment, a decline in production, and an increase in social exclusion (Pochmann 2017). The established approach of "sectorial development" was replaced by the new "territorial approach." Promoted by directives from the OECD and legitimized by the World Bank's publication of the report "The New Vision of Rural Development," it advocated a new growth model based on multi-sectoriality, the decentralization of decision making, emphasis on the regional dimension of development over a national focus, incentives for, and control of, productive processes and, above all, labor flexibilization (Favareto 2007). A wealth of studies analyzed the consequences and contradictions of this approach. They stressed that it engendered not only the enhanced exploitation of local human and natural resources, but also the phenomenon of "commodification of local culture" whereby socio-economic development is subordinated to the transformation of local products and social relations into appealing commodities for the global market (Harvey 2004; Leite 2005). In this new context, the focus on a local/regional approach fostered a new period of primitive accumulation that intensified the exploitation of small family farmers and their subordination to corporate market-based designs (Pochmann 2017).

In Brazil, the expansion of the regime of flexible accumulation and the implementation of neoliberal policies accompanied the growing opposition to the dictatorial regime. This broad-based movement resulted in the democratization of the country embodied in the enactment of the 1988 Constitution. Dense with contradictions and social tension, these years saw the coexistence of the effects of "conservative modernization" promoted by the previous regime, neoliberal deregulation, and pressure to address the issues that affected the country's underdeveloped rural space. The time's social unrest featured the growth of new social movements such as the landless workers movement (*Trabalhadores Sem Terra* or MST), environmentalism, the movements of indigenous people and *quilombolas* (people of color) and the feminist movement. Along with the movement of the people displaced by the construction of dams *(Movimento dos Atingidos por Barragens)*, these movements brought together the protest of different urban and rural groups that suffered the negative consequences of the conservative modernization policies and the economic crises of the second half of the twentieth century (Honneth 2009; Scherer-Warren 2007).

Because of the pressure exerted by these rural social movements, the State, under the administration of President Fernando Henrique Cardoso, began to implement public policies directed at improving the conditions of small-scale farming. One of the results of this effort was the creation of a new—for Brazil—political subject of rights: the family farmer. This social figure included a variety of established groups, such as *quilombolas* (Afro-Brazilians), native populations, settlers of the land reform, peoples of the rivers (*ribeirinhos*) and peasants that claimed rights to land, autonomy, and independence by means of different struggles, such as land occupation and land expropriation. Cardoso's objectives were to restructure state intervention and promote private initiatives. Following ideas promoted under the neoliberal Washington Consensus, Cardoso viewed in the partnership between the State and the private sector a way to stimulate not only the economy but also social development. To these ends, he reformulated the Program for the Support of Small Rural Production (PROVAP) and created PRONAF (National Program for the Strengthening of Family Farming) which implemented technical, financial, and infrastructure subsidies for family farmers. In 2000 and as part of this process, the Ministry for the Development of Agriculture (*Ministério do Desenvolvimento Agrário*) was created.

Changes in production of key agri-food commodities are telling of the actual results generated by the alliance between state and private capital. Cassava and beans are, historically, crops central to the life of peasants. From the 1970s and throughout the 1990s, however, their production dropped dramatically, indicating the overwhelming expulsion of peasants from the land following the restructuring of state intervention. The production of rice and corn, conversely, increased sharply over the same period. While both these crops are important components of the traditional production of family farms, they are also in demand in the international market as they are employed as inputs for other export-oriented products. The expansion of corn is a case in point as this crop is used not only for direct consumption but also as feed for cattle and as a component for many processed foods. These increases accompanied the exponential expansion of the production of other export-oriented commodities such as coffee, sugarcane, and soybeans. These are crops whose global demand sharply increased and was largely met by the growth of corporate farming. In essence and despite pronouncements in support of family farming, the 1990s ended with a crisis of the family farm sector and the strengthening of corporate agriculture as Brazil positioned itself to be one of the major producers and exporters of crops in high demand in the global market.

A PERIOD OF CONTRADICTIONS: FAMILY FARMING AND THE STATE BETWEEN THE NEO-DEVELOPMENTALISM OF THE 2000s AND CONTEMPORARY NEOLIBERALISM

After a decade of deregulation policies that engendered poverty growth, rising unemployment and, above all, the organized protest of social movements, the PT won the Presidential elections and formed its first government in 2003. Its Neo-developmentalist program was directed at improving the socio-economic conditions of the working classes and the poor and at promoting a productive transformation designed to reduce inequality between regions and social classes and create employment, income growth and upward social mobility. In this model, the role of the State was to redistribute wealth and maintain equity and equality (Cepeda 2012: 84). In the case of agri-food, the goal was to implement measures that would increase the income and the productive capacity of family farms. This project centered on two programs: the 2003 Zero Hunger Program (*Fome Zero*) and the 2007 Growth Acceleration Program (*Programa de Aceleração do Crescimento* or PAC). Countering the policy of the "end of developmentalism" established in the 1990s, the State took center stage in the regulation and management of agri-food. In addition to injecting a significant amount of capital in farming through the Harvest Plan for Family Agriculture (*Plano Safra para a Agricultura Familiar)*, it created the Food Acquisition Program (*Programa de Aquisição de Alimentos* or PAA) that, as part of the Zero Hunger program, was a renewed version of established price support programs. Through the PAA, the State promoted the participation of family farmers in the formal market and ways to reduce self-consumption in favor of cash generating uses of farm outputs. The PAA consisted of state guaranteed purchases of crops designed to generate a minimum income for farmers. Additionally, the State distributed the acquired farm products to segments of the population in need of food assistance. Supported by the cooperation of state institutions and NGOs, the distribution of these farm products involved actions such as the distribution of milk to pregnant women, children, nursing mothers, and the elderly. This also included the provision of food items to public supported institutions such as state university cafeterias, prisons, hospitals, police academies, and the purchase of seeds from organizations of family farmers. It also required that 30 percent of all school meals be purchased from family farmers (Grisa, Schmitt, Mattei, Maluf and Leite 2011). Simultaneously, however, the PT implemented another set of measures that supported export-oriented corporate firms. In summary, these measures consisted of: 1) support to agribusiness as a way of stabilizing the balance of payments; 2) public investment for infrastructure that supported agribusiness; 3) legislative changes that facilitated the domestic expansion of agribusiness and 4) the State's direct investment in domestic companies that operated in agri-food.

1) Since the Cardoso government, economic and political measures have been implemented to address the deficit of the balance of payments and the associated capital flight. The implementation of these measures was continued and in some instances deepened by the Lula Administration as it supported investment in infrastructure for agribusiness, public-private partnership in science and technology linked to the interests of the corporate agro-export sector, the reduction of regulation on the use and acquisition of land and the expansion of credit for large agri-food firms. In effect, between 2000 and 2010, there was a 148 percent increase in public support for agri-food. Two-thirds of this support consisted of transfers of public monetary and

fiscal resources to the private sector while the rest was mostly disbursed in the form of subsidies that also largely benefitted the corporate sector (Delgado 2012). This investment was functional to the growth of production for the export of commodities such as soybeans, corn, sugar, alcohol, meats, wood pulp, and minerals that were deemed central for the economic growth of Brazil (Paulilo, Ramos Filho and Montenegro 2015). In the context of the re-primarization (emphasis on agriculture and mining) of foreign trade, the State was responsible for not only the financing of operations but also the regulation of production and marketing. It established standards and procedures that coordinated economic activities, financing conditions and certified traceable quality criteria that met market requirements. The State was also instrumental in the expansion of the production of commodities demanded by the global market. Ultimately, during this period, the State financed, regulated, and promoted agribusiness internationally, as indicated by the episodes in which Lula defended sugarcane and beef agribusiness on charges of overexploitation of labor and adulteration of exported products.

By virtue of this and other episodes, President Lula became known as the "ethanol ambassador" to indicate the support that his administration granted to corporate agri-food. Under his administration, sugarcane production continued to increase in the Southeast, forcing the production of soybeans and livestock to be relocated to the Center-West and North of the country. Increased exports, rural credit, and loose land policies engendered land price increases, the private appropriation of public lands, and the expropriation of peasant and traditional people's land that promoted a new cycle of permanent primitive accumulation. Simultaneously, the State neglected to oversee the social function originally assigned to land property and reduced the number of land expropriations for land reform purposes (Delgado 2012). After a timid increase between 2003 and 2006, land expropriations sharply decreased until the end of the Dilma Rousseff Administration in 2016.

2) The high level of investment in infrastructure is another mechanism that was employed to transfer public resources directly to large agri-food corporations. An instance of this process is represented by the investment in the PAC program that injected capital into the sectors of sanitation, housing, transport, energy, and water resources. In the 2007–2010 first phase, this investment totaled 675 billion reals, while in the second 2011–2014 phase this amount rose to 955 billion reals. The majority of this investment went to the energy sector followed by social and urban infrastructure and logistics. In addition to responding to the legitimate demand of part of the local population, investment in energy was functional to the increased demand for energy from the agri-food and mining sectors. Investment in logistics directly benefited the agri-food corporate firms that expanded operations to the Midwest, North, and Northeast of the country. This investment was crucial in promoting the circulation of products within the interior of the country and towards

important shipping ports servicing foreign markets. In addition to the PAC and beginning in 2004, the national investment bank, BNDES, has injected considerable amounts of capital for the development of infrastructure, such as the construction of highways, pipelines, and hydroelectric dams, that fostered the export of Brazilian agri-food products to neighboring countries like Paraguay, Ecuador, and Venezuela (Assis 2014; Paulilo, Ramos Filho, and Montenegro 2015: 312).

These and similar programs aimed at developing new poles of agricultural production. Engineered through the partnership of federal agencies and agri-food research centers, these poles were created to attract investment to enhance the capacity of Brazilian agriculture to meet the global demand for agri-food commodities. MATOPIBA (an acronym that refers to the states that are contained in the pole: Maranhão, Tocantins, Piauí, and Bahia), is an area of 33 million hectares that, because of the State's investment in infrastructure, became an important pole of production for soybeans, corn, cotton, and sugar cane. The implantation of this pole attracted 26 transnational corporations—mostly from the United States—that invested in the purchase of land. Particularly after the 2008 global financial crisis, this land, however, was employed more as a financial asset rather than a factor of production and used as a tool for financial speculations rather than the production of commodities (Aguiar, Lima Filho, and Torres Jr. 2013; Pitta, Boechat, and Mendonça 2017). More importantly, this investment and the associated expansion of production fueled a violent process of expropriation of peasants and indigenous tribes along with the acceleration of the exploitation of natural resources and degradation of the environment (CIMI 2016). In addition to investments in infrastructure and financial support for corporate agriculture in the region, the State took a leading role in the promotion of developmental policies through the implementation of the 2015 Agricultural Development Plan of MATOPIBA. It consists of the establishment of a management committee for the region and the enactment of public policies that increased agricultural production and natural resource exploitation for export.

An additional pole of agricultural development, SEALBA, includes a portion of the states of Sergipe, Alagoas, and Bahia. According to a 2016 analysis carried out by Embrapa, the State's investment in this pole enhanced the production of commodities destined for the global market. Conversely, productions that are more valuable for the domestic market are declining and forecasted to be further reduced in the future. Moreover, the study suggests that state intervention in partnership with private actors is essential in the rationalization of production processes and leads to a more efficient use of human and natural resources (Embrapa 2016: 33). In essence, the State's economic intervention for the expansion of agri-food production for export reinforces the role of agriculture in the Brazilian economy and society as the sector that defines the regional and national territory and the country's employment. However, and in the context of globalization, this intervention permits that a significant portion of this investment is captured by corporate actors to the detriment of local family farmers and farm workers (Ianni 2013: 243).

3) The PT Administration enacted legislation but also abstained from implementing required legislative changes that ultimately resulted in deregulation that favored corporate agriculture. Two items can be briefly mentioned to illustrate this point. The first refers to the inaction of the Brazilian State in terms of updating productivity indexes that are employed to identify land to be expropriated for Land Reform. These are poorly exploited tracts of land that are part of latifundia and that are considered better used by landless peasants and farm workers. By failing to update the productivity indexes employed to identify these tracts of land, the State de-facto slowed down, and in some instances limited, the implementation of the very Land Reform that it so eloquently supported. The second item consists of the reduction of the "Permanent Preservation Area" (*Área de Preservação Permanente*) and the simultaneous change in the legal interpretation of the concept of the Forest Reserve (*Reserva Florestal)*. These are ecologically protected areas that, for their environmental importance, are excluded for commercial use. The PT Administration's policies contributed to reduce the size of these protected spaces and opened them to agri-food companies and the extractive industries (Sauer and França 2012).

4) Finally, the fourth set of measures implemented by the State under the PT refers to direct investment in private companies. Countering the processes of deregulation and privatization that occurred in the 1990s, under the PT Administration, the State invested in private agri-food companies and became either their majority owner or minority partner (Pochmann, 2017; Bonanno in this volume). According to Lazzarini and Musacchio (2015), this is a global phenomenon that includes instances such as the Agricultural Bank of China and JBS in Brazil. In the particular case of Brazil, the State owns shares in companies that control between 40 and 60 percent of the value traded in the world market. In the case of JBS, the state investment bank, BNDES, invested 3.5 billion reals in the purchase of debt securities convertible into shares that allowed JBS to acquire the US company Pilgrim's Pride in 2009 (Bonanno in this volume). Additionally, the State operated to acquire a number of other domestic companies such as Vale, Braskem, and Raízen, with the objective of transforming them into leaders in their respective markets (Cossi 2013). In essence, the strategy of the Brazilian State was to identify "champion companies" that, through the injection of large quantities of public capital, could achieve dominance in the global market and economy. In essence, this strategy signaled the alliance between the PT and the domestic bourgeoisie cemented through the effort of the State to transform

fractions of the domestic bourgeoisie into members of the global capitalist class (Bugiato 2016).

Contradictions

The two primary objectives pursued by the PT Administration during this period are contradictory. State actions centered on the strengthening of family farming and economic development, imbued with the broader goal of reducing inequality and eliminating poverty. This effort contradicts the implementation of state initiatives in support of corporate agri-food that took place through the mobilization of financial incentives and the implementation of measures that deregulate the sector. The PT never articulated a rationale that could explain the coexistence of such opposite policies and constantly maintained its alliance to the ideals of social justice and the elimination of social inequality and poverty.

As President Dilma Rousseff was impeached and stripped of her power in 2016, many identify this change of government as a coup d'état of the conservative and neoliberal right. In effect, the short-lived government of the then Vice President Michel Temer implemented a series of measures that followed the tenets of Neoliberalism as they aimed at dismantling the social state and at curbing state intervention for economic development. The first major reform, PEC 55, cut public spending in a number of areas for a period of twenty years. Implemented in 2017, the second major reform, the Labor Reform, promoted the flexibilization of labor by allowing irregular work and diminishing the rights of labor. As far as policies for agricultural production are concerned, the first step was an administrative reform that transferred key agencies from the now extinct Ministry of Agrarian Development to Civil House. This action was followed by the end of the Harvest Plan (Plano Safra) that provided funds for family agriculture and the reduction by 40 percent of the budget of the Food Acquisition Program that resulted in a reduction of 55 percent of the public served.

WHAT SOVEREIGNTY? FAMILY FARMERS BESIEGED BETWEEN NEO-DEVELOPMENTALISM AND NEOLIBERALISM

The actions of the PT State were part of that long-standing general project of the political left to emancipate Brazil from its dependence on global capital and the hegemonic North and terminate the underdevelopment and dependency of the global South. This quest of the Brazilian left and the PT as its political representative, begs the question of whether the actions of the State—and, indeed, state capitalism—actually strengthened the national economy and its weakest actors within the broader scenario of neoliberalism.

Hence, the actual realization of national sovereignty emerges as a legitimate question that can elucidate the role of the Brazilian State under the PT. More specifically, I feel that it is legitimate to ask if the actions of the Brazilian State have been based on this principle and if they have been effective in producing actual sovereignty. The legitimacy of this questioning rests on the historical evidence that sovereignty is a constitutive principle of the modern nation-state. Yet, and while the nation-state has retained the power to regulate its territory economically, politically, and socially, the expansion of globalization, the related growth of the influence of international regulatory agencies, and the overwhelming power gained by transnational corporations provide this questioning with additional relevance.

The definition of sovereignty that I would like to use reads accordingly:

> [O]n its *internal side*, sovereignty represents the capacity to maintain peace among all components of society, in order to allow the State to guarantee social order and to face up to other States on the international scene. In this way, it manifests itself in a position of supremacy in relation to the other social forces present in the political arena. In its *external side*, it is based on relations of equilibrium—always unstable and questionable—between the different States, an equilibrium that has a powerful instrument in the war, which is now rationalized through the treaties of international law, which put States in a position of formal equality in the context of an international legal order (emphasis added) (Miranda 2004: 87).

Considering its *external side*, the policies adopted by the PT government did not improve the country's position of dependence and subordination that reaffirms the place of Brazil in the international division of labor as a supplier of raw materials and labor at low costs. This is a historical role that the country has played since colonial times and that has been repeated throughout key periods of its history such as the 1930s–1950s developmentalist era, the conservative modernization of the 1960s and 1970s and the neoliberalization of the 1990s. The re-primarization of exports, the opening of the land market to international actors, direct and indirect investment in the production and marketing of agribusiness-driven exports along with de-industrialization, escalated the heteronomy of the State and of the national economy. These conditions emerged as real threats to the possibility of building sovereignty. Efforts to favor the domestic bourgeoisie by expanding the conditions for the advantageous insertion of domestic companies in the international market proved to be fragile and contradictory. Despite state support, they were too weak to outcompete established large transnational corporations. Additionally, their association with the State did not form a coherent political alliance and project in which the generation of global profit could have been meaningfully redirected to support the domestic economy and its social components. In effect, this association created dissatisfaction in business circles and the dissatisfied national bourgeoisie was among the political subjects that orchestrated the coup against the PT and its Neo-developmentalism.

In the case of the *internal side* of the production of sovereignty, the different forms of state support of corporate agri-food promoted not only the drainage of an important part of the national wealth but also the subordination and overexploitation of human and natural resources that resulted in the weakening of local and regional economies. This outcome contradicts the expected results of the implementation of the policies of valorization of territories that characterized the PT Neo-developmentalist program. This weakening of the local economy is exemplified by numerous empirical case studies including that of the municipality of Jales in the state of San Paulo. This is an area dominated by small family farmers that produce fruit and milk for the domestic market (Melo 2013). These family farmers were negatively affected by the expansion of the production of sugar cane and alcohol that subordinated them to large corporate entities and weakened their conditions of social reproduction. Additionally, the crisis of family farming also affected the local economy that supported them. The vertical and transnational structure of large-scale production bypasses local actors and does not produce conditions that allow the existing local economy to benefit from gains accrued by the corporate sector (Melo 2013).

Simultaneously and to some extent, public policies in support of family farming provided a buffer against the negative consequences that the local economy suffered from the expansion of corporate agri-food. A number of investigations indicate that farmers support policies for family agriculture and oppose recent cuts to these and related policies (Melo 2013). Despite this support and the contribution that these policies generated for family farming, their problems are numerous and point to the increasing subordination of family farming to corporate agriculture. In essence, they can be summarized accordingly. First, disproportionally large farms were the beneficiary of these policies as they captured the greater quantity of financial assistance provided by the government. The political project to expand family farming production and transform subsistence farming into market-oriented production overwhelmingly translated into support for those farms that were already producing for the market. In effect, the greater quantity of money went towards the production of global commodities such as corn and soybeans. Second, the promised technical assistance to all family farms that never materialized as technical support either was selected or simply lacked. Third, limited financial support and technical assistance engendered indebtedness that, in numerous cases, led to the loss of farms. Fourth, financial support was concentrated in the South and Southwest penalizing regions that historically needed a greater influx of resources. Finally, these policies remained largely outside the traditional rationale that motivated the actions of peasants and their desire to remain on the land (Grisa et al. 2011; Favareto 2007; Melo 2013; Montenegro 2015; Paula, Gomez and Tracz 2017).

Additional problems were associated with the implementation of price support programs and the limits of the land reform. As far as price support programs are concerned, they involved corruption as local power brokers controlled the disbursement of funds, never transcended their anti-poverty character and did not establish conditions that would enhance the ability of family farmers to compete. As for the land reform, its limits can be summarized in its very slow pace, the limited expropriation of unutilized land, and the rampant speculation that accompanied the redistribution of land. These and related conditions resulted in increased land prices, social instability, and the expansion of physical violence against landless peasants and small farmers that characterized rural regions (Paulilo, Ramos and Montenegro, 2015).

CONCLUSIONS

The research question of this book addresses the topic of whether the form of state capitalism implemented in Brazil is emancipatory. In specific terms, it refers to the effect of the actions of the government on the Workers' Party and the actual execution of its pronouncements about the fight against poverty, the support of family farming, and justice. The conclusions that this chapter proposes stress the contradictory nature of the agricultural policy of the Brazilian State. It was directed at the improvement of the conditions of small, family agriculture in the hope to transform peasants and landless rural residents into efficient and self-sufficient family farmers. Simultaneously, it promoted corporate agriculture in the hope of inserting Brazilian companies into global circuits of production and gaining from global market competition.

The contradictory nature of this proposal rests on its dualistic approach that calls for the simultaneous support of two very different groups. However, it also rests on the lack of a project that would harmonize these two different objectives and make them compatible. In essence, the PT agricultural policy was risky and this risk was taken without the deployment of control mechanisms that would provide a buffer against the negative consequences of this policy implementation. The result is that, despite the resources mobilized, small family farming is a sector that did not significantly improve during the state capitalism years. It remains under siege by the growth of corporate agriculture and the forces of globalization that promote its growth. In effect, the expansion of corporate agriculture finds its roots in the implementation of neoliberal globalization. However, it is also the result of the policies implemented by the government through large public investment and deregulation. Ultimately, the PT administration overestimated its ability to control global trends and to maneuver in ways that could translate global profits into domestic wealth. These historical bets did not pay off. In the end, this situation is a reminder of the difficulties that nation-states encounter in their dealings with global economic forces. In particular, this is a reminder of the difficulties that the implementation of a socially oriented domestic approach encounters in this corporate dominated neoliberal global era.

BIBLIOGRAPHY

Aguiar, Gustavo Adolpho Maranhão, Rafael Ribeiro Lima Filho, and Alcides de Moura Torres Junior. 2013. "A Ultima Fronteira Agrícola." *Revista Agroanalysis* 33 (5): 15–17.

Assis, Wendell Ficher. 2014. "O Moderno Arcaísmo Nacional: Investimento Estrangeiro Direto e Expropriação Territorial do Agronegócio Canavieiro." *Revista RESR* 52 (2): 285–302.

Bugiato, Caio Martins. 2016. "A Política de Financiamento do BNDES e a Burguesia Brasileira." PhD dissertation. Instituto de Filosofia e Ciências Humanas da Universidade Estadual de Campinas.

Cepeda, Vera Alves. 2012. "Inclusão, Democracia e Novo-Desenvolvimentismo—um Balanço Histórico." *Revista de Estudos Avançados* 26 (75): 77–90.

CIMI. 2016. *MATOPIBA: Destrói a Natureza e Seus Povos*. Goiânia: Conselho Indigenista Missionário.

Cossi, Rafael Ferreira. 2013. *Capitalismo de Estado e Inovação: Facetas da Relação entre Estado e Iniciativa Privada no Desenvolvimento Nacional*. PhD dissertation. San Paulo: Fundação Getúlio Vargas, Escola de Direito de São Paulo.

Delgado, Guilherme Costa. 2012. *Do Capital Financeiro na Agricultura à Economia do Agronegócio: Mudanças Cíclicas em Meio Século (1965–2012)*. Porto Alegre: UFRGS.

Embrapa. 2016. *Perspectiva Geral Para a Introdução da Soja nos Sistemas de Produção Agrícolas da Região da SEALBA*. Londrina: Embrapa Soja.

Favareto, Arilson. 2007. *Paradigmas do Desenvolvimento Rural em Questão*. São Paulo: Iglu.

Grisa, Catia, Claudia Job Schmitt, Lauro Francisco Mattei, Renato Sergio Maluf, and Sergio Pereira Leite. 2011. "Contribuições do Programa de Aquisição de Alimentos à Segurança Alimentar e Nutricional e à Criação de Mercados Para a Agricultura Familiar." *Agriculturas* 3: 34–41.

Harvey, David. 2004. *O Novo Imperialismo*. São Paulo: Edições Loyola.

Honneth, Axel. 2009. *Lutas por Reconhecimento: A Gramática Moral dos Conflitos Sociais*. São Paulo: Editora 34.

Ianni, Octávio. 2013. *Origens Agrárias do Estado Brasileiro*. San Paulo: Brasiliense.

Lazzarini, Sergio G., and Aldo Musacchio. 2015. *Reiventando o Capitalismo de Estado. O Leviatã nos Negócios: Brasil e Outros Países*. San Paulo: Portfolio-Penguim.

Leite, Sérgio Pereira. 2005. "Estado, Padrão de Desenvolvimento e Agricultura: o Caso Brasileiro," *Estudos Sociedade e Agricultura* 13 (2): 280–332.

Melo, Beatriz Medeiros de. 2013. "História e Memória na Contramão da Expansão Canavieira: um Estudo das Formas de Resistência dos Sitiantes do Extremo Noroeste Paulista." PhD dissertation. Universidade Federal de São Carlos. São Carlos.

Miranda, Napoleão. 2004. "Globalização, Soberania Nacional e Direito Internacional." *CEJ* 27: 86–94.

Montenegro, Jorge. 2015. "Reconversión Silenciosa de la Producción y Comercialización Campesina: Lectura Multiescalar de las Políticas Públicas Implementadas en Brasil." *Geonordeste* 26 (1): 124–149.

Paula, Adriano Makux, Jorge Rámon Montenegro Gómez, and Caroline Aparecida Marchioro Tracz. 2017. "Novo Ciclo Neoliberal no Brasil: Desmontando as Políticas Públicas para a Agricultura Familiar." *Revista Pegada* 18 (1): 57–88.

Paulilo, Eliane Tomasi, Eraldo da Silva Ramos Filho, and Jorge Montenegro. 2015. "As Resistências e os Limites do Modelo Primário Exportador no Brasil." *Revista Geonordeste* 26 (2): 308–318.

Pitta, Fábio Teixeira, Cássio Arruda Boechat, and Maria Luisa Mendonça. 2017. "A Produção do Espaço na Região da MATOPIBA: Violência, Transnacionais Imobiliárias e Capital Fictício." *Revista Estudos Internacionais* 5 (2): 155–179.

Pochmann, Marcio. 2017. "Estado e Capitalismo no Brasil: A Inflexão Atual no Padrão das Políticas Púbicas do Ciclo Político da Nova República." *Revista Educação & Sociedade* 38 (139): 309–330.

Sauer, Sergio, and Franciney Carreiro França. 2012. "Código Florestal, Função Socioambiental da Terra e Soberania Alimentar." *Caderno CRH* 25 (65): 285–307.

Scherer-Warren, Ilse. 2007. "A Política dos Movimentos Sociais para o Mundo Rural. *Estudos Sociedade Agricultura* 15 (1): 5–22.

Chapter Eight

Neoliberalism and Neo-Developmentalism as Promoters of Capitalist Aquaculture in Brazil

The Case of the State of Pernambuco

José Ignácio Vega Fernández

International scholars, institutions, and businesses in the aquaculture and fishing sector employ the term "Blue Revolution" to refer to a process of productive transformation similar to the so-called "Green Revolution" that took place in agriculture (Ramalho 2015: 522, 540). In both instances, the large-scale production of homogeneous commodities for the international food market and domestic mass consumption entails the intensive deployment of inputs that translates into the use of genetically modified species, phytosanitary packages, and industrially produced feed. As stressed by Cavalcanti (1997; 1999), in the case of fruit grown in the San Francisco Valley of Brazil, all this is accompanied by the use of wage labor and the transformation of previously common, public areas of artisanal fishing (e.g., mangroves and rivers) into privately owned aquaculture operations (in captivity cultivation of aquatic life forms).

This chapter discusses the role that the Brazilian national policy for the development of fisheries and aquaculture played in the growth of capitalist aquaculture and its principal consequences on artisanal fishing. In order to do so, the chapter situates the expansion of aquaculture in Pernambuco in the socio-historical context that permitted the growth of this sector in Brazil and its relationship with the international fishing industry and neoliberal globalization. The objective is to analyze the expansion of aquaculture by understanding it as a reflection of the neoliberal globalization of agri-food and as a source of conflict that, in the case of Brazil, is a specific manifestation of the contradictory implementation of the model known as neo-developmentalism (Boito and Berringer 2012; 2013; Santos and Milanez 2009; 2014). To this end, the chapter analyzes the relationship among the State, market, society, and capital that enabled the emergence and expansion of capitalist aquaculture in Brazil and in the Northeastern region. This makes it possible to problematize the continuities and ruptures of neo-developmentalism with neoliberalism and to discuss to what extent the neo-developmental model adopted by the Brazilian State has represented a real opposition to neoliberalism.

As a first step, the chapter discusses the socio-historical context that allowed the expansion of capitalist aquaculture in Brazil and in Pernambuco. This discussion is based on the analysis of the primary institutions that have overseen fishing and aquaculture in recent decades. Their evolution contemplates a socio-historical path that goes first through the developmental period of the 1960s centered on the role played by the Superintendence of Fisheries Development or SUDEPE. Second, it involves the conservative environmentalism of the Brazilian Institute for the Environment (IBAMA) during the neoliberal era of the 1990s. And finally, it covers the neo-developmental period featuring the government of the Workers' Party (PT) that began in 2003. That year saw the establishment of the Special Secretariat for Aquaculture and Fisheries (SEAP-PR) that, in 2009, was transformed into the Ministry of Fisheries and Aquaculture (MAP). Also in 2009, Act No. 11.959, also known as the Fishery Act, was approved, creating the basis for the National Policy for the Sustainable Development of Aquaculture and Fisheries. The neo-developmental period of the PT administration ended in 2016 with the parliamentary coup d'état orchestrated against President Dilma Rousseff that led to the resumption of an openly neoliberal developmental model.

The following portion of the chapter focuses on the principal achievements of the national fishery policy in Pernambuco beginning with the analysis of the expansion of capitalist aquaculture in that state. Finally, some conclusions concerning the consequences of this state-promoted Blue Revolution are discussed. The aim is to problematize the relationship between state intervention and the fishing sector in order to analyze to what extent this intervention contributed to the autonomy of artisanal fishermen, the main fish producers in Brazil, or whether it engendered the dependence of this sector to the demands of capitalist aquaculture and the international fish market.

THE SOCIOPOLITICAL CONTEXT OF THE BLUE REVOLUTION: THE DEVELOPMENT POLICIES OF FISHERIES AND AQUACULTURE, FROM SUDEPE TO MPA

Until the establishment of SUDEPE in the 1960s, there was virtually no policy in Brazil to promote a capitalist oriented fishing industry. In effect, prior to this decade, fishing had not achieved a significant commercial scale, except in some areas of the South and Southeast of the country. Largely coinciding with the years of the military dictatorship (1964–1985), the period of the SUDEPE (1962–1968) was characterized by the control of the navy over commercial fishermen and the implementation of a paternalistic and conservative form of developmentalism (Azevedo and Pierri 2014; Ramalho 2014). Symbolized by the National Fisheries Development Plans (PNDP), the developmental era policies centered on the public financing of the industrial fishing fleet. As a result, the capitalist sector experienced a boom during the 1970s, followed, however, by a crisis of overfishing and the consequent bankruptcy of many of these companies. In order to survive, some relocated to states, such as Pará and Maranhão, where an abundance of fish existed. However, only a relatively small number of operations was able to successfully stay in business (Diegues 1983; 1995; 1999; Timm 1975).

In 1989, the closing down of SUDEPE coincided with the emergence of the neoliberal state model. Represented by the two-term presidency of Fernando Henrique Cardoso of the Brazilian Social Democracy Party (PSDB [1995–2003]), the introduction of neoliberal policies left the IBAMA responsible for the fishing sector. An environmental institution, IBAMA, however, did not implement a specific policy directed at the development of capitalist fishing and aquaculture. This role was played by the Department of Fisheries and Aquaculture (DPA) within the Ministry of Agriculture, Livestock and Food Supply (MAPA) (Azevedo and Pierri 2013; Dias-Neto 2010; Ramalho 2014). In this context, capitalist fishing and aquaculture received institutional support and credit through the Northeast Development Superintendence (SUDENE) and financial entities such as Banco do Nordeste do Brasil (BNB).[1] According to public statements, including those made by the former president of the Brazilian Association of Shrimp Breeders (ABCC), Itamar Rocha, the sector benefited from 374 million reals in financial support, of which nearly 80 percent came from the coffers of the Banco do Nordeste do Brasil (BNB) (Ramalho 2014, 2015).

During the 1990s and through the first years of the 2000s, aquaculture, and specifically shrimp farming, grew significantly despite the lack of a specific supervising institution and charges that the establishment of aquaculture farms contaminated the environment. These activities further received institutional support, as there was widespread agreement that they could generate significant economic gains. According to Ramalho (2014: 42), "there was a favorable conjuncture" for the sector's expansion due to the strong foreign demand and the implementation of market liberalization policies. This situation generated "rapid economic gains for those who invested in the business as well as massive support for research from public institutions . . . [and] . . . it facilitated the sector's expansion in Permanent Preservation Areas (APPs), such as mangroves, with the approval of environmental agencies" (Ramalho 2014: 42). In the case of Pernambuco, a significant example was the establishment of the largest shrimp farm in the state made possible through the deforestation of a large number of hectares of mangroves in the estuary of the rivers Goiana and Megao. Paradoxically, the state of Pernambuco's environmental protection agency authorized this deforestation.

The vast majority of political and financial support went to capitalist fishery and aquaculture farms mainly through the granting of credit and subsidies for the acquisition of diesel oil. According to the Pluriannual Plan of the second Cardoso term, the program for the establishment of 46 aquaculture farms could count on 65.4 million reals and contributed to the expansion of shrimp farming, especially in the Northeast region, but it also generated serious consequences for artisanal fishing (Azevedo 2012). New legislation, such as the Decree No. 2.896, of December 9, 1998, further jeopardized the activities of artisanal fisheries as it promoted the privatization of public waters for the development of aquaculture farms.

Additionally, receiving funding from international sources—such as the World Bank and the Latin-American Development Bank (Scardua, Burtzstyn 2003 in Azevedo, 2012)—the implementation of a variety of plans—such as the National Coastal Management Plan (*Plano Nacional de Gerenciamento Costeiro*) and the National System of Units for the Conservation of Nature (*Sistema Nacional de Unidades de Conservação da Natureza*)—created a global neoliberal framework for the regulation of fisheries. This framework implied the integration of local fisheries into global markets and the loss of the centrality of the State in the regulation of economic activities. This function was now decentered to market relations with the objectives of improving efficiency and competitiveness. As the PT took control of the government in 2013, it continued this global neoliberal policy despite pronouncements about the introduction of a new neo-developmental approach. In effect, PT sponsored legislative measures, such as the 2009 Fishery Law, showing remarkable continuity with legislation introduced during the Cardoso administration. In this context, the legal framework for the expansion of capitalist aquaculture and the concomitant privatization of public waters was not only maintained but also reinforced.

As the Lula administration took office, this policy continuity featured the creation of the SEAP-PR in 2003. It also involved important institutional moves that centralized developmental policies and strengthened the expansion of the capitalist sector with aquaculture as its primary focus. The expansion of shrimp farming itself represented the basis of the division of development and labor in the Brazilian fishing industry that placed the Northeast as the primary region for the growth of this form of aquaculture. The conditions for the growth of the blue revolution in Brazil were, de-facto, set in place.

Particularly beginning with the creation of SEAP-PR, the specificities of the model for economic development that accompanied the modernization of fisheries can be analyzed through theories that problematize the character of the expansion of neoliberalism in Brazil and the ruptures and continuities of this model with respect to neo-developmentalism. Neo-developmentalism has as its premises unlimited growth as the sole way to socio-economic well-being, economic expansion as synonymous with development, and the focus on international markets and the complementarity between the State and the market as central concepts. In the case of Brazil, this meant a "resumption of the proposal of state intervention in favor of the development of Brazilian capitalism" (Boito 2012: 32). As indicated above, a critical portion of the literature emphasizes some elements of continuity between neoliberalism and neo-developmentalism. It sees this continuity, either as a version of liberalism or as a liberal-mercantilist fusion that follows a compromise between the strategic guidelines of the liberal model of the periphery and the active action of the State as a stabilizing factor within the economy and society. The primary element of rupture with neoliberalism is the existence of a—albeit limited—wealth redistribution element (Santos and Milanez 2013; 2014). The specificities of this model are articulated in terms of the support of aquaculture as a sector generating unlimited economic growth, the development of international competitiveness, and a positive contribution to the balance of trade.

The political actions and structural project of SEAP-PR elevated the interests of the capitalist aquaculture sector to the level of national institutional objectives. An analysis of the first Sustainable Development Plan for Fisheries and Aquaculture reveals that the SEAP-PR objectives were to raise production by 50 percent, triple the commercial surplus and modernize the production chain. Specifically to aquaculture and capitalist fishing, this plan's goals were to increase aquaculture production by 100 percent in three years and the production of capitalist fishing by 30 percent. Simultaneously, SEAP-PR advocated a more active intervention of the State in order to "allow the control of its activity and agility in the establishment of developmental policies, thus guaranteeing its sustainability;" for this it contemplated the development of technological packages, credit, and insurance for aquaculture (Brasil 2003:1).

Accordingly, this institution was key in the consolidation of the social dynamics that subordinated artisanal fishing to the sector's capitalist expansion. To this end, it proposed the conversion of artisanal fishing to aquaculture farms as a solution to the crisis of this group of fishermen. Counting on the support of the sector's capitalist elites, the proposal of SEAP-PR contemplated the use of technological and scientific resources that promoted large-scale production for the national and international markets. Mendonça and Valencio (2008) summarize the role of SEAP and its political actions towards artisanal fisheries as follows:

> For SEAP-PR, aquaculture is not a real strategy to support the artisanal fishing sector, but it is a mechanism for its extinction. In its first term and throughout the nation, the Lula government proposed a credit policy for the sector that encouraged a progressive conversion of artisanal fishing into aquaculture. It proposed the technical argument that such a policy was an alternative to the overfishing practiced by artisanal fishermen. Aside from the fact that there are differences in methods and interpretations about the technical criteria employed to determine overfishing, the absence of artisanal fishermen in the process of expert valuation of stocks, the absence of expert considerations of the traditional knowledge regarding the status of fishing and the absence of a dialogue between these forms of knowledge, make the proposal of a less radical alternative than aquaculture impossible (Mendonça and Valencio 2008: 112).

In this way, we can see that the institutional approach toward fisheries promoted by SEAP-PR represents a continuity with that of the institutions responsible for fisheries in previous periods. On the one hand, there is a rhetoric—accompanied by paternalistic policies—that stresses the protection, recognition, and promotion of the artisanal fishing sector. On the other hand, the material conditions for the implementation of the dominant view of the capitalist expansion of aquaculture are created. The National Plan for Sustainable Development of More Fisheries and Aquaculture (*Plano Nacional de Desenvolvimento Sustentável Mais Pesca e Aquicultura*) published by SEAP-PR in 2008 is a key document that highlights the strategic plan of this institution and establishes the guidelines by which the entire policy for fisheries, its actions, and its objectives are established. In a contradictory way, the plan recognizes the importance of artisanal fishing, highlighting that the more than six hundred thousand artisanal fishermen are responsible for more than 60 percent of production. However, it also stresses that aquaculture represents the primary form of sustainable development capable of "meeting the growing demand for food and the generation of jobs and income" (Brasil 2008: 2, 7).

This plan reflects the contradictory policy of the PT that, in theory, expresses support for small-scale fishing and, in practice, places aquaculture at the center of its policies and promotes its capitalist expansion in communities where artisanal fishing is practiced. The same text states that policies should aim at social inclusion and the valuation of traditional fishing communities, pointing to family aquaculture as the main form of income generation and autonomy. Accordingly, the claims of converting artisanal fishermen into family fish farmers and exercising social inclusion proposed by SEAP-PR translate into processes of social and cultural assimilation by which artisanal fishing is considered obsolete. It is seen as an entity in need of being replaced by aquaculture farming as a necessary step to meet the demands of a modernized sector. In this context, the policy of the PT promoted not only the reconversion of traditional fishermen to aquaculture farmers but also the insertion of these new operations into the capitalist global system of food production.

The strengthening of the institutional project carried out by SEAP-PR was continued through the creation of a ministry focused specifically on aquaculture and fisheries, the MPA. In a move that implied a greater institutional and budgetary support for the promotion for aquaculture, SEAP-PR played an important role. Its staff worked with FAO to prepare a technical advisory report to guide the creation of MAP that was viewed as part of the solution to the problems of fishery and aquaculture policies in the country. The report was employed by the SEAP-PR technicians and managers to form a parliamentary front and to initiate the legislative process for the creation of the MPA (Dias Neto 2010). Shortly after the creation of the MPA, the government enacted the Fishery Act, which created the National Policy for the Sustainable Development of Aquaculture and Fisheries.

As a way to promote the sector, the Fishery Act established credit for the development of fishing and aquaculture activities and granted the private use of public waters and lands for the exercise of aquaculture. As a way to regulate the sector, it implemented a number of plans, such as the Aquaculture Development Plans, Aquaculture Parks and Areas, and the National Use of Common Waters Authorization System (Brasil 2009). Once the Fishery Act was passed, the MPA introduced a territorial policy called "Fishery and Aquaculture Territories" that established the process of organization of aquaculture. This policy identified the growth of production as its primary objective and aquaculture as its primary tool to achieve this objective. In Pernambuco and in its coastal areas, it consisted mainly of the expansion of shrimp farms. In the interior, it involved a more intensive growth as exemplified by the case of the "São Francisco Aquaculture Pole" characterized by aquaculture farms of tilapia. Overall, this policy translated into an expansion of capitalist aquaculture through a productivist bias that, following earlier modernization models, prioritized large-scale production for export, competitiveness at the international level and the logic of capitalist development linked to technological advances and the insertion of artisanal fisheries into global markets (Brasil 2009).

Accordingly, the aquaculture conversion initiated by SEAP-PR was continued by the MPA. The primary aspect of the MPA's policy was a project for the expansion of aquaculture that created the material conditions for the transformation of the common territories for artisanal fishing into areas of private capitalist production that strengthened the expansion of capitalist fisheries. We will now see the consequences of the policies implemented by MPA policies beginning with the analysis of the expansion of aquaculture in the state of Pernambuco. This will allow us to understand the consolidation and expansion of capitalist fisheries and, ultimately, of the so-called "Blue Revolution" promoted by the interventions of the Brazilian State.

THE CHARACTERISTICS OF THE "BLUE REVOLUTION" IN THE STATE OF PERNAMBUCO: THE EXPANSION OF INTENSIVE SHRIMP AND TILAPIA MONOCULTURES ON LARGE AQUACULTURE FARMS

The Northeast of Brazil, in general, and the state of Pernambuco, in particular, occupy a primary and strategic place in the expansion of aquaculture production as they are considered pillars of the growth of the "blue revolution." Accordingly, the study of the expansion of aquaculture in this state is an important tool to understand the contradictions and conflicts arising from this growth. The rhetoric of the principal plans for the promotion of fisheries and aquaculture (Fishery and Aquaculture Territories [*Territórios da Pesca e da Aquicultura*], Plan More Fisheries and Aquaculture—SEAP, 2008 [*Plano Mais Pesca e Aquicultura*—SEAP, 2008] and the Fisheries and Aquaculture Production 2012/2013/2014—MPA Plans [*Planos Safra da Pesca e Aquicultura 2012/2013/2014—MPA*]) combines the potentials of aquaculture in the Northeast and the consequent expansion of aquaculture with the reduction of social inequalities and the eradication of poverty. According to these plans, the North and Northeast of Brazil, that is, regions with great potentials for aquaculture, have the resources to develop these potentials and, as such, they will see a reduction of social inequalities and the end of poverty for many families (Brasil 2012).

As indicated above, in the case of Pernambuco, the expansion of capitalist aquaculture took place predominantly on the coast through the growth of shrimp farming practiced in mangroves and estuaries. In the interior, it took place through the production of tilapia in freshwater tanks. Existing statistics indicate that in 2007, fish production in this state was about 20,000 metric tons, with fishing responsible for 15,159.5 metric tons and aquaculture for only 4,141 metric tons (Brasil 2007). According to the 2011 Statistical Bulletin of Fisheries and Aquaculture, production increased to more than 27.6 thousand metric tons of which fishing contribution remained virtually constant with 14,894 metric tons. However, aquaculture production grew significantly to 12,798 metric tons (Brasil 2011). To be sure, the extent of this growth does not take into account the possible underestimation of artisanal fishery production as data collection does not include a large portion of the landing places of artisanal fishermen. Simultaneously, it clearly reveals the consequences of the strong institutional support that capitalist aquaculture received during these years.

This institutional support emerged primarily through the establishment and leasing of aquaculture parks and areas and the implementation of credit policies. The main credit plan was the Fishery and Aquaculture Production Plan (*Plano Safra da Pesca e Aquicultura*) that aimed at stimulating national fish production by expanding credit supply, reducing interest rates, and increasing payment grace periods. It was the reflection of a state-promoted neo-developmental policy that wanted to capitalize on the sector by subordinating its development to the interests and logic of capitalist aquaculture. The differences between the lines of credit offered are obvious. In the case of large firms, credit lines ranged from 130,000 reals to 30,000,000 reals. In the case of small producers and artisanal fishermen, these lines did not exceed 2,500 reals.

The availability and leasing of aquaculture areas in the state of Pernambuco can be used as indicators of the growth of the sector. In the reservoirs of hydroelectric power plants of Moxotó and Itaparica located in Petrolândia-PE, San Francisco region, a total of 23 aquaculture areas were made available by the MPA for a total of 126.21 hectares. Of these, 103.83 hectares were allocated for capitalist aquaculture, meaning that 82.27 percent of the total area was exclusively assigned for large-scale aquaculture. Only 22.3 hectares, or 17.73 percent of the total, were devoted to family aquaculture. The two main companies that monopolized the bids for the use of this land were *Netuno Internacional* and *Pescanova.* Largely supported by international capital, these two companies now occupy 57.82 hectares or 45.59 percent of the total land available in these reservoirs. It can be concluded, therefore, that the aquaculture project promoted by the MPA was almost exclusively aimed at the growth of capitalist aquaculture (Fernández 2015).

Another instance of the support and promotion that the MPA provided to the expansion of capitalist aquaculture in Pernambuco was the first Aquaculture Seminar of the state of Pernambuco that was held in December 2014. It brought together representatives of the institutions that promoted the event—such as the San Francisco and Parnaíba Valley Development Company (*Companhia de Desenvolvimento dos Vales do São Francisco e do Parnaíba or CODEVASF*), the Agricultural Defense and Inspection Agency (*Agência de Defesa e Fiscalização Agropecuária or ADAGRO*), the Prefecture of Petrolândia and the Agronomic Research Institute (*Instituto de Pesquisas Agronômicas or IPA*), financial institutions—such as the National Bank of Brazil (BNB)—and aquaculture and industry associations. The primary objective of the seminar was to assist aquaculture firms located within the fifteen municipalities of the San Francisco Meso-region with the use of the water of the local reservoirs. Referred to in the region as the "Aquaculture Pole of Pernambuco" and the "Aquaculture Showcase of the State," representatives of the MPA continually emphasized the importance of the aquaculture production of these municipalities. In addition, they and other seminar participants often described aquaculture as the only way to think about improving fish production in Brazil. The words of one invited MPA representative reflect this posture as he stated, "There is no other way to reach the production estimated by the FAO, other than aquaculture production" (Fernández, 2015: 86, 87).

In addition to farms located in the interior of the state, numerous aquaculture farms operate in areas near the coast, such as mangroves and river estuaries. According to data compiled by MCR LLC., the largest consulting and aquaculture technical assistance firm operating in Pernambuco, the number of hectares of mangroves deforested for the creation of aquaculture farms totals 926.70. However, within this large area, only 0.6 percent of all farms are family-operated while 75 percent are large capitalist farms operating 100 hectares or more (MCR 2014). This situation indicates not only a dualistic distribution of aquaculture farms but also the capitalist nature of aquaculture in the region. Accordingly, the primary achievement of the state-promoted "Blue Revolution" is an exponential growth in capitalist aquaculture and the subsequent conversion of common fishing areas into private use areas dominated by large capitalist farms. Ultimately, and despite pronouncements stressing that state intervention was aimed at the expansion of artisanal fishing operations and the promotion of their autonomy, state intervention contributed to the crisis of artisanal fishing and the concomitant development of capitalist aquaculture.

CONCLUSIONS

The evolution of the national policy about fisheries and aquaculture shows the continuity of the policy implemented by the PT with those of the previous administrations as state intervention has consistently promoted the development of capitalist operations and the subordination of artisanal fishing to capitalist aquaculture. This practice was initiated under the SUDEPE in the 1960s, continued throughout the neoliberal period of the 1990s, and remained in place after the creation of the Special Secretariat of Aquaculture and Fisheries and the MPA in 2003 and 2009 respectively. It ultimately contradicts State pronouncements in favor of the development and autonomy of artisanal fishing operations, reflects political programs of previous neoliberal and conservative administrations, and shows the contradictory, ambivalent, and limited nature of the actions of the Brazilian State.

During the 1970s and 1980s, SUDEPE supported a form of vertically imposed authoritarianism that, advancing the time's national developmentalist project, viewed artisanal fishing as outdated and in need of drastic reforms. Led by state investments, these reforms promoted the creation and growth of large capitalist fishing operations. In the 1990s and with IBAMA supervising the national policy for fisheries, the adoption of neoliberal and conservative policies further facilitated the development of capitalist aquaculture. A significant number of capitalist aquaculture farms were established with the objective of producing for the international market. While successful in economic terms, this process led to the devastation of thousands of hectares of mangroves and the identification of capitalist aquaculture as the preferred form of production for fisheries.

Beginning in 2003, the creation of SEAP-PR set in motion a political process that increased the power of this institution over fisheries and aquaculture. While SEAP-PR addressed some of the environmental problems engendered by the aggressive deforestation of mangroves associated with the growth of aquaculture, it also entered in an alliance with capitalist aquaculture groups. The latter were able to extend their hegemony over this institution that continued the authoritarian and vertically oriented policy of previous administrations. This time, though, one of the primary objectives was to promote competitiveness in the sector through the introduction of practices based on flexible accumulation. In a contradictory fashion, this process was accompanied by a discourse that stressed the importance of social participation and sustainable development converting aquaculture into a symbol for the greater presence in international markets and, simultaneously, for the promotion of environmentally and socially sustainable production. With the transferring of SEAP-PR under the MPA and the enactment of the Fishery Act in 2009, the strengthening of the aquaculture project initiated under SEAP-PR came to full fruition. In this context, the 2009 Fishery Act promoted the figure of the family aquaculture farmer as a key to achieving the goal of converting traditional fishermen into aquaculture farmers. Yet, this policy led to increased production rather than the prosperity of family operations. At the political-institutional level, the alliance between the MPA and the capitalist sector strengthened, moving the actions of this ministry closer to the interests of the capitalist sector and distancing them from the democratic and politically popular support of artisanal fishing.

The analysis of the policies for fisheries and aquaculture implemented since 2003 underscores the link between the political strategies adopted and the class structure in which antagonistic modes of production clashes. Following the evidence, the proposed political change resulting from the popular mobilization that elected the PT governments did not engender a structural change in the mode of production and development model. The promised change from developmentalism and the neoliberal proposal of the privatization of public waters simply did not occur. Conversely, continuity from previous political economic systems characterized the PT years. Although the neo-developmentalism of the PT administrations differed from the neoliberalism of the PSDB governments as the State played an active role in the economy and an important stabilizing socio-economic function based on redistributive policies, it ultimately fostered the development of the Brazilian capitalist sector.

The existence of artisanal fishing in the state of Pernambuco does not depend exclusively on specific policies for fisheries and aquaculture. However, it depends on the existing model for socio-economic development. This means that the subordination of artisanal fishing to capitalist production is inherent to a model that logically promotes socioeconomic dynamics that feed into the expansion of capitalist structures of production. These constraining dynamics are manifested both in the concrete case of the capitalist aquaculture expansion promoted by the political actions of MPA and in other policies and projects aiming at the conversion of public spaces into private enclaves. In this sense, the neo-developmental model that was adopted under the PT administrations did not represent a barrier to the neoliberalism implemented in Brazil in the previous decade by the Brazilian Social Democracy Party (PSDB). Neoliberalism and neo-developmentalism in Brazil have worked in favor of the privatization of fisheries by expanding capitalist networks in fishing areas and converting them into constant capital for aquaculture production. In the end, this continuity between neoliberalism and neo-developmentalism is the result of the weaknesses and ambiguities of state capitalism and the power of the neoliberal forces in Brazil.

NOTE

1. To be sure, access to information about companies that benefitted from these financing activities is restricted and often unavailable, as the names of each of these companies are not published in the BNDES (the Brazilian Development Bank) database. In this official database, only quantitative data on the total value of the financing of fishery and aquaculture companies appear. However, representatives of capitalist aquaculture provided qualitative accounts of the importance of this public support through BNDES financing.

BIBLIOGRAPHY

Azevedo, Natália Tavares. 2012. "Política Nacional para o Setor Pesqueiro no Brasil (2003–2011)." PhD thesis in Programa de Pós-graduação em Meio Ambiente e Desenvolvimento. UFPR. Curitiba.

Azevedo, Natália Tavares, and Naína Pierri. 2013. "A Política Pesqueira Atual no Brasil: A Escolha pelo Crescimento Produtivo em Detrimento da Pesca Artesanal." *Samudra Report* 64 (1): 34–41.

Boito Jr., Armando, and Tatiane Berringer. 2012. *A Frente Neodesenvolvimentista e a Política Externa nos Governos Lula e Dilma.* Campinas: Mimeo.

———. 2013. "Brasil: Classes Sociais, Neodesenvolvimentismo e Política Externa nos Governos Lula e Dilma." *Revista de Sociologia e Política* (47): 94–109.

Boito Jr., Armando. 2012. "As Bases Políticas do Neodesenvolvimentismo. FGV—SP." https://bibliotecadigital.fgv.br/dspace/bitstream/handle/10438/16866/Painel%203%20-%20Novo%20Desenv%20BR%20-%20Boito%20-%20Bases%20Pol%20Neodesenv%20-%20PAPER.pdf. Accessed June 20, 2018.

Brasil. 2003. *Caderno de Resoluções da 1ª Conferência Nacional de Aquicultura e Pesca.* Brasília: Secretaria Especial de Aquicultura e Pesca.

———. 2007. Ministério do Meio Ambiente. Instituto Brasileiro do Meio Ambiente e dos Recursos Naturais Renováveis. Estatística da Pesca 2007. https://www.ibama.gov.br/sophia/cnia/livros/estatisticadepescadigital.pdf. Accessed May 2018.

———. 2008. *Mais Pesca e Aquicultura—Plano de Desenvolvimento Sustentável: uma rede de ações para o desenvolvimento do setor.* Brasília: Secretaria Especial de Aquicultura e Pesca

———. 2009. Lei nº 11.959, de 29 de junho de 2009 sobre a *Politica Nacional de Desenvolvimento Sustentável da Aquicultura e da Pesca.* http://www.planalto.gov.br/ccivil_03/_ato2007-2010/2009/lei/l11959.htm. Accessed June 20, 2018.

———. 2011. Ministério da Pesca e da Aquicultura. Boletim Estatístico da Pesca e da Aquicultura de 2011. http://www.icmbio.gov.br/cepsul/images/stories/biblioteca/download/estatistica/est_2011_bol__bra.pdf. Accessed May 15, 2018.

———. 2012. Plano Safra da Pesca e Aquicultura 2012/2013/2014. Brasília: Ministério da Pesca e da Aquicultura. http://junjiabe.com/files/Plano-Safra-da-Pesca-e-Aquicultura.pdf. Accessed June 25, 2018.

Cavalcanti, Josefa Salete Barbosa. 1999. "Globalização e Processos Sociais na Fruticultura de Exportação do Vale Do São Francisco." In Josefa Salete Barbosa Cavalcanti (Ed.), *Globalização, Trabalho, Meio Ambiente. Mudanças Socioeconômicas em Regiões Frutícolas para Exportação* (pp. 123–170). Recife: ED.UFPE.

———. 1997. "Frutas Para o Mercado Global." *Estudos Avançados USP* 29: 79–93.

Dias Neto, José. 2010. *"Gestão do Uso dos Recursos Pesqueiros Marinhos no Brasil."* Rio de Janeiro: Instituto Brasileiro do Meio Ambiente e dos Recursos Naturas Renováveis.

Diegues, Antônio Carlos. 1983. *Pescadores, Camponeses e Trabalhadores do Mar.* São Paulo, Ática.

———. 1995. *Povos e mares: leituras em sócio-antropologia marítima.* São Paulo, Nupaub.

———. 1999. "A Sócio—Antropologia das Comunidades de Pescadores Marítimos no Brasil." *Revista Etnográfica* (2): 361–375.

Fernández, José Ignácio Vega. 2015. *A Política Nacional de Desenvolvimento Sustentável da Pesca e da Aquicultura e Seus Impactos Sobre a Pesca Artesanal no Estado de Pernambuco.* Dissertação de mestrado no Programa de Pos-Graduação em Sociologia. Recide, PE: PPGS-UFPE.

MCR, Aquacultura Ltda. 2014. Portfólio. http://mcraquacultura.com.br/portifolio/. Accessed May 2, 2018.

Mendonça, Sandro Augusto Teixeira, and Norma Valencio. 2008. "The Role of Modernity in the Disruption of the Tradition: The Policies of the SEAP as Dissolution of the Way of Life of Artisanal Fisheries." *Boletim do Instituto de Pesca Sao Paulo* 34 (1): 107–116.

Ramalho, Cristiano Wellington Noberto. 2014. "Estado, Pescadores e Desenvolvimento Nacional: Da Reserva Naval à Aquícola." *Revista Ruris* 8 (1): 31–62.

———. 2015. "Ideologia e Aquicultura: Uma das Faces da Revolução Azul." *Contemporânea* 5 (2): 521–544.

Santos, Rodrigo Salles Pereira, and Bruno Milanez. 2014. *Neodesenvolvimentismo às Avessas? Uma Análise do Atual Modelo de Desenvolvimento Brasileiro.* Rio de Janeiro. https://www.researchgate.net/profile/Bruno_Milanez/publication/274638633_Neodesenvolvimentismo_as_avessas_Uma_analise_do_atual_modelo_de_desenvolvimento_brasileiro/links/552453e10cf2caf11bfcc65c/Neodesenvolvimentismo-as-avessas-Uma-analise-do-atual-modelo-de-desenvolvimento-brasileiro.pdf?origin=publication_detail. Accessed May 20, 2017.

———. 2013. "Neodesenvolvimentismo e Neoextrativismo: Duas Faces da Mesma Moeda?" 37o. Encontro Anual da ANPOCS, Anais do 37o. Encontro Anual da ANPOCS. http://www.

ufjf.br/poemas/files/2014/07/Milanez-2013-Neodesenvolvimentismo-e-neoextrativismo-duas-faces-da-mesma-moeda.pdf. Accessed February 15, 2017.

———. 2009. "Eixos de Desenvolvimento Econômico e a Geração de Conflitos Socioambientais no Brasil: Desafios para a Sustentabilidade e a Justiça Ambiental." *Ciência e Saúde Coletiva* (14): 1983–1993.

Timm, J. U. C. S. 1975. *Sudepe: 12 Anos de Frustrações no Desenvolvimento da Pesca.* http://www.icmbio.gov.br/cepsul/images/stories/biblioteca/download/trabalhos_tecnicos/pub_1975_sudepe_12_anos_frustacoes_desenvolvimento_pesca_parte_1.pdf. Accessed June 5, 2018.

Conclusion

The Political and Structural Limits of State Capitalism in Brazil

Alessandro Bonanno and
Josefa Salete Barbosa Cavalcanti

Is state capitalism an effective emancipatory tool to address the socio-economic consequences of neoliberal globalization? This is the research question that this book addresses. Employing the case of the agri-food sector, the chapters included in this volume probed pertinent topics and offered specific analyses on the role of the PT administrations that ruled Brazil from 2003 to 2016 on a state capitalism model. This concluding chapter provides an overall answer to the book's research question that is a synthesis of, but also advances, the conclusions reached by each of the chapters. It takes into consideration the politically centered nature of the analyses presented in the previous pages by focusing on the evaluations of the policies implemented by the PT Administrations of Presidents Lula and Dilma Rousseff that the book's contributors offered. In addition, however, it reviews the structural conditions that framed the implementation of these policies. More specifically, it acknowledges the limited independence of the State and the fact that its actions take place in a context—neoliberal globalization—that is controlled by transnational capital and the transnational capitalist class.

Employing this theoretical framework, this concluding chapter identifies seven basic conclusions. The first stresses that *neoliberal globalization is an unsustainable regime. This unsustainability promoted demands for change that provided the impetus for the constitution and strengthening of the social movements that supported the electoral victory of the Workers' Party in 2002 and the establishment of its 2003–2016 presidential administrations*. The second conclusion dwells on the analytical observation that the conditions of the relative development of Brazil are rooted on established processes of exploitation that were not altered by the various administrations that controlled the presidency in the post-World War II era. It follows that it is highly difficult to rectify structural conditions that are constitutive of the functioning of the global market by simply acting at the political level in one country. Accordingly, the second conclusion about the emancipatory dimension of the role of the State under the PT administrations states that *the PT created expectations that were too unrealistic in regard to the historical and structural nature of the problems that faced Brazil.* A corollary of this second conclusion is that it is equally significant that the PT accepted the challenge to alter the historical and structural conditions that were the origins of the problems of Brazil

The book chapters underscore the characteristics of the PT program concerning agri-food. They all stress the efforts of the State to improve the conditions of small family agriculturalists and to distribute land to landless peasants without an effective land reform. These efforts accompanied initiatives that increased the availability of food to poor segments of the rural and urban populations. Accordingly, the third conclusion is that *the intervention of the Brazilian State in favor of small family farming and the peasantry contributed to the improvement of the socio-economic conditions of these social groups*. The fourth conclusion acknowledges that these *actions of the State were not free of problems as financial and technical support earmarked for family agriculture went to a greater extent to larger farms and monoculture production for export and that the redistribution of land and the recognition of land rights did not achieve the levels hoped for.* The analyses included in the book document that *the PT administrations invested in domestic agri-food companies with the hope that their growth and insertion into global circuits of production would benefit not only these companies but also other components of the Brazilian society. This action generated a number of contradictions and ultimately did not achieve the desired results.* This is the fifth conclusion of the book.

In the case of agri-food, the fundamental challenge that the Brazilian State faced was that of addressing the classic agrarian question or improving the socio-economic conditions of those who work on the land. This classic question is the subject of a great number of scientific works (e.g., Kautsky 1988 [1899]; Chayanov 1986; Weber 1958). Many of them stress that the different ideological and cultural characteristics of farmers and peasants for their way of thinking and worldview do not necessarily conform to the productivist rationality that dominates society and is assumed in capitalist economics. The sixth conclusion pertains to this issue and indicates that state efforts to improve the conditions of agriculturalists fell short of establishing alternatives to productivism—or giving priority to the expansion of production and productivity. In effect, *there was relatively very little alternative in the policies implemented by the PT as they ultimately followed those very productivist approaches that have been so central in the development of capitalist agri-food.* The seventh and final conclusion reached in this chapter refers to the structural limits of the action of the State. While the ability of the nation-state to act independently is often assumed, in reality, there are structural limitations that constrain these actions. These limitations are best exemplified by the theory of the relative autonomy of the State that stresses that the State needs to simultaneously promote the accumulation of capital and social legitimation. Following this theory, we contend that *the contradictory actions of the Brazilian State cannot be simply attributed to the will of the PT administrations themselves.* They are the result of the existence of the above-mentioned structural constraints. Moreover, the consequences of the existence of these constraints depend on the strength of the social forces that operate in society. Accordingly, as progressive social movements provided support to emancipatory actions of the State, the reaction of pro-capital forces significantly shaped the events that led to the end of the PT administration and the type of implementation of emancipatory actions in agri-food. This last conclusion, therefore, indicates that state capitalism is a limited form of opposition to neoliberal globalization. However, the extent of its success (or failure) depends upon the strength of the social movements that support state actions. *It depends on the status of the contested terrain of capitalist social relations.*

These arguments are articulated in three separate sections that follow this introduction. In the first section, the first five conclusions are illustrated through a brief review of the events that led to the establishment of the PT administrations and the implementation of its agri-food policies. The second section of the chapter discusses the failed resolution of the agrarian question that is followed by the actions of the Brazilian State. A review of the fundamental components of the classic debate on the agrarian question is presented along with the argument that led to the sixth conclusion of the book. The third and final section addresses the question of the structural limits of the action of the State under neoliberal global capitalism. It probes the extent to which state capitalism implies an autonomous acting state. Employing the relative autonomy of state theory, this section indicates how the structural limits to the autonomy of the State can be mitigated by the support of strong social movements. These considerations constitute the background for the seventh and last conclusion of the book.

STATE CAPITALISM IN BRAZILIAN AGRI-FOOD: THE CONTRADICTIONS OF AMBITIOUS PROGRAMS

The objective of this volume is to probe the issue of whether the implementation of state capitalism is an effective instrument to combat the negative consequences generated by decades of neoliberal globalization. This question requires a number of specifications—see introduction—that primarily pertain to the meanings of the key concepts that define this task. In particular, the concepts of "effective instrument" and "neoliberal globalization" require some additional discussion. The understanding of "effective instrument" that the book's contributors employed refers to the actions of the Brazilian State and its implementation of a set of political, economic and social measures that were emancipatory for the lower and working classes in Brazilian agri-food. The extent to which these measures were indeed emancipatory is the essential goal of the volume. In more specific terms, however, the chapters presented in the previous pages focus on the ability of the State to address the struggle of small family producers, peasants, indigenous groups and other minorities to remain on the land, have their right to the land recognized and make a living from their work in farming.

Simultaneously, the meaning of "neoliberal globalization" (and of its associated concepts of neoliberalism, globalization, free market, and deregulation) refers to the post-Fordist era regime that proposes the undisturbed global functioning of the free market as the most appropriate form of socioeconomic organization of society. While primarily a form of regulation of the economy, it has been heralded as an approach that should be applied to all the other spheres of society, including culture and politics. Accordingly, state intervention to address economic and social problems should be limited to the construction of markets. In this context, postures that contemplate state intervention to limit the unwanted consequences of capitalism should be abandoned (Bonanno 2017; Harvey 2005; Mirowski 2014). While the copious debate on the consequences of the application of neoliberal measures at the global level continues, the analyses proposed in this book are explicit about their problematic consequences. The opening of markets, their deregulation, the limits and/or inability of nation-states to regulate global economy flows and the power acquired by global corporations negatively affected small, family agriculturalists and their communities. Joining a significant number of investigations, the chapters presented in this book see *neoliberal globalization as an unsustainable regime that requires change*. This is the first and—in many ways—the most obvious conclusion of the book. Neoliberalism in Brazil generated a number of significant negative consequences and the introduction of a new political course was not only demanded by the public, but also necessary in historical terms.

This was also the declared position of the Workers' Party of Brazil as it took office in 2003 after the electoral victory that brought Lula to the Presidency of the country. The neoliberal regime implemented by the previous administration needed to be changed. To various extents, all the chapters in this volume offer accounts of the meaning of the electoral victory of the PT. It came after decades in which attempts to promote the socio-economic development of Brazil, its agri-food sector, and rural regions largely failed. The post-World War II era of modernization consisted of the adoption of Fordist and Keynesian socio-economic policies in the US-controlled Western world (Keynes 2009 [1936]; Harvey 1999). In this construct, the economy was directed through state planning and intervention that was aimed at achieving equilibrium among the many components of the economy. In essence, it was assumed that the free functioning of the market was not, by itself, capable of reaching these equilibria. Conversely, they could have been established under the direction and action of the State. This core tenet of Keynesianism required the shifting of the responsibility of economic stability from the market to the State. The State, therefore, was endowed with the responsibility to find solutions to the limits (read crises) of the functioning of the market. This politicization of the market endowed the State with great power but also created the conditions for a crisis of legitimation as its intervention in the economy had to be always justified.

Economic Keynesianism was accompanied by a social policy that, in pertinent literature, is referred to as Fordism (Harvey 1999). It required the State to address not only economic issues but also social problems. Accordingly, the State was charged with establishing social pacts that, involving the major social classes in the country, defined the implementation of policies designed to maintain social stability. In the US-dominated Western world, Fordism functioned relatively well during the first three post-World War II decades as the fear of labor uprisings and the socialist threat forced the entrepreneurial class to allow concessions to the middle and lower classes in return for the commitment to continuous membership in the capitalist world (Streeck 2014). In instances in which this commitment was threatened and social stability appeared to be compromised, Fordism often translated into repressive dictatorial regimes, such as those experienced in Latin America by Brazil between 1964 and 1985 and Chile and Argentina in the 1970s. As allegiance to the US-dominated Western world diminished, force and political oppression were deployed to defeat opposition to the US hegemony.

In Brazil, as in other countries of the developing South and Latin America, state management of the economy and society signified the implementation of populist policies. Often articulated in nationalistic terms, these policies mixed left-leaning strategies—such as import substitution—with conservative and paternalistic measures that aimed at reconciling the interests of American multinational capital with those of the local bourgeoisie, the landed oligarchy while paying lip service to the actual well-being of the working and middle classes. As indicated by the book chapters, modernization policies took a top-down approach as the military dictatorship signified political repression and lack of democratic decision-making processes. Simultaneously, the modernization tenet that the State had to invest in the creation of infrastructure and productive units was followed to an important extent in the case of agri-food. As documented in the book, the creation of irrigated areas in the arid Northeast represent a result of the modernization effort carried out by the Brazilian State.

Initiated in the mid-1980s and culminated with the proclamation of the new constitution in 1988, the democratization of the country ended the modernization era and inaugurated the neoliberal phase in the economic history of Brazil and its agri-food sector. The conclusions stressed by the book chapters show the contradictory results generated by the adoption of neoliberal policies. Inaugurated by the end of the 1970s, the neoliberal era signified the implementation of economic measures conceptualized in the 1930s and 1940s but largely disregarded by the scientific and political communities during the following decades (Mirowski and Plehwe 2009; Stedman Jones 2012). Proposing a singular understanding of market economy, neoliberalism required the withdrawal of the State from the management of the economy and society and reliance on the free functioning of the market.

In the case of Brazil and agri-food, the implementation of neoliberalism signified the reversal of conservative modernization that the State implemented in previous decades. The call for the reduction and/or elimination of state intervention found its legitimacy in the need to end the rampant inflation and economic instability that characterized the time economy. Aligned with the interests of the American-led global bourgeoisie but also subordinate to it, the Brazilian elites supported the plans of Presidents Collor de Melo first and Cardoso later to deregulate the economy, privatize public companies and, through these and associated measures, promote foreign direct investment. The increase in interest rates was instrumental in the implementation of this plan. Results of the application of these policies were mixed at best. As inflation was relatively controlled, the privatization of public companies and the opening of the domestic market to foreign investment did not translate into the improvement of employment levels and the socio-economic conditions of significant segments of the local population. In agri-food, the structural, monetary and fiscal policies of the Collor de Melo and Cardoso era made local products more expensive in global markets and permitted cheaper agri-food imports to successfully penetrate the local market.

At the global level, neoliberalism maintained its popularity at the outset of the new century. However, the consistently unstable conditions of the Brazilian economy called for change. This call was answered by the PT victory in the 2002 presidential election. Supported by a set of new ideas, the PT offered a left-leaning response to the Washington Consensus and its more progressive proposal of the Third Way championed by Cardoso. More importantly, the program proposed by the PT wanted to address the conditions that generated the underdevelopment of the global South in general and Brazil in particular. It was a proposal for the emancipation of Brazil and its middle and lower classes. The chapters of the book offer empirical elements that allow us to stress the difficulties associated with this task and the ambitious nature of the PT program. It is highly difficult to rectify structural conditions that are constitutive of the functioning of the global market by simply acting at the political level in one country. Accordingly, a second conclusion that can be reached about the emancipatory dimension of the role of the state under the PT administrations is that *it created expectations that were too unrealistic in regard to the historical and structural nature of the problems that faced Brazil.* Simultaneously, it is equally important to stress the significance of accepting the challenge to alter the historical and structural conditions that were at the origins of the problems of Brazil as the PT did.

The analyses presented in the previous pages underscore the characteristics of the PT program concerning agri-food. They all point out the State's efforts to improve the conditions of small family agriculturalists and to distribute land to landless peasants. These efforts were also accompanied by initiatives to increase the availability of food to poor segments of the rural and urban populations. The progressive nature of these actions is documented and acknowledged. Accordingly, a third conclusion that can be drawn from the investigations presented in this volume is that *the intervention of the Brazilian State in favor of small family farming and the peasantry contributed to the improvement of the socio-economic conditions of these social groups*. Simultaneously, however, the book's contributors stress that these *actions of the State were not free of problems as support for family agriculture went to a greater extent to larger farms, promoted monoculture production for export and the recognition of land rights and land redistribution did not achieve the levels hoped for*. This is the fourth conclusion of the book.

The *contradictory nature of the program implemented by the Workers' Party administrations, however, was not simply limited to its actions about family and peasant agriculture. It involved its program concerning agri-food corporations*. This is the fifth conclusion that we reached. As clearly indicated by the analyses included in the book, the PT administrations invested in domestic agri-food companies with the hope that their growth would benefit not only these companies but also other components of Brazilian society. Labeled as the strategy of "champion companies," it involved the identification of local firms and the adoption of financial measures that would allow their growth through the insertion into global circuits of production. The instance of the company JBS discussed in depth in the chapter by Bonanno and mentioned in other chapters (see Medeiros de Melo in this volume) is a case in point. The analysis of this case shows that state investment contributed to transform an otherwise marginal domestic company into a global giant that could rival with other large transnational corporations in meat production. Simultaneously, however, the economic success of the company did not translate into commensurate social and political benefits for other social groups. To the contrary, this company's actions failed socially as they did not conform to the PT objectives of improving labor conditions, labor practices, local communities, and protecting the environment. Politically, they proved to be quite questionable as the company's executives became embroiled in the corruption scandals that engulfed Brazil in the mid-2010s.

The uncharted character of the Brazilian State's strategy emerged from the analyses presented in the book. As indicated above, the actions of the Brazilian State were ambitious as they aimed at altering historically established structural conditions. Their unchartered character refers to the claim of addressing the demands of subordinate groups without having an effective strategy to alter the power relations and structural conditions that generated the socio-economic position of these groups. More specifically, the PT administrations selected global competitiveness as the underlying strategy to advance not only the conditions of family agriculturalist and peasants but also those of local companies. Family farmers were asked to become more competitive through the improvement of their production and productivity. Similarly, Brazilian companies were required to enhance their competitive position in global circuits. In both these cases, the State employed market relation-based strategies to promote these groups' statuses despite the fact that their conditions were the outcomes of the very functioning of market relations. In the case of family farmers and peasants, their marginal socio-economic status was the result of the expansion of capitalist relations in the Brazilian countryside and the centrifugal forces associated with this expansion. In the case of Brazilian companies, the State subscribed to the neoliberal tenet that the growth of corporate profit is beneficial to broader segments of society. Known as "trickledown economics," this theory remains highly questionable (Krugman 2013; Stiglitz 2016).

THE FAILED RESOLUTION OF THE AGRARIAN QUESTION

The issues pertaining to agriculture in Brazil are about the conditions of the many—politically and economically weak—social groups that are part of agri-food. In this regard, these issues are still very much linked to the historical *agrarian question*. Formulated at the end of the nineteenth century, the classic agrarian question refers to the conditions of people working in agriculture. Its original theorization is proposed in the seminal book *Die Agrarfrage* (the Agrarian Question) by Karl Kautsky (Kautsky 1988 [1899]). Like in the case of the PT, Kautsky's objective was to formulate a political strategy for the betterment of the working classes in agriculture. He criticized both the free market theory of the evolution of agriculture and the orthodox Marxist theory of the centralization of capital whereby farming evolves, following the same patterns typical of manufacturing. In a striking parallel, the program of the PT administrations planned to oppose free market approaches to the development of agri-food and rural regions. However, it also intended to offer an alternative to leftist approaches that failed in the past.

The classic free market (laissez-faire) theory saw the co-existence of family farms and large industrial farms as a constant feature of capitalist agriculture due to a steady range of new entries into farming coupled with the tendency of some farms to grow and develop into large operations. These conditions, this theory contends, reproduce a multifaceted farming sector in which open competition allows small and medium farms to expand and transform into large industrial firms featuring mechanization and the use of industrial inputs and wage labor. Some of these farms, however, also experience problems and, eventually, exit the sector. This theory concludes that the pursuit of self-interest on the part of farmers would guarantee the existence not only of efficient forms of production but also of the sustainable use of natural resources (Smith 1981 [1776]). The orthodox Marxist view of farming proposed the theory of the proletarianization of family farmers and the concomitant emergence of green-factories whereby urban manufacturing's capital concentration and centralization would be reproduced in the farming sector (Lenin 1961 [1908]). In this view, the disappearance of family producers is inevitable, as they would be transformed into wage laborers. Accordingly, policies designed to improve the living conditions of farmers were to be discouraged for they simply delayed their unavoidable proletarianization (Lenin 1961 [1908]).

For Kautsky, and like-minded social democrats, both these positions were incorrect, as they did not contextualize the existence of family farmers and peasants in the overall evolution of capitalism and its necessary equilibria. Kautsky contended that family farming performs several functions in the capitalist economy. One of them is that of a reservoir of labor for large farms and for the manufacturing sector. As additional labor is needed in manufacturing and large farm agriculture, family farm and peasant labor are released to satisfy this demand. The opposite occurs in periods of crisis when surplus labor is retained on the farm contributing to social and economic stability. Following this analysis, Kautsky concluded that, because of the functions that they perform, family farms would continue to persist despite economic hardship and capital centralization.

Theorists sympathetic to the position of Kautsky proposed additional arguments about the relevance of family farming. In this vein, some argued that family farmers and peasants' paramount desire to own land allows them to endure high levels of socio-economic hardship. This is the case of the theory proposed by Max Weber. He contended that peasant farming is characterized by high levels of labor self-exploitation. This is a condition, he continued, that allows peasants to pursue the ownership of farmland. Rather than following an economic rationality, peasants obey a different logic that privileges their desire to become owners of their farms (Weber 1958). Alexander Chayanov's *Theory of Peasant Economy* (1986) offers another instance of the different logic that typifies the behavior of small farm holders. For Chayanov, peasants are primarily interested in subsistence production. Accordingly, the quantity of per-capita labor performed on the farm is a function of the number of family members and their ages. The younger and more numerous the children in the family are, the more labor is necessary to support them. Once these children become adults and can work on the farm, peasants diminish the per capita quantity of labor performed. In essence, for Chayanov, peasants are not interested in generating surplus value and, therefore, it would be difficult for them to follow the logic of capitalist accumulation.

The resolution of the agrarian question has been historically difficult. It requires solutions that are not only economic in nature, but that also address social and cultural aspects of the lives of agriculturalists. In effect, Kautsky, Chayanov, Weber and like-minded theorists contended that the overall position of small farm holders and peasants in the totality of the economy and their culturally-based attitudes ought to occupy central positions in plans that could effectively address the future of people who work on the land. In the past and in the case of advanced societies, a successful solution of the agrarian question has never been found. Family farms have been experiencing a de-facto constant state of crisis that repeated attempts to address it have not been able to ease. These attempts have been based either on technical measures designed to improve these farms' productivity and production and/or on assistance measures that support their persistence through various forms of transfer payments. The latter are also production-based, such as the cases of the very popular price support programs and set aside programs. In essence and historically, the solution of the agrarian question has been sought through assorted types of measures that did not contemplate any type of rationality other than the dominant productivism. This is precisely at the center of the critiques that theorists such as Kautsky, Chayanov, and Weber advanced. They stressed the gap between culturally-based alternative ways of thinking that defined the existence of small farmers and peasants and the productivist rationality that motored the expansion of capitalist social relations.

To be sure, the failure of these anti-crisis measures is not simply cultural. It is predominantly economic. The project of transforming underproducing and/or subsistence farms into operations that can successfully compete in local and global markets contradicts established critiques—such as the classic Marxian theory—and supporting empirical evidence that stresses the overwhelming importance of the processes of concentration and centralization of capital. In effect, the history of contemporary agriculture has featured the drastic reduction of the number of farms and the concomitant concentration of land and assets in the hands of the selected group of large farms. This process has been paralleled by the centralization of capital in the agri-food sector in the hand of a limited number of large transnational corporations whereby the entire farming sector is controlled by corporate entities that operate in the input, transformation, and financial sectors. These are historical processes that the measures mentioned above have neither been able to halt nor mitigate. Measures in support of family farms and the peasantry have also been resisted politically—as other economic sectors and actors vie for state support and the use of finite state resources—and ideologically—as support of family agriculture has often been charged with creating unwanted surpluses and waste. Simultaneously, these measures have been seen as contributing to the fiscal crisis of the State for the State is charged with spending too much in support of a sector where the persistence of family farms is largely based on the availability of off-farm employment and many young farmers are reluctant to continue working on the farm.

As illustrated in the book chapters, the actions of the Brazilian State under the PT administrations followed, to a significant extent, the same patterns applied in the advanced North. The Brazilian State provided financial support to family farms through technical assistance and economic incentives aimed at increasing production and productivity and established measures that limited the negative consequences of price fluctuations. All these efforts fell short of establishing conditions that would contemplate alternative views of the role of family farmers and peasants as claimed by theorists of the agrarian question. In effect, *there was relatively very little alternative in the policies implemented by the PT as they ultimately followed those very productivist approaches that have been so central in the development of capitalist agri-food*. This is the sixth conclusion of the book.

THE QUESTION OF THE SOCIAL DEMOCRACY IN CONTEMPORARY GLOBAL CAPITALISM

The conformity to productivist policies displayed by the Brazilian State under the PT begs the ultimate question of whether social democratic policies can be emancipatory in the context of the contemporary neoliberal globalization. The analyses presented in the chapters allow conclusions that point to the partially progressive but also contradictory role played by the State and the equally partial and contradictory emancipatory dimension represented by state capitalism. Accordingly, a plausible answer to this question is that, to some extent, state capitalism offers an alternative to the various forms of neoliberalism that have been proposed since the 1990s. It is certainly possible that a future progressive administration in Brazil could rectify the contradictory policies implemented by the PT between 2003 and 2016 and offer an effective emancipatory policy for Brazil. Yet, this hypothetical administration would also have to come to terms with the structural conditions of neoliberal globalization and their limiting effects on the emancipatory actions of a social democratic State. In short, the essential question is whether a social democratic State could address the conditions that limit its emancipatory actions under global neoliberal capitalism.

The basic argument presented here rests on theorizations of previous historical instances of state intervention-based social democratic experiments and the dominant trends that define global neoliberal capitalism. In this context, the essential issue is about the extent to which the State can exercise autonomy vis-à-vis the ruling domestic and—more importantly under neoliberal globalization—global capitalist ruling class. More specifically, the question is about whether the State can implement policies that are not supported by, and/or run counter to the interests of, the ruling capitalist class. In classic literature on the autonomy of the State, the most satisfactory answer to the question of state autonomy stresses that the State can exercise only a "relative" autonomy (e.g., Habermas 1975; Offe and Ronge 1979).[1] This argument indicates that the State in its national and supranational forms is not financially autonomous. That is, it does not control the origins of the financial resources that it needs to function. Conversely, it is the ruling capitalist class that create and control these resources. The ruling capitalist class generates profit through the management of their enterprises and pays wages and salaries to labor. The State taxes profits, wages and salaries and through this taxation obtains its own resources. Accordingly, the availability of state financial resources depends on the continuous and successful accomplishment of the process of capital accumulation.

Historically, however, the ability of the State to assist the bourgeoisie has limited the State's dependent position. Accordingly, the bourgeoisie counts on the State to further its agenda domestically and internationally. This support includes the control of social and political oppositions, the resolution of issues that emerge internationally and the investment of state resources in activities that directly benefit the ruling class. In the case of Brazil as well as other countries of the South, the State further performs the role of organizer/promoter of economic activities as it assists a relatively weak domestic bourgeoisie. Over the years and since the creation of the Brazilian nation, the

State has often acted as a broker in processes of domestic capital accumulation. Following this theory, the actions of the PT could be read in terms of the limits that the State faced in regard to the availability of economic resources and the necessity to promote the process of accumulation of capital. Accordingly , it is possible to view the pro-corporate actions of the Brazilian State as attempts to satisfy the structural requirement of capital accumulation rather than exquisitely independent political actions. In other words, this theory would preclude the State from acting in ways that would limit the interests of the capitalist class and their profit-generating actions.

To be sure, the relationship between the State and the capitalist ruling class is not simply a relationship of dependence of the former on any specific fraction of the latter. The theory of relative autonomy of the State indicates that the State does not tend to necessarily support any single fraction of the capitalist class. Rather, it is interested in the well-being of the entire capitalist class as one of its fundamental objectives is the continuation of the entire process of accumulation of capital. This is the case because the generation of economic resources that the State appropriates through taxation is not simply carried out by one or more specific fractions of the capitalist class. It is generated by all economic activities involving all the components of the capitalist class. Moreover, the protection of the entire economy safeguards the State against crises that involve specific sectors. This situation, however, does not prevent the State from identifying specific capitalist class fractions that, at any given time, guarantee greater sources of capital accumulation.

Accordingly, the State is interested in providing greater support to companies and economic sectors that have equally greater potentials to generate profit. In the case of Brazil, chapters of the book document the State's support of fractions of the local bourgeoisie that are involved in the exploitation of natural resources (extraction and agri-food). These companies are those that guarantee more resources for the Brazilian State and are part of the position that Brazil occupies in the international division of labor. Additionally, this position responds to the interests of the global bourgeoisie and its policy to exploit less expensive natural resources available worldwide (Harvey 2003). Following these considerations, the PT administration's policy in support of agri-food and extraction companies and their insertion in global circuits fit the requirements indicated by this theory.

The relationship between the State and the global bourgeoisie has assumed particular importance under neoliberal globalization. In effect, as recently as the end of the twentieth century, most of the literature on the role of the State in the economy and society addressed the question of the State in domestic terms. In these constructs, the class question involved almost exclusively the domestic bourgeoisie. In the case of the less developed countries, it contemplated the interaction between the State, the local bourgeoisie and the interests of American capital. This situation changed with the development of globalization and the emergence of a transnational capitalist class (TCC) (Sklair 20; Robinson 2014). While the TCC has not reached the same levels of unity of established national bourgeoisies, its political program of global deregulation of the economy and support of neoliberalism have characterized the early decades of the twenty-first century. Accordingly, the interests of the transnational capitalist class consist of claims about the desirability of the free circulation of capital and labor and the elimination of barriers to the mobility of capital. In the case of Brazil, the PT attempts to promote the insertion of Brazilian companies in global circuits and the support of agri-food production for these international circuits are compatible with the agenda of the TCC.

The relative autonomy of the State theory also specifies the relationship between the State and all the other social classes present in society. This relationship is defined not only by the requirement of the accumulation of capital but also by the requirement to maintain an adequate level of legitimacy on the part of the State. This means that the actions of the State ought to appear legitimate and just in the opinion of the voting population. It follows that the State is also required to provide enough support to the interests of the lower classes in order to obtain their backing in political elections while it needs to support the process of capital accumulation. A relevant issue to mention here is that, despite its power, the ruling capitalist class is a numerical minority in the national population and therefore attention to the opinion of the general population assumes significant importance. In essence, the reproduction of class power goes through the process of receiving support from subordinate classes.[2] In the case of Brazil, the State was required to support the accumulation of capital and, therefore, the interests of the ruling capitalist class, particularly in the extraction and agri-food sectors. Simultaneously, it was required to create conditions that legitimize its actions to the general population. This goal was accomplished through economic (economic legitimation) and ideological (ideological legitimation) interventions. Policies in support of family farmers, peasants and poor segments of society addressed the issue of legitimation economically. Pronouncements in favor of the emancipation of the lower classes and for the reduction of socio-economic inequality in the country constituted the sources of ideological legitimation.

State policies that promote capital accumulation and legitimate the actions of the State are limited by the finite nature of state financial resources. In classic literature, this situation is referred to as the "fiscal crisis of the State" whereby, as the State attempts to accomplish its role as the promoter of the accumulation of capital and supporter of subordinate classes, it encounters difficulties in financing both projects (O'Connor 1974). In recent decades, the fiscal crisis of the State has been countered through measures of fiscal austerity (i.e., the reduction and/or elimination of spending programs) and fiscal responsibility (i.e., the establishment of a specific ceiling to state spending). In both instances, the neoliberal concept that the State should not intervene in the economy and society is advocated. However, as this ideological posture is heralded as effective and necessary, state spending in favor of corporations has expanded worldwide, contributing to the development of the phenomenon of corporate welfare (Bennett 2015). In the case of Brazil and as illustrated in the chapters presented above, state spending for family farms, peasants, and the land redistribution was restructured in favor of capitalized farms while greater amounts were invested for the international expansion of Brazilian companies.

To be sure, the relative autonomy of the State theory should not be interpreted in strict structuralist terms. In effect, this theory criticizes structuralist approaches for viewing structural trends as determining the actions of social groups. In essence, for structuralists, the economic conditions that determine the reproduction of capital are those that, in the *last instance*, determine the status of all the spheres of society including the polity and ideology (Althusser and Balibar 1979 [1968]). According to the relative autonomy of the State theory, conversely, the structural requirements that condition the actions of the State are mediated by social classes that act to advance their interests. Accordingly, under Fordism, the state requirement to advance capital accumulation was mediated by the strength of the working class movement and the relative weakness of the capitalist ruling class (Streeck 2014; Harvey 1990). Once the strength of the working class diminished in the mid-1970s, the resurgence of the capitalist class pushed the State to promote forms of capital accumulation and social legitimation that favored capital over labor (Streeck 2014; Bonanno 2017).

Following this aspect of the theory of the relative autonomy of the State and the analyses presented above, it can be concluded that the extent to which state capitalism in Brazil was emancipatory was affected not only by structural conditions but also by the strength of the Brazilian progressive social movements and the concomitant responses of the dominant classes. More specifically, the strength of social movements that promoted the democratization of social relations in agri-food and in the country and that fought for the land reform, the recognition of the rights of indigenous populations, and the reduction of poverty provided impetus to the emancipatory actions of the State. However, as structural limitations persisted, the response of the ruling capitalist class promoted discourses that, first, limited proposed transformations in agri-food and society and, later, created conditions that overtly discredited the emancipatory plan of the PT administrations. These considerations allow us to reach the seventh and final conclusion of the book. *The containment of the actions of progressive social movements by pro-capital social forces limited the ability of the Brazilian State to implement a truly emancipatory agenda. Accordingly, the contradictory actions of the*

Brazilian State cannot be simply attributed to the will of the PT administrations. They were the result of the specific forms of class contestation that defined capitalist social relations in Brazil.

NOTES

1. In the long-standing debate on the role of the State under mature capitalism, the theory of the relative autonomy of the State is accompanied by two additional, often used, yet inadequate, theories. The first is the *instrumental theory of the State* (Miliband 1973; Poulantzas 1978). In its various forms, it argues that the State directly responds to either the directives of the capitalist class or to the structural conditions imposed by the functioning of the capitalist system. The fundamental limit of this theory rests on its inability to account for instances in which the State acts in favor of subordinate classes. A second and equally inadequate theory is the *theory of the autonomy of the State* (Skocpol 1979; Skocpol and Finegold 1982). The limit of this theory is twofold. First, it does not provide an argument for the separation between the officialdom of the State and the ruling class. Second, it is impossible to accept its assertion that the State under capitalism is not part of a class system. Ultimately, capitalism is a class system.

2. In classic sociological literature, this phenomenon is explained through the concept of hegemony (Gramsci 2011). It stresses that the stable rule of the capitalist class in a given society is established through the implementation of political projects that support the interests of the ruling class but also are accepted by subordinate classes. In many instances, the support that the capitalist State provides to the lower class is largely stated rather than actual (Streeck 2014).

BIBLIOGRAPHY

Althusser, Louis and Etienne Balibar. 1979 [1968]. *Reading Capital*. London: Verso.

Bennett, James. 2015. *Corporate Welfare*. New York: Routledge.

Bonanno, Alessandro. 2017. *The Legitimation Crisis of Neoliberalism*. New York: Palgrave-Macmillan.

Chayanov, Alexander. 1986. *The Theory of Peasant Economy*. Madison: University of Wisconsin Press.

Gramsci, Antonio. 2011. *Prison Notebooks*. New York: Columbia University Press.

Habermas, Jürgen. 1975. *Legitimation Crisis*. Boston: Beacon Press.

Harvey, David. 2005. *A Brief History of Neoliberalism*. Oxford: Oxford University Press.

———. 2003. *The New Imperialism*. New York: Oxford University Press.

———.1990. *The Condition of Postmodernity*. Oxford: Blackwell.

Kautsky, Karl. 1988 [1899]. *The Agrarian Question*. London: Pluto Press.

Keynes, John Maynard. 2009 [1936]. *The General Theory of Employment, Interest and Money*. New York: Classic Books America.

Krugman, Paul. 2013. *End this Depression Now*. New York: W.W. Norton.

Lenin, Vladimir Ilich. 1961 [1908]. *Theory of the Agrarian Question*. London: International Publishers.

Miliband, Ralph. 1973. "Poulantzas and the Capitalist State." *New Left Review* 82: 83–92.

Mirowski, Philip. 2014. *Never Let a Serious Crisis Go to Waste*. London: Verso.

Mirowski, Philip and Dieter Plehwe (Eds.). 2009. *The Road from Mont Pèlerin: The Making of the Neoliberal Thought Collective*. Cambridge, MA: Harvard University Press.

O'Connor, James. 1974. *The Fiscal Crisis of the State*. New York: St. Martin's Press.

Offe, Claus and Volker Ronge. 1979. "Theses on the Theory of the State." Pp. 345–356 in J. W. Frieberg. *Critical Sociology*. New York: Irvington Press.

Poulantzas, Nicos. 1978. *State, Power and Socialism*. London: New Left Books.

Robinson, William. 2014. *Global Capitalism and the Crisis of Humanity*. New York: Cambridge University Press.
Sklair, Leslie. 2001. *The Transnational Capitalist Class*. Oxford: Blackwell.
Skocpol, Theda. 1979. States and Social Revolutions. Cambridge: Cambridge University Press.
Skocpol, Theda, and Kenneth Finegold. 1982. "State Capacity and Economic Intervention in the Early New Deal." *Political Science Quarterly* 97: 255–278.
Smith, Adam. 1981 [1776]. *An Inquiry into the Nature and Causes of the Wealth of Nations*. Indianapolis, IN: Liberty Classics.
Stedman Jones, Daniel. 2012. *Masters of the Universe*. Princeton, NJ: Princeton University Press.
Stiglitz, Joseph. 2016. *The Great Divide: Unequal Societies and What We Can do about Them*. New York: W. W. Norton.
Streeck, Wolfgang. 2014. *Buying Time. The Delayed Crisis of Democratic Capitalism*. New York and London: Verso.
Weber, Max. 1958. "Capitalism and Rural Society in Germany." Pp. 363–385 in Hans H. Gerth and C. Wright Mills (Eds.), *Form Max Weber: Essays in Sociology, Capitalism and Rural Society in Germany*. New York: Oxford University Press.

Index

agrarian question, 162, 163, 164, 165, 170, 171
agribusiness, 45, 47–48, 50, 52, 53, 54, 56, 56n1, 69, 70, 71, 79, 85, 86, 87, 88, 89, 94, 95, 97, 102, 103, 117, 124, 127, 129, 137, 142
agriculture, 1, 2, 3, 4, 8, 10, 12–13, 30, 45, 47, 48, 49, 52, 55, 56, 59, 61, 63, 65, 66, 67, 69, 71, 82, 83, 85, 94, 95, 96, 99, 101, 103, 105, 107, 108n2, 113, 114, 115, 117, 118–119, 120, 121, 122, 123, 125, 129, 133, 135, 136, 137, 139–140, 141, 143, 144, 147, 149, 162, 167, 168–169, 171
agri-food, 1–3, 4–5, 5, 6, 8, 9, 11–13, 17, 19, 28, 29, 36, 49, 54, 55, 59, 61, 62, 63, 66, 71, 73, 77, 78, 82, 85, 88, 93, 94, 96, 113, 115, 120, 124, 125, 126, 127, 128, 133, 136, 137–140, 141, 143, 147, 161, 162–164, 165, 166, 167, 168, 171, 173, 174
agroecology, 10, 59, 63, 67–70, 70
aquaculture, 12, 13, 147–150, 152–158, 158n1
artificial negativity, 4

BNDES (Brazilian development bank), 6, 7, 18, 19, 22, 26, 29–32, 32, 33, 34, 36–37, 51, 125, 138, 140, 158n1
Bolsa Familia, 50, 52, 107, 128
bourgeoisie, 2, 6, 7, 18, 21, 124, 128, 129, 140, 142, 165, 166, 172, 173
Brazilian Real, 47, 124

capitalist class, 4, 5, 6, 141, 172–173, 173, 174, 175, 176n1, 176n2
Cardoso, Fernando Henrique, 8, 9, 10, 18, 26, 27, 45, 46–47, 48, 52, 54, 55, 61, 64, 66, 74n1, 95, 115, 124, 135, 137, 149, 150, 166
Cédula da Terra (Ticket to the Land), 49, 64
centralization of capital in agri-food, 168, 171
certification, 11, 78, 79–80, 81, 82, 84, 86, 87, 114, 124, 126, 127
Collor de Mello, Fernando, 7, 26, 115
concentration of land ownership, 65, 97, 121, 171
conservative modernization, 77, 135, 142, 166
CONTAG, 60–61, 62, 67, 69, 74n3, 103

Deregulation, 2, 12, 18, 23, 24, 46, 82, 115, 128, 134, 135, 136, 140, 144, 164, 173
developmentalism and neo-developmentalism, 12, 45, 50, 53, 54, 54–55, 56, 82, 83, 85, 89, 133, 137, 141, 142, 147, 149, 151, 157, 158

emancipatory, vii, 1, 3, 4, 5, 8, 9, 10, 17, 36, 38, 59, 61, 72, 73, 79, 89, 114, 133, 161, 162, 164, 166, 171, 175
EMBRAPA (Brazilian Agricultural Research Corporation), 77, 78, 97, 101, 118, 139
environment, 2, 10, 11, 19, 30, 34, 36, 61, 65, 67, 70, 73, 86, 87–88, 94, 97, 98, 105, 126, 129, 139, 148, 149, 167; environmental, 32, 53, 69, 71, 80, 87–88, 93, 96, 101, 105, 107, 126, 140, 149, 157; environmentalism, 135, 148

family farmers, 10, 12, 14, 49, 52, 55, 56, 60, 82, 97, 99, 100, 105, 106, 108, 108n1, 114, 120–121, 129, 133, 134, 135, 137, 139, 141, 143, 144, 168, 169–170, 171, 174
farming communities, 5
feminism, 59, 67, 69, 72, 73
Fome Zero (no more hunger), 8, 51, 137
Fordism, 5, 6, 7, 18, 19, 21, 23, 23–24, 25, 165, 175
free market, 22, 23, 38, 53, 81, 88, 164, 168, 169
fruit production, 11, 12, 77, 79, 83, 84, 85, 115, 120, 120–121, 123, 124, 125, 127

global corporations. *See* transnational corporations
global sourcing, 2, 24, 34, 37
globalization, vii, 1–2, 3, 5, 8, 9, 13, 24, 63, 78, 79, 80, 82, 116, 139, 141, 144, 147, 161, 162, 164, 171, 172, 173
governance, 21, 24, 55, 80, 81
governmentality, 11, 50, 79, 81, 85, 88

hypermobility of capital, 2, 25

import substitution, 6, 21, 22, 30, 82
indigenous people, 8, 9, 32, 53, 99, 135, 139, 164, 175
inequality, 14, 24, 30, 31, 37, 46, 54, 72, 127, 128, 129, 136–137, 141, 174
inflation, 7, 23, 26, 46, 47, 49, 50, 53–54, 55, 102, 124, 127, 134, 166

JBS, 9, 17, 19, 28, 29, 30, 32–34, 34–35, 36–37, 37, 56n1, 140, 167

Juazeiro, 77, 113, 117, 121, 125

Keynesianism, 6, 20, 165

Labor, 2, 4, 9, 10, 20, 21, 25, 28, 34, 53, 59, 60, 63, 65, 66, 69, 72, 82, 83, 86, 87, 89, 93, 94, 97, 101, 102, 103, 114, 115, 116, 124, 125, 126, 127, 128, 129, 133, 141, 142, 147, 150, 165, 168, 169, 170, 172, 173, 175
laissez-faire, 19, 20, 23, 81, 169
land reform, 2, 48–49, 52, 53, 54, 59, 61, 63–65, 66, 73, 128, 135, 138, 140, 144, 166, 175
landless peasants (Sem Terra). *See* peasants
legitimation, 5, 49, 81, 163, 165, 174, 175
Lula (Luiz Inácio Lula da Silva), 8, 10, 14, 17, 18–19, 26, 27, 30, 31, 35, 36, 45, 46, 49, 50, 51, 52, 54, 54–55, 61, 63, 64, 66, 73, 85, 95, 98, 99, 105, 107, 108, 124, 133, 137, 138, 150, 152, 161, 165

March of the Daisies, 10, 59–61, 62–63, 63–66, 67–69, 70–72, 73, 74n4
Ministry of Agrarian Development (MDA), 8, 14, 52, 55, 68, 95, 96, 99, 108n1, 134
Modernization, 21, 47, 52, 78, 82, 83, 88, 101, 114, 115, 117, 118, 151, 153, 165, 166; Conservative, 77, 135, 142, 166

natural resources, 51, 53, 63, 65, 73, 80, 88, 99, 101, 107, 115, 117, 118, 133, 134, 139, 143, 169, 173
Neoliberalism, 5, 7, 9, 10, 12–13, 18, 23, 24, 25, 48, 49, 53, 54, 55, 56, 79, 81, 82, 83, 84, 85, 120, 122, 124, 133, 134, 136, 141, 147, 151, 157, 158, 164, 166, 171, 173
networks, 1, 2, 78, 83, 158
NGOs, 32, 67, 68, 71, 80, 99, 137

oil palm, 11, 93, 94, 95–96, 97–98, 98, 100–101, 102, 103, 104, 105, 106, 107–108

PADRSS, 60, 64, 67, 68

Parliamentary Front of the Palma (FPP), 103, 104
peasants, 8, 9, 135, 136, 139, 140, 143, 144, 162, 164, 167, 168, 169–170, 171, 174
Petrobras, 6, 18, 50, 51, 55
Petrolina, 77, 85, 87, 113, 117, 121, 122, 123, 125, 128
poverty, 12, 27, 48, 49, 50, 52, 54, 55, 63, 94, 128, 129, 133, 136, 141, 144, 154, 175
PRONAF, 48, 49, 52, 95, 100, 108n1, 135
PT (*Partido dos Trabalhadores*), 8–9, 9–10, 11, 12–13, 17, 18, 19, 24, 26, 27, 32, 36, 37, 38, 45, 49, 53, 54, 55, 56, 57, 59, 61, 66, 70, 71, 73, 79, 82, 85, 88, 94, 95, 99, 114, 115, 124, 127–128, 129, 133, 136, 137, 140, 141, 142, 143, 144, 148, 150, 152, 156, 157, 158, 161–163, 165, 166–168, 168, 171, 172, 173, 175

Quilombolas, 9, 101, 116, 135

Real Plan, 46
resistance to corporate agri-food, 2–4, 11, 13, 24, 48, 61, 73, 107, 108
Rousseff Dilma, 2, 8, 10, 17, 19, 26, 27, 30, 36, 45, 52, 55, 61, 63, 66, 69, 73, 74n1, 95, 128, 133, 138, 141, 148, 161
rural violence, 48, 63, 65–66, 69, 104, 144
rural women, 10, 59, 60–61, 62–63, 63, 64–65, 66, 67–69, 70–71, 72–73, 74n2–74n4, 87, 127, 137

San Francisco Valley, 6, 11, 12, 77, 78, 82–84, 84–85, 85, 86, 88, 89, 104, 113, 114–115, 116, 117, 118, 119, 120, 121, 122–123, 124, 125, 126, 129
sector chamber, 94, 102, 103, 108
state: Brazilian, 1, 6, 7, 8–9, 10, 12, 13, 17–18, 22, 29, 30, 31, 35, 36, 37, 45, 48, 51, 59, 61, 71, 77, 78, 79, 83, 85, 86, 89, 94, 97, 104, 115, 116, 117, 118, 119, 129, 133, 140, 141, 144, 147, 153, 156, 162–163, 164, 165, 167, 168, 171, 173, 175; -capitalism, 1, 9, 13, 17, 18, 19, 20, 36, 37, 38, 55, 114, 129, 133, 141, 144, 158, 161, 162–164, 171, 175; developmental, 10, 45, 53, 54, 56; emancipatory role of, 1, 8, 9, 10, 17, 36, 38, 59, 73, 79, 89, 114, 129, 133, 134, 161, 162, 164, 167, 171, 175; -intervention, 1, 4, 5, 5–6, 7, 9, 11, 12, 13, 17, 18–19, 19, 20, 21, 23, 24, 26, 27, 34, 35, 36, 37, 37–38, 46, 55, 77, 78, 81, 82, 83, 84–86, 86, 88, 89, 94, 103, 114, 115, 116, 118, 119, 120, 123, 125, 128, 129, 134, 135, 136, 139, 141, 148, 151, 156, 162, 164, 165, 166, 167, 172; -owned companies, 6, 7–8, 18, 20, 22, 25, 26, 30, 45, 82, 125; -theory, 163, 168, 172–173, 174, 175, 176n1
SUDEPE Superintendence of Fisheries Development, 148, 149, 156, 157

Technology, 30, 50, 65, 67, 126, 137
trade unions, 20, 24, 25, 60, 97, 127, 128
transnational corporations (TNCs), 1, 2, 8, 13, 17, 19, 28, 32, 63, 80, 89, 120, 128, 129, 139, 141, 142, 168, 171
transnational capitalist class, 1, 161, 173
trickle-down economics, 24, 37, 168

wages, 3, 46, 50, 53, 120, 127, 128, 172
Washington consensus, 49, 134, 135, 166
workers, 3, 10, 12, 19, 33, 45, 55, 60, 61, 65, 67, 74n2, 85, 86, 102, 103, 114, 116, 126, 127–128, 133, 135, 139, 140
Workers' Party. *See* PT

About the Editors and Contributors

ABOUT THE EDITORS

Alessandro Bonanno (PhD, sociology, University of Kentucky, 1985) is Texas State University System Regents' Professor and Distinguished Professor of Sociology at Sam Houston State University, United States. Focusing on agri-food, Bonanno studies the neoliberal globalization of the economy and society. In particular, he investigates the impact that neoliberal globalization has on democracy, labor relations and the emancipatory options of subordinate groups. Dr. Bonanno is the author of numerous publications that appeared in English and other major languages. His most recent books are: *The Legitimation Crisis of Neoliberalism* (2017), *Resistance to the Neoliberal Agri-Food Regime: A Critical Analysis* (2018) and *Geographical Indications in the Development and Democratization of Global Agri-Food* (2019).

Josefa Salete Barbosa Cavalcanti (PhD, sociology, University of Manchester, 1982) continued her education through postdoctoral experiences at the University of Wisconsin–Madison and Cardiff University. She was also a visiting professor at universities in Europe, North America, and South America. From 2014 to 2018, Cavalcanti served on the executive committee of the International Sociological Association's Research Committee on Sociology of Agriculture and Food (RC-40) and on the board of the Brazilian Sociological Association. Currently, she is professor in the Department of Sociology and the postgraduation program in sociology at the Federal University of Pernambuco, Brazil, and holds a productivity scholarship from the National Council for Scientific and Technological Development (CNPq), Brazil. She studies the globalization of agriculture and food and social inequalities, with an emphasis on migrant rural labor. The primary themes of her research include: sociology of agriculture and food, rural development, peasant societies, and gender division of labor. She is the coeditor (with Alessandro Bonanno) of *Labor Relations in Globalized Food, 2014* and author of numerous articles and books that appear in English, Portuguese, and other major languages.

ABOUT THE CONTRIBUTORS

Andrea Butto is associate professor in the Department of Social Sciences at the Rural Federal University of Pernambuco, Brazil.

José Ignácio Vega Fernández is a PhD candidate in the postgraduate program in sociology at the Federal University of Pernambuco, Recife, Brazil.

Stéphane Gérard Emile Guéneau is visiting professor at the Federal University of Maranhão, Brazil, in the Research Centre for International Development.

Catia Grisa is assistant professor in the Graduate Center of Rural Development at the Federal University of Rio Grande do Sul, Brazil.

Beatriz Medeiros de Melo is associate professor in the Federal Institute of Alagoas, Alagoas Brazil.

Dalva Maria da Mota is researcher at EMBRAPA (the Brazilian Agricultural Research Center) Eastern Amazonia, Belém, Brazil.

Guilherme J. Mota Silva is associate professor at the Federal Institute of Education, Science, and Technology, Bahia, Brazil.

Moisés Mourão Júnior is researcher at EMBRAPA (the Brazilian Agricultural Research Center) Eastern Amazonia, Belém, Brazil.

Paulo Niederle is associate professor in the Graduate Center of Sociology at the Federal University of Rio Grande do Sul, Brazil.

Cinthia Regina Nunes Reis is associate professor of sociology in Department of Education and Philosophy at the State University of Maranhão, Brazil.

Heribert Schmitz is associate professor of sociology at the Federal University of Pará, Belém, Brazil.

www.ingramcontent.com/pod-product-compliance
Ingram Content Group UK Ltd.
Pitfield, Milton Keynes, MK11 3LW, UK
UKHW041123071026
15587UKWH00009B/140

9 781498 589895